The Corridors of Time · X ·

TIMES AND PLACES

By the late HAROLD PEAKE and
HERBERT JOHN FLEURE

OXFORD
AT THE CLARENDON PRESS
1956

Oxford University Press, Amen House, London E.C.4

GLASGOW NEW YORK TORONTO MELBOURNE WELLINGTON
BOMBAY CALCUTTA MADRAS KARACHI CAPE TOWN IBADAN

———

PRINTED IN GREAT BRITAIN

HAROLD JOHN EDWARD PEAKE

HAROLD JOHN EDWARD PEAKE, son of Rev. J. Peake, Vicar of Ellesmere, was born in 1867 and died in 1946. An early training at Leicester in estate management gave him an insight into matters of land-tenure and land-use on an historical basis. After his marriage with Miss Charlotte Bayliss they found it possible to go round the world, spending some time on a ranch in British Columbia; and from this came the insight into prehistoric pastoralism utilized in many papers and in some of the chapters in this series. Settling at Boxford in 1899, Mr. and Mrs. Peake exemplified the valuable British tradition of the use of leisure, without professional commitments, for intellectual and public work. Their house was a centre of light and leading not only for the district, with its rehearsals for village plays and pageants, its many committees and charities, but also for many younger workers who came for refreshment from the wit and wisdom that was always generously at our disposal in walks up and down the beautiful garden or talks over the wood fire in the open hearth. Peake became honorary curator of Newbury Museum and gave it some remarkable features, especially a chronological sequence in which each century from 3000 B.C. had equal space for exhibits and maps. He was Chairman of the Governors of Newbury Grammar School and a member of the Berkshire County Education Committee, Chairman and later President of Newbury General Hospital, a member of the Council of the Society of Antiquaries of London, President and Huxley Medallist of the Royal Anthropological Institute, and President of the Anthropological Section of the British Association for the advancement of science.

His chronological series at Newbury Museum was designed to show how inadequate are our books that quote a few remarks from Caesar's *Gallic War* and then go on to Anglo-Saxon invasions supposedly obliterating earlier populations. A result of his museum work was pleasantly shown when a school inspector spoke of things that had happened 'very long ago' and a Newbury child interjected: 'Oh but that was quite lately, in the La Tène period.'

A keen observer and helper of many good causes, Peake deliberately kept away from sect and party, his mind was too objective and he could not 'put his conscience in pawn'. The objective mind was humorously in evidence when a foreign guest, going to stay with him as so many did, asked, as the train passed, what Newbury racecourse might be. 'That', said Peake, 'is a temple of our national religion.' Lecturing on some prehistoric subject he would lead us up to the dawn of history and, with a twinkle, break off because, as he put it, the story thereafter got blurred by the prejudices of men who write records. Peake was one of the pioneers of the geographical study of early man and his achievements, and he encouraged many efforts to make distribution-maps of implements, pottery, and other matters, being convinced of the importance of diffusion of culture and of its hybridization. His idea of, and his work on, the *Catalogue of British Bronze Implements* remains as a monument, indeed a landmark, in the evolution of prehistoric studies. His wide knowledge made him chary of any support of the Neo-Diffusionists who, under Sir Grafton Elliot Smith and Dr. Perry, pleaded for diffusion from ancient Egypt by 'Children of the Sun'. Peake sometimes said that he found it difficult to look at the world through a 'Perryscope', but he appreciated the stimulus the venturesome hypotheses of Elliot Smith and those of Ellsworth Huntington gave to discussion and research. He tried to keep his own working hypotheses from getting the mastery of his mind, and his views evolved considerably in the course of fifty years of work. Always he sought to unite a careful distributional and typological study of remains of antiquity with a vivid appreciation of the lives and the craftsmanship of the people concerned. He made ancient times and ancient men come alive to the student and was careful to include himself and all others in the products of cultural evolution. In a series of museum exhibits of primate types leading towards man, the last term in the series, the significant feature indicating *homo sapiens* was not a skeleton but a mirror! Two subjects which received his special attention were the origins of cereal cultivation and (in partnership with his friend H. H. Coghlan) the early phases of metallurgy.

Peake's published work, in addition to 'The Corridors of Time' and many papers in the *Journal of the Royal Anthropological Institute*, in *Man*, in the *Transactions of the Newbury Field Club*, and in the *Victoria County History of Berkshire*, include *The English Village* (1922), *The Bronze Age and the Celtic World* (1923), *Origins of Agriculture* (1926), *The Flood* (1930), and *Early Steps in Human Progress* (1933).

Those who knew Mr. and Mrs. Peake will realize the appropriateness of a grateful mention of Misses Wilson and Plumb, their household staff for over forty-five years and helpers in many efforts of Westbrook House, including amateur drama and prehistoric inquiries.

PREFACE

THE present volume is planned as a conclusion to the series of 'Corridors of Time' and it has to begin with an appreciation of the senior member of the partnership, Harold Peake, who died in 1946.

The book falls naturally into two parts. Part I includes the first three chapters and attempts a broad sketch of the work of recent years on man in the Old Stone Age.

It has been the writers' belief in compiling the 'Corridors' that south-west Asia was the region in which man made the great step forward from dependence on hunting and collecting to food production by cereal cultivation; and to this the keeping of domestic animals was soon added. While there may have been small attempts at cultivation begun independently elsewhere, and there were probably several more or less independent beginnings of domestication of animals, the spread of food production from south-west Asia and Egypt and its consequences remain major features of the story of mankind. In Part II of this book therefore the attempt has been made to trace this spread of food production into a number of regions and to follow life in those regions in very broad outline from that beginning onwards.

The Americas with their largely distinct problems have not been included in the survey.

Circumstances beyond the control of the surviving author have delayed the issue of this last volume for several years. The continuous effort to adjust it to new data has been difficult, but it is hoped that not many statements are seriously out of date.

ACKNOWLEDGEMENTS

MANY thanks are due to the authors, editors, and publishers of the following works and journals for permission to reproduce figures: *The South African Ape Man*, by R. Broom and G. W. H. Schepers (Transvaal Museum, Pretoria) for fig. 1; *The Queen's Medical Magazine* (The University Club, Birmingham) for fig. 2; *Zeitschr. f. Morph. und Anthr.*, vol. xxxv (Stuttgart, Schweizerbart) for fig. 3; *Journal of the Royal Anthropological Institute of Great Britain and Ireland*, vol. lxviii for fig. 4; *Stone Age of Mount Carmel*, vol. ii by T. D. McCown and Sir Arthur Keith (Clarendon Press) for fig. 5; *Les Hommes fossiles*, by M. Boule (Masson et Cie, Paris) for fig. 6; *Tools and the Man*, by W. B. Wright (G. Bell & Sons) for figs. 7, 8A, 9, 10, 13, 14, 16, 17, and 30; *A Guide to the Antiquities of the Stone Age* (British Museum) for figs. 8B, 53, and 54; *Manuel d'Archeologie préhistorique celtique et gallo-romaine*, by J. Déchelette (Alphonse Picard, Paris) for figs. 15, 18, 22, and 25; *Reallexikon der Vorgeschichte*, vols. i, ii, v, vii, viii, ix (Walter de Gruyter & Co., Berlin) for figs. 19, 23, 26, 29, 40, 43, 45, 47, 48, and 49; *Les Combarelles aux Eyzies*, by Capitan, Breuil and Peyrony (Masson et Cie, Paris) for fig. 20; *Lascaux Cave Paintings*, by F. Windels (Faber & Faber) for fig. 21; *Peintures Rupestres schématiques*, vol. iv by the Abbé Breuil (Lagny) for fig. 24; *Men of the Old Stone Age*, by H. Fairfield Osborn (G. Bell & Sons) for figs. 27 and 28; *Malta and the Mediterranean Race*, by R. N. Bradley (T. Fisher Unwin) for fig. 46; *The Temple of Deir el Bahari*, by E. Naville 'Memoirs of the Egypt Exploration Society', No. 12 for figs. 41 and 42; *Corpus of Prehistoric Pottery*, by Professor Sir Flinders Petrie (Bernard Quaritch Ltd.) for fig. 37; *From Tribe to Empire*, by A. Moret (La Renaissance du Livre, Paris) for fig. 38; *Prehistoric Cheshire*, by W. J. Varley and J. W. Jackson (Cheshire Rural Community Council, Chester) for fig. 51; *Mohenjo-Daro and the Indus Civi-*

lization, vol. iii, by Sir John Marshall (Arthur Probsthain) for figs. 55, 56, 57, and 58; *Prehistoric Pottery in China*, by G. D. Wu (The Courtauld Institute of Art, University of London) for fig. 61; *Birth of China*, by H. G. Creel (Jonathan Cape) for figs. 62 and 63; *Anthropos*, by R. Heine-Geldern, vols. 23 and 27 (Anthropos Institute, Fribourg, Switzerland) for figs. 64, 65, 66, 67, and 69; *Nias*, by E. E. W. Schröder (E. J. Brill, Leiden) for figs. 68 and 70; *The Caroline Islands*, by F. W. Christian (Methuen & Co. Ltd.) for figs. 71, 72, and 74; *Eastern Pacific Lands*, by F. W. Christian (R. Scott) for fig. 73; *Early Steps in Human Progress*, by H. J. E. Peake (Sampson Low, Marston & Co. Ltd.) for fig. 11 (Drill, Saw, Plough and Flint and pyrites for making fire).

CONTENTS

LIST OF ILLUSTRATIONS

PART I

THE EVOLUTION OF MAN

I

THE story of man's evolution has become more detailed, and more complex, through discoveries during the past thirty or more years (1924–54), especially in Java, China, South Africa, and East Africa. A new means of testing the relative ages of fossil bones, applicable under some circumstances only, has also enriched our knowledge. But no discoveries, as yet, have pushed man's origin much beyond the transition from Pliocene to Pleistocene, say a million years ago. And it is only under special conditions that fossil remains of early man or his nearest forebears are preserved. It is widely agreed that the chimpanzee and gorilla have many characteristics in common with man and that these characteristics possessed in common are too numerous to be all due to what is called convergence, that is to changes tending from diverse beginnings towards increased resemblances. One must, however, say that an animal hardly above the Lemurs, the Tarsius, has the forward look and the holding up of the head as well as the general features of the hand showing likeness to man. A separate branch of the tree of ascent might possibly have grown from near Tarsius to man, as Wood-Jones has urged. Morton has argued in support of this view that the long tarsal bone of man is a feature that persists as a heritage from small ancestors. It is to be contrasted with the strong, short tarsus of the great apes. There is little serious evidence, and, to appreciate this difficulty, we must realize that, except man, the primates, i.e. lemurs, monkeys, and apes, are animals of the warm wet forests, in which dead bodies would rot quickly and bones would dissolve. Man became man partly through venturing out into grass-lands away from the tree cover, and there, again, the remains of the dead without definite burial would soon be lost. So fossils of the earliest men are very rare, and, moreover, the number of 'men' was probably small.

Apes and some monkeys use stones for nut-cracking, and we must think that our ancestors also used them, but, until they had learned to shape them, these stones gave no evidence of man. We may, at any rate, say that man and the chimpanzee and gorilla have some kind of cousinly relationship, and that their divergence from one another is due largely to man's shift to open country and the apes' continuance in the woodlands even if they move along the ground a good deal, as do some monkeys also.

The higher apes and man have a pre-natal life of about nine months and are able to breed at most seasons. Their sexual life is thus a matter of closer association than it is among many other animals; and the prolongation of pre-natal life from seven to nine months has resulted in increase of what were already the last stages of growth, namely, special growth of the head and brain. As an illustration of that special growth one might say that, while many animals have a small range of meaningful diversity in the sounds they make, the chimpanzee is said by some naturalists to have a much wider range of calls. Also some chimpanzees are able to do things which imply adaptation of means to foreseen ends, adaptation involving something very near reason.

In South Africa, Dart, Broom, Robinson, and their colleagues have found a number of specimens, mostly embedded in limestone in the Transvaal, and, now, the names *Australopithecus Plesianthropus*, and *Telanthropus* are given. The tendency has been to date these fossils to the transition from the Pliocene to the Pleistocene Age, but Breuil has recently inclined to allocate them to the Pliocene; the accompanying fauna on the whole seems to favour this view. There is much discussion as to their relationship to both apes and man, and that question must be left to specialists to work out as more specimens become available. The ascending branch of the lower jaw has a rather human

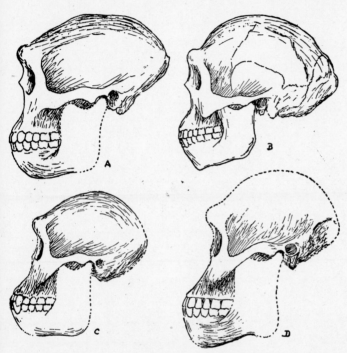

Fig. 1. Side-views of early skulls (after Broom): Scale *c.* 0:22 linear.
A. *Pithecanthropus erectus*, Dubois, Java. B. *Sinanthropus pekinensis*, Black, N. China. C. *Plesianthropus transvaalensis*, Broom, Sterkfontein, Transvaal. D. *Paranthropus robustus*, Broom, Kromdraai, Transvaal.

character and the canine teeth are not very large. Apes have a gap between the canine teeth and their neighbours for interlocking of the canines of the upper and lower jaws; in the South African specimens that gap or diastema is very small and not very important functionally. That, again, tends towards the human condition. The pelvic girdle also is rather human than ape-like. It is further claimed that *Australopithecus prometheus* was able to use fire, the claim being based on remains of burnt bones including those of this species itself. That a being contemporary with *Australopithecus* used fire thus seems likely to be established, and, if this is so, it is probable that this *Australopithecus* itself was responsible. He would, therefore, deserve the specific name of *prometheus*, if he was the earliest fire-user. The utilization of fire was one of the most important steps towards the human status; it involves continuous care for maintenance as well as care in arrangement in order to secure a foreseen result. It is probable that at this early stage the art of making fire was not known, fire could only be maintained.

Kohl-Larsen, in 1938 at Lake Njara, found a fragment of an upper jaw of a large form related to apes and men. This has been called *Meganthropus* and the same name has been used for a fragment of a lower jaw from Java, while three fragments of a large jaw from Java have had the name *Pithecanthropus robustus* given them. Von Koenigswald bought three large near-human teeth in a medicine shop in Hong Kong, and it is believed that they came originally from Shansi; they have been given the name *Gigantopithecus*. It is most probable that these large forms are long-extinct side branches of the genealogical tree of man and throw little light on our ancestry. The *Australopithecus* group is more important; they seem to have walked erect, or nearly erect, on the ground, and may have used fire, as well as stones and probably bones as weapons. They were at any rate not very far from human status, as le Gros Clark has well argued.

Though the name *Pithecanthropus* has been used in connexion with fragments of large jaws as just mentioned, it really belongs to skulls and skeletons mostly of the Pleistocene, and often said to be Lower Pleistocene, from Java. The first was found by

Dubois in 1891, the three others many years afterwards. (One of the three is the one mentioned above.) Unfortunately, these finds were made in such circumstances as precluded the possibility of collecting any evidence of implements, &c. Davidson Black, however, from 1927 onwards, investigated a site of long occupation at Chou Kou Tien near Peking. Considerable portions of skulls attributable to fourteen people, together with many fragments of bone and numerous teeth, have been studied. That they are closely related to the Java *Pithecanthropus* is very clear, though the name of *Sinanthropus* has been used for them. Some of them have a rather higher forehead than the Java *Pithecanthropus*. Flake implements and fire-hearths have been found. The dating of these finds of *Pithecanthropus* and *Sinanthropus* is Pleistocene, but whether we should say Lower or Middle is not certain. We know that the above-mentioned Chou Kou Tien finds come from before the Upper Pleistocene.

Twenty years ago Leakey found in Kenya a jaw and skull at Kanem and Kanjera, said to be in association with Acheulean tools and certainly approaching *homo sapiens*. These specimens are very ancient, but Boswell has doubts about detailed dating.

In Europe the lower jaw found in the Mauer sands in a quarry near Heidelberg is generally allowed to be Lower Pleistocene in date. It is very large as compared with that of modern man, but apparently it fits the skull from Broken Hill, Rhodesia, which is discussed below. (Fig. 2).

A girl's skull (adolescent) from Steinheim in the Murr valley, Germany, is Lower or Middle Pleistocene. It is usually ascribed to the Riss Ice Age or to some milder phase within that broad period. In some ways it suggests a trend towards the type of modern humanity in the large sense, i.e. to *homo sapiens*. Here one may interpolate that young forms, and especially young females, are likely to show most clearly resemblances between types; it is largely by changes in the late stages of growth that

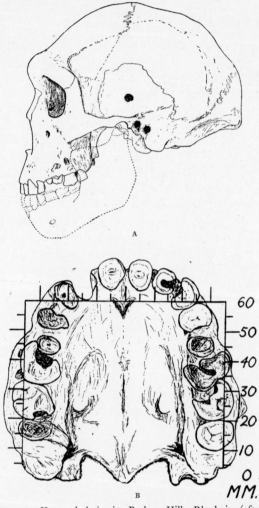

FIG. 2. *Homo rhodesiensis*, Broken Hill, Rhodesia (after
Brash). A. Skull, to which has been added the outline of the
Heidelberg lower jaw: Scale *c.* 0·3 linear. B. Palate of *homo
rhodesiensis*: Scale *c.* 0·75 linear. The rectangle shows
the limits within which a similar scale drawing of a palate
of modern man would lie

new types come into existence, and these late stages of growth are longer continued and more pronounced in the male than in the female.

A portion of a skull found at Swanscombe, Kent, and described by A. T. Marston, has had its Early Pleistocene date confirmed recently by Oakley, who has worked out means of

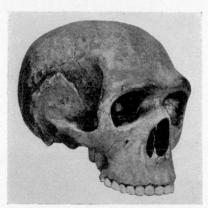

Fig. 3. Skull (young female). Steinheim, Germany.

estimating age, under certain restrictions, by a quantitative analysis of the fluorine absorbed by bones from the earth since their burial. Bones of post-Pleistocene date rarely have as much as 0·3 per cent. of absorbed fluorine, whereas the Swanscombe skull had 2 per cent. in one part and 1·9 per cent. in another. The formerly much-discussed Galley Hill skeleton gave a maximum figure of 0·4 per cent., so is likely to be Late Pleistocene or later. The test of fluorine content is limited by the fact that it is to some extent related to conditions on each site. Unfortunately only the back part of the Swanscombe skull remained when it came under scientific observation, but on the whole that suggests a trend towards the type of *homo sapiens*;

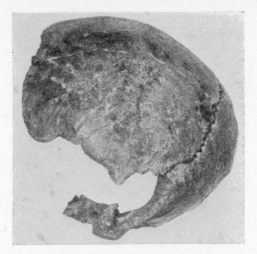

A

B

FIG. 4. Two views of the Swanscombe skull-fragment:
Scale *c.* 0·4 linear. (After the Report of the Swanscombe
Committee, 1938.) A. Side view. B. Inner surface.

in fact, some would incorporate it completely in that sub-species.

It was found in a deposit that contains Acheulean hand-axes (see below), and many think it is associated with them. Acceptance of this would further confirm the early date of the skull.

More recently portions of two skulls have been found at Fontéchevade in western France associated with late Acheulean (Tayacian) flints. This suggests an early date. They have been supposed to show a trend towards the *homo sapiens* type.

From the Middle Pleistocene of Europe we have some skulls usually grouped together as the Neandertal type, so called because the first of them to be studied was found at Neandertal, near Bonn, in the Rhineland, in 1856. Recognition of it as a type came only after controversy in which the theory of its then supposed pathological character played a large part. Once it was recognized as a type it became obvious that a female skull found at Gibraltar in 1848 must be considered related. In 1908 a most important specimen was found at La Chapelle-aux-Saints and it has become the standard of the Neandertal type, thanks to its good and almost complete preservation.

This type has a higher forehead than is found in the *Pithecanthropus* group, but much lower than that in *homo sapiens*, from which it is also distinguished by the heavy arched brows making a bar or torus right across over the eyes. The jaws and teeth are also large, and it is doubtful whether the type habitually walked erect if one may judge from the curving of the femur. The La Chapelle-aux-Saints specimen had a strongly projecting jaw, but it is not certain that this feature is universal for the type. Skulls from Shkul, Palestine, have more or less Neandertal characters, with a suggestion of intermediacy between *homo sapiens* and *neandertalensis*. If the latter group is to be looked upon as a Pleistocene specialization in very cold regions from an earlier *sapiens* stem, the Palestinian finds—notably the skull called

Shkul IV—may even be specimens of *sapiens* slightly modified towards the *neandertalensis* type. Broken Hill, Rhodesia, has yielded a skull with very strong brows and low forehead that belongs in the main to this group, and according to some ob-

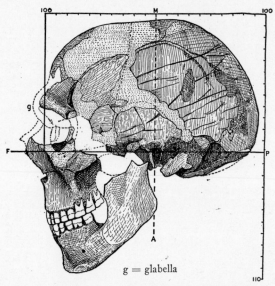

g = glabella

FIG. 5. Skull known as Shkul IV (male). Mt. Carmel, Palestine.

servers also shows hints of the trend towards *homo sapiens*. A skull from Eyassi (North Tanganyika) is somewhat similar, but less extreme and may be female. It is probably Middle Pleistocene. The Steinheim skull mentioned above is sometimes taken to be a juvenile example of a Neandertal type, and this well illustrates the impossibility of making sharp distinctions. A further and important illustration of the same difficulty is that a group of skulls of Middle or Late Pleistocene date from

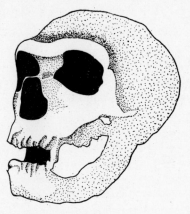

The skull and jaw of the man of La Chapelle-aux-Saints.

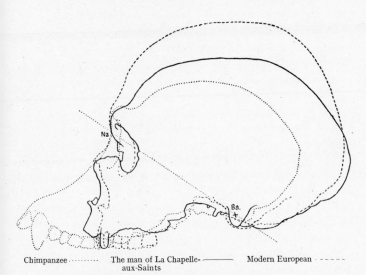

Chimpanzee ········· The man of La Chapelle- ——— Modern European - - - - -
aux-Saints

Diagrammatic longitudinal sections of skulls.

Fig. 6

Ngandong, Java, often referred to as *homo soloensis*, and rather more like *homo sapiens* than are any of the Neandertal type specimens. Some observers link the Ngandong group with the Australian blackfellows.

If *homo sapiens* or a type approaching him was in existence in Middle Pleistocene and even in some phase of Lower Pleistocene times, we may perhaps think of a fully characterized *homo sapiens* such as Combe Capelle or Cro Magnon (see Chap. 2) as one extreme and of the man of La Chapelle-aux-Saints as another extreme. Other specimens would then range between them with a tendency towards the *homo sapiens* type becoming general at the end of the Middle Pleistocene.

Thirty years ago it was supposed that no *homo sapiens* existed before the Late Pleistocene, and it was known that no Neandertal type had been found from any deposit after the Middle Pleistocene. There thus seemed a once-for-all replacement. The non-occurrence of a Neandertal type after the end of the Middle Pleistocene is still a proper inference, if we accept datings as at present, but it seems possible to think that *homo sapiens* was in existence before the end of the Middle Pleistocene, perhaps before its beginning, at least in a preliminary form. This way of looking at the matter avoids old and difficult hypotheses of the supposed descent of *homo sapiens* from Neandertal ancestors.

The Neandertal group with the powerful bony development is somehow related to the cold period of the early Würm phase of the Ice Age, illustrating a development which seems in the cases of several animals to have been one possible response to an icy environment. One must be careful to say 'one possible response' and to avoid classing it as a necessary and general one.

With the beginning of the Late Pleistocene Age varieties of *homo sapiens* became the only types of man known, always supposing that datings generally accepted are maintained. Men in the Late Pleistocene were evidently much like modern men.

Some had brow ridges fairly marked but much reduced in comparison with older types, others had very little of them left. Nearly all walked erect, and the forward projection of mouth and jaws, if it occurred at all, was relatively slight, while the chin was better developed than in other types. More is said about this in Chapter 2.

One of the most notable facts concerning mankind is its adaptability, by artificial protection through skins and fires in the case of cold, to every climate on earth except that of the Antarctic continent, and with this its mobility, especially in the early nomad hunting stage, and the accompanying possibilities of occasional intermingling over wide areas and so of limiting large-scale regional differentiation. At the same time inbreeding within the small groups of that time must have been common.

Evidence from tools is far more abundant than evidence from bones, but is specially incomplete in that wood, which early man no doubt used, is almost never preserved. Bone, horn, and ivory were all used, and objects made from them by men of the later part of the Old Stone Age are found. A pointed wooden instrument said to date from the Mindel-Riss interglacial has, however, been found at Clacton-on-Sea, Essex.

The earliest fabricated tools were probably pebbles chipped to give an edge; the chips knocked off might be used as well. Men later prepared nodules of flint, or blocks of chert or obsidian, or, with more difficulty, might at need make tools of quartz or other rocks.

Men have shaped implements both by knocking chips off a stone core which latter they intended to use, and by further shaping of the chips with the intention of using them. The earlier cores shaped by knocking off large chips from both sides were formerly called Chellean, from Chelles near Paris, but are now named Abbevillean from Abbeville on the Somme in northern France, where they are found in numbers. The later, more

finely chipped hand-axes, usually shaped from flint or other
blocks, are called Acheulean from St. Acheul near Amiens in
northern France. It is thought that these finer tools were often
shaped by well-aimed blows from a hard wood or bone mallet.
M. Coutil in France experimented to show this, and Dr. Leakey
has confirmed and extended his conclusions.

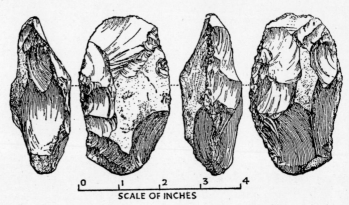

SCALE OF INCHES

FIG. 7. An implement of the earlier part of the Abbevillean–Acheulean
series; made on a flint core, both faces worked.

The fineness of the better Acheulean workmanship suggests it
was *homo sapiens* who was concerned, and, if the Swanscombe
and Kanjera skulls were really associated with Acheulean implements there is some support for this view. The distribution of
rough flakes in many parts of Eurasia where they are found without core tools suggests their link with some hominid types rather
than with *homo sapiens*.

One may envisage drifts of mankind using biface core tools
(Abbevillean and Acheulean) from the open lands of Africa,
north of lat. 10° N., in various directions:

(a) Especially in the drier periods, southwards to the southern
end of Africa, carrying culture elements from the north

probably to survive for long ages in the far end of the continent, but avoiding the equatorial rain forest to a large extent. That forest was of larger extent in many phases of the Pleistocene.

(*b*) Especially in the warmer periods, northwards to Europe. We now feel confident, following Vaufrey, that there was

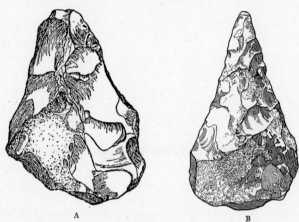

A   B

FIG. 8. Hand-axes of flint. A. Early (Abbevillean) type.
B. Later (Acheulean) type.

no land-bridge across from Africa to Italy in the Pleistocene. As regards the Straits of Gibraltar, Vaufrey believes they have been open all through the Pleistocene; W. B. Wright, on the other hand, thought the land-bridge was probably finally submerged during the Pleistocene period, so the makers of biface implements, in his view, might conceivably have got across by land. In any case, however, the Straits were probably narrower than they now are, and it may not have been impossible to get across on floats of some kind.

(*c*) Eastwards to India and probably to the nearer East Indies, which may have been parts of the Asiatic continent during periods of low ocean-levels. As the present cliff edges of western India and southern Arabia are probably due to faulting late in or even after the Pleistocene, the connexions from Arabia eastwards to India may have been easier than they now are, especially when sea-level was lower.

A very striking feature of the biface tools is their abundance in, and comparative uniformity over, the wide area in which they do occur. Chisel-like tools or cleavers seem to be common where rhyolite and quartzite are the typical materials, especially in Africa; they flake appropriately. But chisel-like implements are also known from Europe and Britain, though flint does not flake very suitably for this, and the type is uncommon. Another striking feature is the slowness of change of style in these tools, and this suggests that the weight of custom lay heavily upon the minds of their makers. Recently, Harpur Kelley has urged that the core-users also sometimes used the sharp flakes they had chipped off. Many agree. However we may argue concerning the mentality, equipment, and activities of these early peoples, we must recognize the fact that some of their implements rise to the level of real artistic achievements.

The dating of these industries in terms of the ice ages has advanced in recent years with more detailed study of sequences of deposits in glacial and periglacial areas. Reid Moir and Sainty have found flints which they claim had been shaped by men; and these come from the uppermost Crag deposits in Norfolk, which have been considered Pliocene but are probably contemporary with the Günz Ice Age. The Rostro-carinates, or bird-beak flints, are perhaps somewhat later, and Zeuner thinks they belong to the Günz-Mindel interglacial interval, but Barnes does not think they are implements at all. Zeuner believes the Acheulean appeared in Europe in the Mindel-Riss interglacial;

it continued beyond the Riss into the Riss-Würm interval in Britain and western Europe.

Within recent years the study of flake implements, typically worked on one side and therefore called uniface, has shown that many are contemporary with biface tools and occur in the same regions, as well as here and there over the interior of Eurasia, which the makers of the biface tools did not reach. Some of the

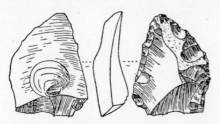

FIG. 9. A Clactonian flake, Clacton-on-Sea,
Essex: Scale 4/9.

roughest flakes have been found at Clacton (Fig. 9), in Essex, and this industry is thence called Clactonian; a flake was simply struck off, sometimes after a certain amount of preliminary chipping. The industry seems to have been independent of the Acheulean and to have developed, or reached Britain in the Mindel-Riss interglacial. Later it became modified into the rather rough Tayacian.

More developed flakes have been named Levalloisian (Fig. 10) and Mousterian, names which have been used with a good many diverse meanings by different researchers, the later developments being largely the result of Breuil's studies. To make these better flake implements the surface of the core was often chipped in steps to produce a convex surface which can be likened to a tortoise carapace, whence the name tortoise-core. Then, along one side of the prospective implement, chips were taken out, to form a 'striking platform'. Next the platform was struck against an anvil, or a mallet blow was given against the platform. As a consequence a flake was detached and, if the preliminary flaking of the surface of the core had been skilfully planned, the flake struck off had sharp edges. In what Breuil calls the Mousterian industry that preliminary flaking was so devised in many cases as to give the flake a sharp point and a triangular form, and the sides of the triangle adjacent to that point were often made regular and sharp by secondary chipping. Other industries mainly dependent on preparation of a block-surface for striking off an implement are characteristic of parts of Africa.

FIG. 10. A Levalloisian flake, Montières, France: Scale 4/9.

It will be noted that these industries relied on the final blow to detach a sharp-edged flake, the underside of which would show no chipping, but in flint does usually show a rounded elevation, called bulb of percussion, near the striking platform in the case of Levallois tools. Apparently the Levallois industry developed during the Riss glaciation or in milder intervals within that period; it continued through the Riss-Würm interglacial and on into the interval between the first and second phases of the Würm. The 'tortoise-core' mentioned above is a special feature of this industry. It is probable that wood or bone mallets were often used in making Levallois and Mousterian flakes.

In numerous cases biface and uniface implements have been found within the same region, but authentic records of finding the two kinds together, or of finding a compromise between the two, are rare until well on in the sequence. But it is only too well known that until about thirty years ago some collectors often threw away flakes and kept only core tools. Late Acheulean biface tools, especially in North Africa, are often worked on large flakes, and there are cases of flake tools that look completely Acheulean on one face but have the other unworked. Late and small Acheulean points of the Riss-Würm interglacial or the first interlude in the Würm series have been called Tayacian and Micoquian, another name used with various meanings by different writers. It is just possible that some of the small flakes were hafted on wood. There are, along with these flakes, others that herald the advent of the Upper Palaeolithic cultures to be discussed in Chapter 2. Various types of early flint tools are known from the Monsoon lands of southern and eastern Asia and a feature here is a pebble chipped to form a rough chopper.

Spain has a varied assortment of uniface tools as well as of the biface types. In North Africa, apart from Egypt, we find that the flake industry of Levalloisian or Mousterian type, accompanied by some evidence of influence from Acheulean fashions, had a considerable development. A peculiarity here added later on, is the chipping of a tang or stem at the mid-point of the base of a finely chipped triangular point. The industry with this type of tool is known as Aterian, and its age has been the subject of many discussions. It has even been considered Neolithic, but, in some cases, circumstantial evidence points to its greater age; it has not been found in caves. One suspects that it lasted in use for a long time, beginning early with crude flaking, and developing, with external contacts, into more elaborate forms. Miss Caton Thompson and Miss Gardner have proved that the Aterian industry in the Kharga Oasis belongs to the Late Palaeolithic Age, and that it handed on some of its fashions to later times in Egypt. It should be added here that tanged or stemmed points occur at some Late Palaeolithic and Mesolithic stations in Europe (they are well known at Font Robert in France).

Some stations have yielded bone implements along with flake tools, and worked bone has been found with core tools in Alsace. In the Alps and Bavaria very ancient stations, in caves containing bone tools, have been described; these include the Drachenloch, 2,445 metres above sea-level, Wildkirchli, 1,500 metres above sea-level, both near St. Gall in Switzerland, Drachenhohle, 1,000 metres above sea-level in Steiermark, and one about 500 metres above sea-level near Nürnberg. A few very poor stone tools, mainly of quartzite and other crystalline rocks, do occur; but the men who made them hunted the cave-bears and used bone in the main. Whatever may be the truth about other men of the Old Stone Age, there can be no doubt that the cave-bear hunters co-operated in groups. The Drachen-loch is a cave with three chambers, two of which had small walls built of limestone slabs at a distance from the cave wall, the intervening space containing many skulls of bears, some of which bear evidence of mortal wounds. Sometimes one or two limb bones were also found, but it is evident that these were not parts of complete skeletons accidentally accumulated. Near the entrance to one of the chambers the collection of bones behind a wall was covered by large slabs forming a stone box or cist, and here the contained bear-skulls were set out in order, as were some limb bones, again not complete skeletons. Other collections, of what we can but suggest were hunting trophies or offerings, could be traced elsewhere in the caves in a disturbed state. Evidence of the same kind is available from south Germany, and here one might mention the offerings of parts of the bear made in modern times by hunters among the Ainu of north Japan. Jaws, without other skeletal parts, of extinct animals have been found in caves occupied by early man in south India, and these also give the impression of having been trophies or offerings.

Apart from these few cases it is noteworthy that nearly all traces of men of the earlier phases of the Old Stone Age, that is of the phases described in this chapter, are from stations in the open, not stations in caves, which are the typical spots for tools of the later phases of that age.

As there are indications that flint edges remained in use down to the Middle Ages, and perhaps later in some localities, it is evident that care must be exercised in dating any finds, especially as the flints used in historic times have often been of the roughest description. Flakes knocked off a block have often been used without further shaping.

We read the evidence of early implements in general as indicating a Eurasiatic region of flaking (uniface) and an Afro-Arabian region using cores (biface) and flakes, the latter region extending northwards in western Europe as far as Britain, and eastwards in south Asia as far as India. The two cultures had a zone of apparent contact and overlap in Britain, France, and North Africa, and there one gets exchange of ideas, the Acheulean point and the Mousterian approaching one another. The use of flakes was becoming universal, and diversity of shape, in conformity with diversity of purpose for scraping, cutting, and boring, began to appear. This heralds the coming of the Upper Palaeolithic cultures, the fashions of the later part of the Old Stone Age, during which phase the glaciers were in the main definitively receding and climate was about to enter upon a new series of changes.

It still seems probable that the core-using cultures discussed in this chapter did not reach the New World, but the flake cultures penetrated into America and Africa and survived there into later times. They apparently also contributed elements to the Australian cultures which are still lingering on at the present time.

The fact that peoples using, for the most part, flake implements of stone still survive in Australia has suggested to some that they are, as it were, survivals from the middle phase of the Old Stone Age. Such arguments, however, are dangerous. Into the Australian cultures there have drifted strays with ideas from later cultural developments, such as the idea of stone hammers, shaped by rubbing and provided with a groove to hold a leather band for hafting. If items of material equipment have come in, such as the hammer and the canoe, ideas affecting social life may also have arrived from elsewhere. There is another danger. The Australian blackfellows, the Semang of Malaya, and others, are lowly folk with what appears to be a stagnant or retrogressive type of life; many of the people of the Old Stone Age were, on the other hand, on the highway to a more elaborate equipment.

One may hint that the zones of contact between peoples who used mainly hand-axes, with flakes as merely subsidiary tools, and peoples who depended mainly on flake implements may have been the scenes on which important steps in cultural evolution occurred. Professor Dorothy Garrod in Palestine has recently gathered evidence of the occurrence together of Levallois-Mousterian flakes and of blades like those of the Late Palaeolithic, but she has found no transitional forms. She inclines to the hypothesis that, at these Palestinian stations, the blade technique of the Late Palaeolithic was invented by people who had hitherto used mainly Levallois flakes. She suggests the name Emireh for this Palestinian culture. One should add here that only when hard-edged tools had come into use for skinning and cutting up beasts could hunting of the larger animals have become important and it must have been a co-operative activity. Elaboration of scrapers and borers made it possible to use skins for wraps. Fine pointed flakes made it more possible to shape bone and ivory.

It should be added that careful search has revealed here and there traces of very ancient sites, at which have been found evidences of fire and remains of animals, sometimes of extinct types. It would be dangerous to argue from this that we are in the presence of very early cultures that used only such perishable material as wood, but the occurrence today of lowly forest peoples, who use only vegetable materials for making implements, prevents us from ruling out such a possibility in the past.

The further discussion of the Late Palaeolithic phase will be taken up in Chapter 2.

The next of man's primal features to be mentioned is, in a sense, the most important of all. Man is a social being and group-life is a feature of all living men. Our evidence from the past also suggests group-life, the indications being well marked in the South African near-men and Chou Kou Tien hominids, admitting, of course, that the law of probabilities has worked so as to give us also isolated finds of individuals. Moreover, there is considerable probability that, from an early phase, the human group was larger than what we should call the simple family-man, wife, and children. We know, thus far, practically nothing of our ancestors while they were still at the stage of merely collecting food, but we seem justified in arguing that, at any rate when they became groundlings of the open country, the group took to increasedly carnivorous habits and so hunting came to have increased importance. Leakey, at Olorgesailie in Kenya, has evidence for pitfalls, as a means of trapping large animals, made and used by men still in the phase of using the Abbevillean-Acheulean hand-axes. The erect posture for walking on the ground, with the accompaniment of improved stereoscopic vision, may be combined with the idea of hunting, and in that connexion perhaps of stone- and spear-throwing (i.e. action at a distance) as concomitant factors in the further evolution of the social group.

The human assumption of the upright posture has made the

late stages of pregnancy a greater hindrance to mobility, and has forced the baby to learn to walk, a long process often hardly complete when the child is over two years of age. The groups in which mothers gave babies increased care during the prolonged stage of helplessness had a great advantage for survival, especially as the care of the group's fire was an occupation the mothers could carry on at the same time, while the men might be far away hunting. Hunting, at least of large animals, was an activity inviting, if not even demanding, co-operation of several men and emphasizing differentiation of work according to sex; women, especially with babies, could not possibly endure the physical strain of hunting on foot over large areas.

It was natural that women gathered accessory activities around the primal care of the babies and the almost primal tending of the fire. So women became initiators in many directions, probably skin garments and their softening and sewing, certainly at a later stage pottery, cultivation, and so on. In several cases men have taken over the tasks women had performed, and this has happened especially when men have found means of reducing hand-work. The potter's wheel worked by a treadle is traditionally a male implement. The spade is another partly foot-worked implement used mainly by males, whereas the traditional female implement of cultivation was the digging-stick, often too the hoe. But mention of pottery and of cultivation of the soil takes us far beyond the primary evolution of man, and these are matters further discussed in subsequent chapters.

An important early advance of humanity associated with the erect posture, fire, and hunting, though in its beginnings probably older than these, is the elaboration of language. Observers of the higher apes, especially the chimpanzee, know that they make many different sounds which have meanings, usually of emotional type, attached to them. Rundle has made a catalogue of 200 for the chimpanzee; but this is hardly language as a

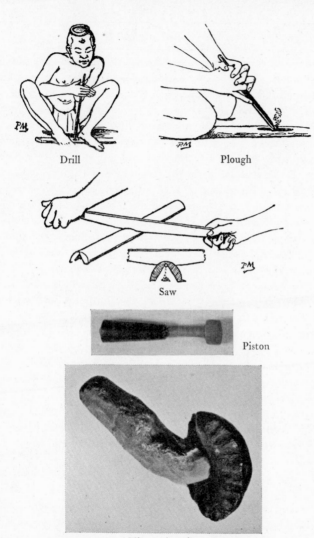

Drill

Plough

Saw

Piston

Flint and pyrite

FIG. 11. Methods of making fire developed after a long period of utilization and maintenance of fire naturally or accidentally ignited.

communication of categorical information or names of things, and some observers are doubtful about a number of these supposedly meaningful sounds.

The shortening of the snout into a mouth and the diminution of the heavy ape-musculature holding the lower jaw in position freed the larynx for more delicate adjustment, and tongue and lips for more differentiated movements. It is probable that this, alongside of the longer association of mother and child, and co-operation of men in hunting as well as social life around the fire, has contributed to the development of speech in early humanity; and the inference has been made, from a cast of the brain, that *Pithecanthropus* could speak in the human sense. No doubt sounds conveying emotional exchanges between mother and child and between man and woman were a large feature in the early evolution of language. One should also bear in mind the importance of resonance in speech and song, a quality highly developed among some peoples with high-arched palate in Europe and Africa. It seems to occur especially among peoples with long, narrow heads and faces and brunet or darker colouring.

The development of language beyond the more purely emotional level to the stage of name-giving was a factor of the greatest importance in intellectual development; it gave the mind counters with which to play, and something to which to pin memories that could be communicated to members of the group, and so helped to transform social life.

In a cave at Monte Circeo, Italy, has been found a skeleton surrounded by specially placed stones. It is generally believed to be late Middle Pleistocene in date. A hole in the skull cap and the removal of part of the skull base suggests that the brain had been removed, probably for a cannibal sacrament, and so it gives us one of the earliest hints of a ritual and of fancies tending towards religion.

It may be said in conclusion here that the prolongation of association of mother and child has been the most important of all factors in humanization and in ethical development generally.

Addendum to Chapter I

CONCERNING THE ICE AGES AND MAN

IN the early volumes of this series written in 1926, the work of Penck and Brückner on the Alps in the Ice Age, and that of de Geer for northern Europe, were made the bases of our chapters. Since that time their work has been carried farther, and we also have a number of attempts at synthesis of results of geological, archaeological, biological, and astronomical observations and calculations. Old views about there having been but one great Ice Age were dying in 1926; they are now almost forgotten, and the numerous ice advances and retreats suggested by James Geikie for Scotland together with the four major Ice Ages inferred by Penck and Brückner for the Alps are accepted and elaborated into a whole succession of phases.

Milankovitch of Belgrade, from observations of solar radiation, has built up calculations of the radiation that was theoretically receivable by the different latitudinal zones of the earth at different periods during the last million years, during which there have been wide oscillations of climate, cold extremes of which are called Ice Ages. Variation in theoretical radiation depends on changes in obliquity of the ecliptic, eccentricity of the earth's orbit and changes in distance of sun from earth at perihelion. He identified from his tables periods of minimum summer irradiation of various latitudinal zones, and estimated that some, at any rate, of these would be epochs when snow and ice accumulated year after year. That accumulation would have further effects: (1) it would cool the sea winds and make them deposit moisture to freeze in its turn, and summers would be made

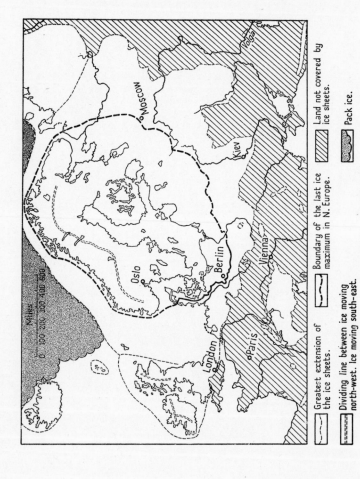

FIG. 12. North Europe and the Ice Ages.

Greatest extension of the ice sheets.

Dividing line between ice moving north-west. Ice moving south-east.

Boundary of the last ice maximum in N. Europe.

Land not covered by ice sheets.

Pack ice.

Miles
0 100 200 300 400 500

MOSCOW
Kiev
Oslo
Berlin
Vienna
London
Paris

colder still; i.e. one would have stormy cyclones coming from the ocean and heavy precipitation on Scandinavia and on mountain ranges in west Britain; (2) it would lock up water as ice and so lower the level of the sea, thus making the land stand out into layers of atmosphere farther removed in this way from the mildening influence of the sea; (3) after the accumulation of ice had gone on for a long time its weight would be sufficient to depress the continent carrying it, and so to raise the relative level of the sea. W. B. Wright in his *Quaternary Ice Age*[1] has dealt in some detail with the combinations of effects under (2) and (3).

Bearing these chief factors in mind and especially the long time-lags involved, we realize that an Ice Age is a phenomenon of many phases. Milankovitch estimated that the last marked period of minimum solar radiation was about 22,100 years ago. De Geer, counting the annual depositions of mud from melting ice from south to north in Sweden, though the last major phase of the Würm Ice Age began to pass away (inception of Daniglacial retreat) about 18,000 years ago. Though this may agree with the Milankovitch estimate of 22,100 years ago for the last major Würm ice-maximum one must have reserves about linking astronomical cycles with seasonal depositions of mud. Dating by proportion of the Carbon Isotope of atomic weight 14, a proportion which apparently diminishes very slowly in organic remains, suggests an estimate of under 20,000 years.

The view that cold summers were the most important factors is said to be borne out by many observations. A large area of north-east Asia is in the same latitude as Greenland, and has a colder winter but a warmer summer. Greenland has had ice-accumulation on a large scale, north-east Asia has none.

Milankovitch states very frankly that his calculations offer no clue to the apparent absence of Ice Ages in the millions of years

[1] 2nd edn., 1937.

between the Pleistocene and the Permo-Carboniferous periods. Perhaps there has been some other secular change of solar activity. Perhaps the accumulations of heat in the earth's interior, due to decomposition of radium, have affected climate either directly or indirectly through the giving off of heat when the internal strain had become too great and mountain building took place. It would further seem that Ice Ages have followed mountain building in the late Tertiary after the rise of the Alps and Himalayas, in the Permo-Carboniferous after the rise of the Hercynian-Variscan mountain systems, in the Devonian, and in the pre-Cambrian geological periods. Mountain building on the large scale raises portions of the earth's crust to heights at which they can accumulate ice.

Soergel, working in Thüringen, between the Alpine and Northern Ice Sheets, has been able to establish in river valleys a succession of changes mainly of two kinds:

(*a*) Accumulation of gravels in cold relatively arid periods.

(*b*) Cutting of valleys and deposition of alluvium on their floors in milder periods.

He has tried to link some of the cold periods with those of ice advance both in the Alps and in northern Europe. In this way, Alpine and north European observations have been brought together, and an elaborate succession of events has been worked out. It has verified and complicated the Penck and Brückner statement of four major Ice Ages in the greater European centres of ice-accumulation.

Breuil, working on the Somme region in northern France, found (1939, *Proceedings of the Prehistoric Society*) not, of course, moraines, but evidence of solifluxion, that is of the slipping down of half-frozen soil along slopes. This has happened in many cases as a consequence of the cracking of frozen material, but Paterson has recently claimed that it also happens under very wet conditions. Breuil identified eleven successive solifluxions, which he thought indicated cold periods, and six intermediate deposits of fluviatile character indicating milder conditions. Breuil's succession can be fitted into the general scheme of Penck and Brückner, Soergel, Milankovitch, &c.

Woldstedt,[1] Zeuner,[2] and Paterson[3] all have attempted continental or world surveys of the Ice Ages; and we are as yet far from agreement as to the factors involved, though there is some approach to concord concerning the sequences of deposits and other evidences.

Milankovitch's tables are thought valuable by Zeuner, who ascribes great influence to successions of cool or cold summers, leading to accumulation of snow and ice in middle and high latitudes. Paterson on the other hand follows, with some modifications, the ingenious theory advanced by Sir George Simpson.[4] This theory starts from the idea of variations in irradiation of the earth from the sun; but supposes that, in a phase in which receivable radiation is increasing, there is a great increase of difference between equatorial and polar conditions with consequent storms and heavy precipitation in high latitudes. This, he thought, was what led to ice-accumulation and an Ice Age.

It is supposed that when the amount of receivable radiation still further increased the accumulated ice melted and gave a mild phase of climate. As the phase of maximum radiation passed, conditions tending towards ice-accumulation would appear once more, and would ultimately pass away when the amount of this radiation was still further reduced and the contrasts between high and low latitudes thus lessened. Whether the cool summers (in middle and high latitudes) of Milankovitch used by Zeuner

---

[1] *Das Eiszeitalter*, 1939.
[2] *Geol. Mag.* 1935; *Proc. Geol. Assoc.* 1937; *Proc. Prehist. Soc.* 1937.
[3] *Trans. Roy. Soc. Edinburgh*, 1940-1.
[4] *Quart. Journ. Meteorol. Soc.* 1934.

and the wet phases inferred by Paterson are really contradictory remains to be examined by climatologists.

Opinion favours Milankovitch and Zeuner, but many have reserves about the 'dating' of the last phases.

The Milankovitch suggestions would carry the implication that each belt of latitude must be studied for its own sake and that one must not argue from the northern to the southern hemisphere because irradiation was different. Paterson, on the other hand, thinks evidences from many regions of both hemispheres point to widespread and general climatic change and he adopts the modified Simpson theory. We are obviously still at an early stage of understanding of the Ice Ages and cannot attempt to create a 'harmony' of the diverse views at this stage. When, however, one remembers that a generation ago there was still a belief, in some quarters, in a one-phase Ice Age, the recent progress of understanding will be appreciated. The agreement on data has developed faster than the agreement on the factors concerned; and that was to be expected.

Note: A few corrections of details from our second volume (*Hunters and Artists*) in the light of new knowledge may be added here. Dating, in years, for the Pleistocene has recently progressed greatly, and the latest tendency has been to reduce the whole period, perhaps to a quarter of a million years.

The identity and importance of the Bühl moraines are now much less clear than they seemed twenty years ago; but the Fennoscandian moraine is obviously very important, and dates from a still-stand of ice rather more than 10,000 years ago, and the Ragunda moraine, deposited when the ice sheet's edge had retreated up to the Scandinavian mountain edge and the sheet was soon to be represented only by northerly and southerly remnants, is about 8,700 years old. The calculations are based upon the counting of seasonal deposits of clay from melt-water of the ice sheets.

2

The Hunters of the Later Old Stone Age

CONTACTS of culture generally lead to advances, and this chapter will try to sketch the great revolution that had its beginnings in the contacts of makers of mainly core (biface) and makers of flake (uniface) tools in south-west Europe, North Africa in a broad sense, and Palestine. Already some biface-type tools (Late Acheulean) had been made from flakes. Core tools became less important, flakes and hafting were elaborated by the finer chipping that had been applied to the making of core tools. With reduction of the Scandinavian ice sheets came changes leading to movements of mankind, now better equipped in mind to meet new circumstances than they were in previous periods of recovery from ice maxima.

Western Europe still had much ice, probably through high precipitation from Atlantic air-currents; but, apparently, the Würm ice sheets spread less in eastern Europe and other inland areas than did their predecessors. As the Würm ice sheets diminished, the north of Africa became more arid, while Palestine, on the other hand, may have profited from the milder cyclones developing in the Mediterranean or insinuating themselves in winter from the Atlantic through southern France or the Straits of Gibraltar. Among periglacial regions, therefore, south-west Europe and Palestine and the loess areas of east-central Europe were likely to offer improved circumstances, while parts of North Africa, on the other hand, were impoverished by droughts. Though the Nile floods kept up a water-supply, the flood-lands were, as yet, undrained, and the possibilities of hunting were limited; Egypt, therefore, was of little account; the arts of cultivation and irrigation were what gave it its prominence much later on. But Huzayyin and others emphasize that, as the present distribution of climates began to establish itself, the summer monsoon rains on the Abyssinian heights began to give Nile floods loaded with dark silt which has made Egypt so fertile. That this was occurring from about 8000 B.C. seems highly probable.

Bobek is inclined to believe that the north-east of Iran and also the ways through to Turkestan escaped glaciation, and G. F. Wright held that there was an extensive sheet of water in the Euxine-Caspian-Aral lowland from the melting of snows in the mountains to the east. The diminishing glaciation of the central Asiatic heights may thus have promoted the utilization of the lowlands in western Asia, but the intense cold on the highland may have hindered the spread of people to the far east and north-east of Asia from farther west.

The hunters of this period in Europe followed over the great stretches of cold grass-lands the herds of bison (*Bison priscus*), also wild cattle (*Bos primigenius*) in the forest glades and on the moister grass-lands, as well as wild horse and, in due course, also wild ass in the drier areas. Deer and wild boar multiplied as forests developed, especially when they had passed beyond the pine and juniper stage. Wild sheep spread in the hills, and near the remains of the ice sheets were found mammoth and reindeer.

It is possible to make some inferences about dwellings. Whereas, in the Early Palaeolithic Age, people wandered about and used sites near rivers and other drinking-places for encampment, it seems likely that the people of the Late Palaeolithic Age had centres to which they returned repeatedly. Willendorf in Austria is a famous case in point, and there is great probability that the decorated caves were cult centres for long periods. The hunters made settlements in the open country in Germany, Austria, and Switzerland, near water but well above flood-level, and there, we imagine, they may have lived in tents during the summer. The tectiform designs in the decorated caves are interpreted by many as drawings of these, but some represent pitfalls. The regions with caves are much less rich in open settlements, and the former in many cases show signs of long occupation, probably especially in winter. Caves may also have served as food stores, and we know they were often sacred places. In both caves and open country stations are found hearths, often hollowed out, sometimes with clay foundations or with the sides baked hard, and stones often surrounded by protective sand, the whole structure being obviously shaped for cooking. Some cases of hollowed-out and stone-floored habitation sites are known from Switzerland and Austria. Evidences of subterranean dwellings have been collected in south Russia: post-holes at Kostenki, hearths and a clay-covered bark chimney at Timonovka, along with flints and geometrical designs on mammoth ivory, and female figurines at Kostenki and Gagarino. Similar subterranean dwellings have been found at Malta in Siberia.

The above sketch suggests that south-west and central Europe and Palestine are likely, on many grounds, to have been centres of special evolution, and finds of tools show that this was the case. Whether the resemblances in tools between these regions indicate more than parallel advances is a moot point. Moravia and some other areas of loess in central Europe and south Russia became important as ice sheets diminished, and their influence on France became well marked; whether there was a cultural connexion between them and south-west Asia is not yet clear.

Hunting large animals involved not only the means of striking from a distance but also the power to work co-operatively and move quickly over long distances. Women and children would hamper such quick and prolonged movement, and, in consequence, the men hunted unaccompanied by their mates, and we thence glean indications of further differentiation of work according to sex. The women and children formed a focus to which the hunters returned; and, where they were available and dry enough, caves were naturally chosen for habitation and for storage of flesh, which was possible in the cold season. It is probable that women tended the fires, which, if we may judge from folk-lore, may have been kindled or brought by a youth who was still unmated. Women and children would prepare the skins they were now using as wraps, scrape and shred sinews for fibres, scrape bones, and do many other things. Mothers and children had opportunities for further and longer association, giving increased opportunities for language-development as well as for the verbal transmission of experience and the handing on of acquired techniques. One wonders whether there were not sometimes pet animals, the beginnings of the art of domestication, of which the dog was, undoubtedly, the first subject.

Caves and rock shelters are often rich in drawings or paintings, chiefly of animals, and the animals are shown sometimes as they appeared in life to the hunters, sometimes as they looked when they lay dead. Among the Birhors, a lowly jungle people of Chota Nagpur, India, the wife of each hunter in whose net a beast has been caught, cleanses a space in front of her house and the dead animal is laid there, after which she performs a ritual before the deer is skinned. Very possibly, ritual practices gathered around the Old Stone Age drawings, often in the depths of dark caves, and we find some of the figures deliberately broken as though this were part of the rite; this is particularly notable in the Magdalenian period. Sometimes the drawings are incised; sometimes, instead of drawing, we find modelling in the round, especially on ivory or in clay. Some of the modellings, notably that of the Tuc d'Audoubert, may have had a real head, or skull, fixed on. Carvings of women, sometimes pregnant, are a feature, while carvings and engravings of men are rare enough in certain cases to suggest that there was a kind of taboo in the matter, but both sexes are represented by engravings at Les Combarelles. We do not know what magical fancies may have gathered around the drawings and models, and some may be just expression of an artist's pleasure; but a few of these artistic efforts suggest a further possibility. At the cavern of Les Trois Frères in southern France, for example, is a representation of a man disguised by having an animal's skin and head above his own. This may be an instance of the well-known practice of a hunter's disguise, but it may have been a ritual mask. It is on the wall of a look-out place, a point of vantage, as though the man were someone of special importance, perhaps the magician of the group. The painted caves, too, and rock surfaces suggest centres of mystery and magical power.

Deliberate burials with accompanying objects and ornaments suggest either ideas of survival beyond death for some, probably, leading personalities, or perhaps notions of reincarnation, especially as the burials are often in a contracted position rather like that of a child in its mother's womb.

At Cogul in Spain a ring of skirted women is shown dancing around a man with enlarged sex organs; size in early drawings often implies emphasis. The petticoat had already, therefore, come into use, and folk-lore implies that it was supposed to allow ancestral spirits access to the womb for rebirth, while at the same time protecting the womb from the 'evil eye'. It is possible that this widespread notion of rebirth of ancestral spirits is linked with the experience that, in our species, sexual union does not lead so regularly to pregnancy as it appears to among the animals that are used by or known to man; an additional factor was, therefore, apparently postulated. Elementary observations of hereditary resemblances may also have been factors here. The origin of male clothing is probably connected with the fact that the assumption of the habit of standing and walking upright set the sex organs between the legs and thus impeded movement; the loin cloth or some alternative could lift them just out of the way. Protection from the evil eye and the beginnings of control, so important once conscious reflection on sex had developed, were, no doubt, additional factors. Some nude peoples in Africa push the male organs upwards in childhood to avoid the impediment above-noted. Needless to say, protection of the body against cold was an important factor in the development of clothes.

Clothing, especially of skins, implies boring holes for fasteners, cutting, and sewing. These activities were dependent on varied tools: borers, knife-blades, awls, bone or ivory needles, and so on; and, whatever aspect of life we take, we find indications of varied tools for different purposes produced often in quantities that suggest the notion of spare parts, a notion that would naturally arise with hafting.

We have seen there is much evidence of more durable settlement than existed in earlier times, and that the cave decorations and many other details suggest corporate aspects in the life of considerable numbers of people even if the population was very sparse. Modern hunter-collector groups rarely attain a density at all approaching one person per square mile. Not only were groups anchored to a considerable extent, subject very probably to seasonal migration, but they also may have had territories they looked upon as their own, and the localization of some types of finds, in Obermaier's view, supports this idea. Hunting groups of the present day, at any rate, have this idea strongly developed. Ornaments include numbers of sea-shells found in the Vezère valley suggest trade or gifts from hand to hand, or, less probably, long migrations. The sorcerer or shaman of the cave look-out at Les Trois Frères suggests there was some notion of leadership. The high level of much of the art suggests that the people of the Late Palaeolithic Age were probably more advanced in equipment and initiative and had more power of thought than have many hunter-collectors of the present day, and frozen winters must have permitted storage of food, which would con-

tribute greatly to the development of forethought and organization and to possible aggregation of population as in the Vezère
valley or on the loess.

The painted caves have, within them, inner chambers most
difficult of access, and especially in these there are many symbols
and drawings. The footprints of youths were found by Bégouen
on the floor of one of these recesses at Montespan that had not
been entered for thousands of years, and by Vallois in several
other caves. The youths had had to go in on their haunches. It
is indeed likely that these dark places were connected with
initiation rites. Such rites are a widespread feature at the present
day among lowly peoples, and there is every reason to suppose
that the ancient hunters also practised them. The burials suggest
strongly an idea of some life after death, and the figurines of
women focus attention upon sex and birth. It is probable that
the widespread notion of rebirth was being developed and, with
it, the notion of a spirit. How far men had gone towards the
idea of spirits in all objects we cannot tell, though some have
imagined that cave drawings give hints of the kindred idea of
totemism, which links the spirits of members of human groups
with those of animals, plants, objects, or phenomena. It is probable, from representations at Cogul, that sex and dancing, as
is generally the case, played a great part in ritual; and that magic,
ritual to secure power over others or over one's circumstances,
was considered very important. Whether anything of the nature
of prayer and the linking of one's personality with the divine
spirit, which is of the essence of later religion, had as yet developed we cannot say.

Implements

In France the early culture of the upper part of the Old
Stone Age has been described by Breuil under the name of
Aurignacian, which, it has recently been proposed, should be

restricted to a phase that is said to have invaded France from
Asia via central Europe and was formerly known as the Middle
Aurignacian. To the earlier phase, and its possible later con-
tinuations, the name Périgordian has been given; and it has
been supposed to be a native development. It is probably wisest
to think for the present that elements native to France and intrusive features from central Europe mingled quite early in
France. The earliest Aurignacian point tools, named from the
French station of Audi, were broad, and the edge curved round
to an asymmetrical point. Later on, an improvement of technique gave a point projecting straight out but still fairly broad;
this was named from the French station of Châtelperron. At
La Ferrassie we get something intermediate between the two,
while at Audi the layer with these points overlies layers with
Mousterian flakes and there is probably a genealogical connexion
between them. Stations said to be of this age have also yielded
flint scrapers with a keel, blades with a sharp cutting edge and
the other edge blunted so that the worker might press with his
finger, gravers (burins) or tools with points kept sharp by striking
off flakelets from the pointed end as it became blunted by use,
some bone points, including a few with a split base, ivory
statuettes of women from Brassempouy, objects (sometimes
called *batons de commandement*) (Fig. 22) with round holes
apparently used for straightening shafts for javelins, and
polishers in bone. The sharp burin made possible work in bone
and ivory and the cutting of wood across the grain.

The Middle Aurignacian, or true Aurignacian in the modern
sense, has a great variety of scrapers and gravers, including
notched implements, but nothing very definitely new in the
matter of points and blades. Flints had by this time become very
abundant, and decorative art was much developed, the statuettes
of women being specially characteristic of central Europe. The
Upper or Late Aurignacian shows finer and sharper points,

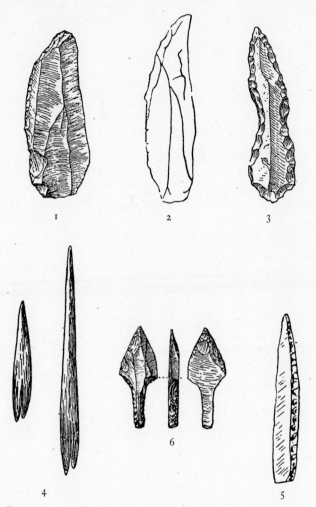

FIG. 13. 1. Audi point ($\frac{1}{2}$) Late Mousterian; Audi France. 2. Châtelperron Point ($\frac{2}{3}$) Early Upper Palaeolithic. 3. Notched blade ($\frac{2}{3}$) Aurignacian. 4. Bone points with grooved bases ($\frac{1}{2}$) Aurignacian. 5. Gravette Point ($\frac{2}{3}$) Post-Aurignacian. 6. Font Robert Point ($\frac{1}{2}$) Post-Aurignacian.

named from La Gravette, and broader points with a special median stem or tang, named from Font Robert, as well as shouldered points with a stem curving out on one flank into the blade, but flint implements were no longer so abundant at this

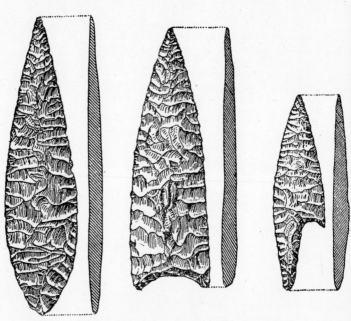

FIG. 14. Solutrean implements ($\frac{2}{3}$), France.

stage. Some of the long blades have one edge blunted to form a back.

Methods of using bone were much improved in this period. The classic areas for all these developments in France are Périgord and other districts in south-west France and on the Riviera coast. We must also mention the north Spanish or Cantabrian coast and some outliers indicating southward extensions in Spain. We have no hint whatever of any incoming of this culture into France from Africa or Spain; on the other hand, near Madrid, Acheulean axes have been found persisting side by side with blades and gravers.

Whatever may be thought concerning spreads of Aurignacian culture from Asia or central Europe to France, or conceivably vice versa, there is no doubt whatever that the next culture, named Solutrean from Solutré in Burgundy, was an intrusion from northern Hungary into western Europe and reached southwest France and north Spain. Its bearers were, apparently, not interested in graphic arts, but they made very fine large flint tools called laurel-leaf-points, and there have been suggestions both that the first makers of these tools owed something to the Mousterian point-makers and through them to the Acheulean core workers, and that they left a heritage to the people of the Neolithic Age. Both these other cultures are, however, very far in time from the Solutrean, and resemblances may be due to similarities of method. The Solutrean invaders spread westward along the steppe or grass-land in a very dry period over areas of loess. They hunted herds of wild horses that multiplied on these grass-lands, and, when the forest grew again, they retreated.

The reindeer had lived in France and the red deer in Spain, and these maintained themselves in their respective regions for a time, but the reindeer gave way to the red deer as temperatures became more moderate. After the retreat of the Solutrean hunters, the old culture of France redeveloped, with the making of long flint knife-blades, often of poor workmanship. Awls and gravers became abundant, but not the scrapers or the points of earlier times. This phase is called the Magdalenian and is subdivided into six periods, the earlier ones of which are poor. In the fourth of these periods, however, ivory and bone points, barbed and sometimes doubtfully called harpoons, became more common. The culture then declined, apparently because the spread of the forest was pushing men out. As Magdalenian stations occur inside the lines of the Würm moraines in Switzer-

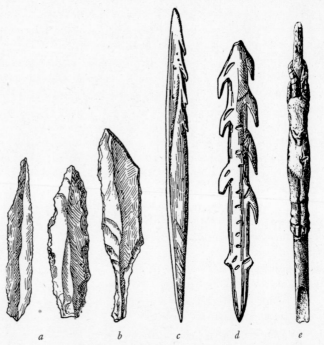

Fig. 15. French Magdalenian implements. *a.* Point. *b.* Implement with tang. *c, d.* Harpoons. *e.* Throwing stick.

land, we have direct evidence of the retreat of the ice and change of climate.

Implements other than French

In Palestine, Professor Dorothy Garrod has found blade tools in layers with Acheulean and Levalloisian or Mousterian implements; then follows the Lower Aurignacian with fairly broad points, gravers, scrapers, and blades with blunted backs, all rather more refined than the corresponding objects from western Europe. From between western Europe and Palestine, on the European side, we have, at present, data from the Crimea which are said to agree, in the main, with those from Palestine,

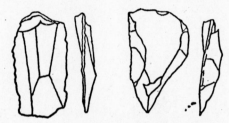

FIG. 16. Late Palaeolithic (Sebilian) flakes,
Fayum, Egypt (⅔).

but evidence of the very early stages is lacking. In Moravia, we have evidence of an industry that begins with a transition from the Mousterian and goes on to a unique development of sculpturing on, and modelling in, ivory, as well as of fine engraving.

On the African side, increasing aridity brought poverty, but it is fairly certain that the Aterian industry continued and handed on its fashions to later times.[1] Egypt appears to have been isolated, and Levalloisian flakes became very small and were increasingly rechipped after the edge had broken. This industry is called Sebilian or Sabylian (Fig 16), and it has no gravers, or burins as they are called, until near the very end. North of Helwan, east of the lower Nile, one finds narrow rather than broad blades, an industry, in fact, probably related to those of south-western

[1] For a discussion of the Aterian industry reference should be made to Gertrude Caton-Thompson's Huxley Memorial Lecture, 1947, Royal Anthropological Institute (vol. 77 of the Institute's *Journal*).

Asia; this relationship has been marked in many later periods in that district.

Inland in south Tunisia and eastern Algeria are found implements much like those of eastern Spain—long thin blades, gravers, and small triangles and trapezoids, the last becoming the most important feature in the late stages. This culture is

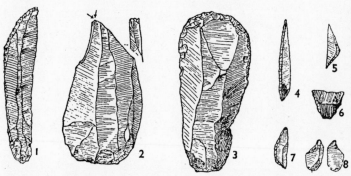

FIG. 17. Capsian implements (Late Palaeolithic), Gafsa, Tunisia ($\frac{2}{3}$).

called Capsian from Gafsa in Tunisia, but some think it came to Africa from Spain; it lasted for a very long time (Fig. 17). Farther west the poor Oranian culture, formerly inappropriately called Ibero-Maurusian though it has no connexion with Spain, has very few of the little geometric-shaped flints.

Italy on the one flank and Britain on the other flank of the Franco-Iberian region had a somewhat reduced development of the Late Palaeolithic cultures; those in Britain have been and are being studied in much detail by Leslie Armstrong. In lands beyond the regions hitherto discussed in this section, the Late Palaeolithic cultures were nearly everywhere delayed and often appeared in an impoverished form. Practically everywhere within and without these regions there ultimately spread the fashion of using very small flakes or chips of geometrical form.

When these become almost the sole implements one calls the culture Tardenoisian, after La Fère-en-Tardenois in France. We shall discuss this further in the section devoted to the aftermath of the Old Stone Age.

In Kenya, Leakey found obsidian flake tools in cave deposits that, he thought, betoken high lake-levels, and therefore, in his very tentative view, a pluvial period to be set beside the Würm Ice Age, but so many changes have occurred in the Kenya Rift Valley that correlations are uncertain. The tools have resemblances to those of the Aurignacian and the Capsian cultures, but, in Kenya, are accompanied by pottery after the early phases. Huzayyin has found, and Miss Caton-Thompson has confirmed his conclusions, a somewhat analogous culture with obsidian flake tools in south Arabia, but there they found it accompanying pottery of the last millennium b.c. It is evident that typology must be used with reserve in dating cultures. Arguments linking typology and date become even more difficult when we consider South Africa, but research there is progressing so fast that we should soon learn a great deal.

Painting, engraving, and sculpture

The increase of initiative and variety noted above in studying implements is still more in evidence in the domain of art, in carving and rubbing, plastic modelling, engraving, and painting. About ten statuettes of women are known from Moravia, a few from Germany, eight from south Russia, and about twenty from Siberia, mostly carved in ivory; well over a dozen have been listed from southern France, and one from Italy. At Laussel, in southern France, six figures of women had been engraved on a limestone block, and at Les Combarelles both men and women are represented, as well as men in animal masks. These carvings and figures of females are mostly stout in body and hips, often have the breasts large, and are shown as being pregnant.

One engraving of this period from England may represent a man. At Vestoniče, in Czechoslovakia, Absolon has found a culture with fine bone tools, harpoons, bodkins, bone spears with a groove for the blood to run down, and bone spoons previously thought to be a Neolithic invention. Some of the implements are marked with notches that imply numeration in fives. Like the

FIG. 18.   Girl's head, in ivory, Brassempouy,
Landes, south-west France.

French artists of the Tuc d'Audoubert cave, these Moravians modelled in soft material—pulverized burnt mammoth bone mixed with fine loam. They made caricature faces, whether for amusement or because of a fear of portraying a perfect representation, a psychological fact of widespread importance. This makes all the more remarkable a wonderful little ivory modelling of a refined and expressive face that Keith and others believe is female.

Breuil has examined a very fine series of cave paintings apparently of Aurignacian age, including notable heads of cattle, at Lascaux in the Dordogne Department of France (Fig. 15). A Solutrean station at Le Roc, Charente, has yielded engraved animal figures perhaps by Aurignacian artists; but the Solutreans were not interested in artistic efforts of this kind.

In the Magdalenian period we find that representations of human figures in France and northern Spain become rare, carvings

Fig. 19. Painting of galloping boar, Altamira Cave, northern Spain.

Fig. 20. *Bos primigenius*, Les Combarelles.

and engravings of animals improve, and paintings on cave-walls become the chief feature of the art of the time. The paintings often represent a hunted animal, but at Font de

Fig. 21. *Bos primigenius*. Bull from Lascaux Cave. A three-branched rod in front of the bull probably has symbolic meaning.

Gaume we have the male reindeer approaching his mate, while at Tuc d'Audoubert, in the Pyrenees, are clay models of a male bison following a female. In the Trois Frères cave nearby, at the back of an outlook spot, is painted a male human figure disguised in an animal's skin (see p. 37). The finest of all Magdalenian collections of cave-paintings is that at Altamira in northern

Spain. Painted cave-walls are often in dark recesses, and remains of stone lamps have been found. The paintings include conventional signs, some of which may be records, while others, found in many places, are thought by Breuil to be representations of the 'tents' the people inhabited in summer; some show pitfalls. Magical value, as well as artists' joy, may attach itself

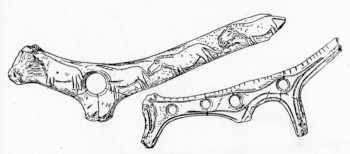

Fig. 22. Decorated and perforated objects in reindeer horn (Magdalenian), called by archaeologists *Batons de commandement* (much reduced).

to these portrayals, and it is hard to think of the figure of the look-out at Les Trois Frères as other than the representation of some shaman who used that point of vantage. The pigments which survive are ochre, either red from hematite ores or yellow from limonite, and black from manganese dioxide or burnt bone, the colours being mixed with grease. We do not know whether some of the plastic or carved figures were originally painted, but a little red ochre has been found on statuettes. Red ochre probably had the magical quality of simulating blood-colour. Sometimes the artist would use a convention, as when he gave the idea of a herd by a large series of horns, but drew bodies only for a few beasts at each end. Some early figures show only two of an animal's four legs, but, later on, the four are shown with some perspective; also the surface on which the animal has been painted may have been shaped to suggest the form of the body. Sometimes, the whole body is filled in with fine lines, sometimes tints are graded to give an idea of relief.

Representations of hands on walls are a special feature of this art, and, apparently, in some cases, a hand was dipped in colour-

FIG. 23. Rock painting (dark red) of archer, Cueva Saltadora, Spain.

ing matter and then pressed against the wall. Often the hand suggests finger-joints cut off, a practice that survives among Australian aboriginal women.

In eastern and southern Spain, rock shelters or surfaces half exposed to daylight show many paintings probably preserved for us by the dryness of the climate. Here there is marked conventionalization as contrasted with the naturalism of many of the cave-paintings in northern Spain and southern France. The pictures include many scenes and human figures (Fig. 25), perhaps a majority of males, climbing a tree for honey, shooting a stag with bow and arrow, and fighting; also, the group of skirted women dancing round a naked youth already mentioned. Size is obviously used for emphasis; sometimes legs are long and thin lines, so placed as to suggest speed; sometimes they are made very thick as though to suggest power, and here one may recall

FIG. 24. Rock paintings, South Africa (after Breuil).

the multiplicity of arms used as a convention in Indian art for this last purpose. Paintings analogous with those of eastern Spain are known from various parts of Africa (Fig. 23), where some of them date from Neolithic and later periods down to the present century in the cases of a few of the efforts by Bushmen of south-west Africa. South Africa also has engravings on stone, often more naturalistic than the paintings, and sometimes showing the widespread taboo against perfect representation; one elephant, for example, is shown with the hind legs of a rhinoceros. The South African provinces of engravings, often naturalistic, and paintings, usually conventionalized, are relatively distinct, as van Riet Lowe has shown. The former are found for the most part nearer the coasts, and the latter more on the high veldt and the Kalahari, but there are overlaps near the Orange River, and west of the Vaal and elsewhere. There is no doubt that the arts of South Africa, rock painting and stone engraving, were begun by peoples with cultures related to those of the later part of the Old Stone Age in North Africa and Spain, and van Riet Lowe thinks that engraving was introduced into South Africa along the west, and rock painting along the east, side of the high plateau in Rhodesia.

The separateness of artistic styles in both South Africa and Europe is a feature of special interest. While we may be sure that the naturalistic cave-paintings of Europe were all made in the late Old Stone Age, which came to an end in France as the climate grew milder and the spread of forests drove men to the shore and to some river banks, we cannot say how long the east Spanish and African arts may have persisted in various places, nor indeed how long a mode of life of the late Old Stone Age may not have continued. In the case of the Bushmen of South Africa it has lasted, with modification, to modern times.

Addendum to Chapter 2

All the remains of man from the later or Upper Palaeolithic period and subsequent times belong to *homo sapiens*, that is, to the same broad group as modern man. Perhaps some types in eastern Asia may carry a little of the *Sinanthropus* inheritance and some from Europe a little of the characters of Neandertal-like men but the resemblances between them all are over-

FIG. 25. Bushman drawing, Hermon, South Africa. Kaffirs pursuing cattle stolen by Bushmen.

whelmingly important whatever the contrasts of skin colour, face, nose, and head-form and blood characteristics.

Nevertheless, diversities have existed from very early times, so far as we can judge from skeletons, and the circumstances of early men were such as would be likely to promote diversity. Early men were not very numerous and, so long as they depended on hunting and collecting, they must live in small and widely scattered groups. Fifty persons of all ages and both sexes would often rank as rather a dangerously large group from the point of view of food-supply. This implies the probability of a great deal of close inbreeding, and close inbreeding is held to tend to limit fertility, so babies might not be very numerous; and, in any case, infant mortality would be very high and expectation of life even for those who survived infancy would not be very long.

In a small inbred group, variations occurring spontaneously might often be doubled as inheritances from both parents, and a rapid succession of generations would promote their accumulation, so natural selection of any valuable variation would work fairly quickly. And natural selection would work especially in connexion with growth, all the more in view of the high mortality rate of juveniles. It is probable that changes in the growth-process account for many of the diversities among mankind. These changes have apparently included important reductions affecting the lower jaw and its musculature as well as the attachment of that musculature to the skull (upper surface of brow ridges, &c.). In Chapter 1 the hypothesis of the existence of a type near *sapiens* in the Lower and Middle Pleistocene periods was shown to be supported by the evidence of the skull fragments from Swanscombe, Kent, and from Fontéchevade in western France. But very little can be inferred from these broken portions of crania. It is in the later Pleistocene that we get evidence on which it is possible to argue a little farther, while, during the Middle Pleistocene, we have indications, so far, chiefly of Neandertal types rather than *sapiens*, save that some specimens from Mt. Carmel may be interpreted as intermediate between *homo Neandertalensis* and *homo sapiens*. From the Upper Pleistocene period of western France Cro Magnon has yielded remains of two men and one woman of the early part of the period (Aurignacian), and Combe Capelle (also Aurignacian) has yielded remains of one man differing quite considerably from the Cro Magnon specimens.

The Combe Capelle skull is relatively higher in the vault, which has a median ridge. The maximum height of the skull from the anterior margin of the *foramen magnum* to the point at the vertex known as the bregma (i.e. the basi-bregmatic height) is greater than the maximum width of the skull. It has a supra-orbital ridge over each eye fairly marked as a forward projection from the base of the forehead, whereas the best preserved specimen from Cro Magnon has none, and the second male specimen only an indication. The female Cro Magnon specimen lacks it completely. The basi-bregmatic height of the best Cro Magnon specimen is estimated at between 132 and 140, while the maximum breadth of the skull is about 149–52 millimetres, i.e. the height is much less than the maximum breadth. The corresponding figures for the Combe Capelle skull are respectively 137 and 134, but the latter figure is subject to some doubt.

The face in the Cro Magnon specimens is short and broad, with very powerful cheek bones. In spite of broad cheek bones the Combe Capelle specimen, on the other hand, has a long face. Its nose is relatively a good deal broader than that of the Cro Magnon men, who also have a stronger chin.

The maximum breadth of the best Cro Magnon skull is estimated at 73·7 to 74·8 per cent. of its maximum length. This ratio is the cranial index. In the Combe Capelle skull this ratio has been estimated at about 67 and in all probability is well below 70. The best Cro Magnon specimen's stature was 1,800 mm., that of Combe Capelle man only 1,550 mm. Grimaldi (Grotte des Enfants) on the French Riviera has yielded four skulls, of which two belong to a very early phase of the Upper Pleistocene. They are the remains of an old woman and a teen-aged lad, so neither of them shows supra-orbital ridges, features rarely found in *homo sapiens* save in full-grown males. Their cranial indices are below 70, noses are broad, and chins weak; the median ridge of the skull is strongly marked and the height probably greater than the maximum breadth. So, while these two skulls have distinctive features, they are on the whole more like Combe Capelle than like Cro Magnon.

On the other hand, the male skeleton found at a higher level in the Grotte des Enfants comes rather nearer to Cro Magnon than to Combe Capelle. The same may probably be said of the female skeleton of the upper level in the same cave. The man was very tall, probably 1,890 mm. (6 ft. 2½ in.).

The Barma Grande Cave at Grimaldi has yielded five skeletons. Two of them show an interesting combination of the high-ridged skull of the Combe Capelle skeleton with some, at least, of the facial characteristics of Cro Magnon man. A third one has suffered much posthumous deformation. The other two are nearer the Combe Capelle type on the whole.

The difference between the Cro Magnon and Combe Capelle men seems partly related to the attachment of the jaw muscles to the skull, more at the sides in the former and rather more above the brow ridges in the latter.

The interesting fact about this is that something near the Combe Capelle type is widespread among modern peoples in certain regions, as will be stated in more detail later in this chapter. Claims have been made that something near the Cro Magnon type survives in a few localities; this will also be mentioned later. Other types will also be discussed, always subject to the reserve that numbers of specimens are small and further discoveries may force revision. At the same time, resemblances between the Combe Capelle type and some large modern samples do in some measure justify the use of the Combe Capelle specimen as a type, apparently distinct to a considerable degree from the Cro Magnon type.

Before proceeding to discuss other types from the Aurignacian phase of the late Old Stone Age it is worth while to refer to some remains from other, later, phases of that period. To the Aurignacian or Solutrean phase belong two male crania from Brno (Brünn), Czechoslovakia. They are high-ridged, very long and narrow, and have strong brow ridges, so may be considered allied to the Combe Capelle specimen. A cranium from Brüx (Czechoslovakia) may be of the same general type but its condition makes it questionable. A high and very narrow male skull from Pschedmost (Czechoslovakia) with strong brow ridges seems, again, of the same general type. A female skull lacks brow ridges, but is high; it is naturally shorter than that of a man, so not so narrow, relatively. A boy's skull from Pschedmost, on the other hand, seems more like the Cro Magnon specimen. The Pschedmost skeletons are considered to be Solutrean. One specimen from Lautsch (Czechoslovakia) is much like the Combe Capelle type, but two others with strong brow ridges seem to have low heads. They also are dated as Solutrean, but one of the Lautsch specimens may be Magdalenian. From the Magdalenian we have something near the Combe Capelle type in a male skull found at Laugerie Basse (France), but something nearer the Cro Magnon in a skull from La Faye Bruniquel (France). The Chancelade (France) skeleton has some resemblances to that of Combe Capelle but has a very narrow nose and is in some respects rather distinct; it has been compared to a modern Greenland Eskimo. Two skulls from Sorde (France) may perhaps not differ much

from the Cro Magnon type as far as the few available details are
a guide.

Two skeletons from Obercassel, near Bonn, German Rhineland, have high-ridged heads and well-marked brow ridges
(less in the female than in the male), but they have the face
short and broad and the stature is low. In these cases, as in the
two from the upper layers of Barma Grande, discussed above,
we seem to have a combination of Cro Magnon and Combe
Capelle characteristics. It is not useful to speculate whether such
a combination is due to mixture or whether the diversities of the
two types provisionally distinguished are the result of differentiation from a common stock allied to specimens from Barma
Grande and Obercassel. The probabilities seem in favour of the
first alternative, but more specimens are needed.

Solutré (Burgundy, France) has yielded a number of specimens
several of which seem not to be inclusible in either of the two
types so far discussed.

In a layer which has been described as Aurignacian, remains of
three men and two women have been found. The head is high
and the face longish in two, but broad and short in two (no data
for the fifth). Here, however, the maximum cranial breadth is
77·9–79·3 per cent. of the maximum cranial length in the three
men, and 77·7 and 83·2 respectively in the two women. The
latter of the women may be of rather later date. Another layer
at Solutré, of uncertain date but almost certainly belonging to
some part of the Upper Pleistocene later than the Aurignacian,
has yielded skulls of eight males and two females from which
measurements could be taken, besides a number of fragments of
others. One male with narrow long head has the head height
considerably less than the maximum breadth and in this respect
agrees with the Cro Magnon specimen, but here the orbit is
higher and less broad. Three males with narrow long heads have
the head height nearly equal to or more than the maximum

breadth and in two cases the brows are prominent. The orbits are rather narrow and in one case distinctly low. On the whole these three may be thought of as analogous in some ways with Combe Capelle man. Four males have the maximum breadth of the skull 79–83·2 per cent. of the maximum length, i.e. are relatively short-headed like some of the Aurignacian skulls from this site.

Oundory, on the Volga in Russia, has yielded two very narrow skulls with strong supra-orbital ridges and retreating foreheads, and Pavlov compared these to the Combe Capelle skull. One is very small but presumably an adult female.

The skeleton of the tall, broad-nosed, narrow-headed man from Asselar (Sahara) might be that of a progenitor of many Bantu. On the other hand the skeletons from Oldoway (Tanganyika) and from Elmenteita (Kenya), though also tall and narrow-headed, are very narrow-nosed. The Boskop skull from South Africa is very long-headed and very large, and skulls from Fish Hoek near Capetown have been thought to be related. A skull from Florisbad is again large but has marked eye-brow ridges and low orbits. All these African skulls are provisionally assigned to the later Palaeolithic. Comparable in date are the skulls of long-headed men from the upper layers of the Chou Kou Tien cave near Peking.

Two skulls from Wadjak (Java) undoubtedly belonging to *homo sapiens* are large, with strong brow ridges and receding foreheads. Two male skulls from Cohuna (Australia) also have strong brow ridges and receding foreheads, very thick skull-cap and long narrow head. A skull from Talgai (Australia) is probably not so old. Possible late Pleistocene skeletons from America include one from Folsom (New Mexico), two from Minnesota and one from the valley of Mexico (Tepexpan). Some of these, including the Tepexpan skull, have had their age estimated by the radio-carbon (C. 14) method mentioned in chapter 5.

From what is thought to be the aftermath of the Old Stone Age a nest of skulls has been found at Ofnet, Bavaria, and data can be gathered from about fourteen adult skulls, of which ten are female and four are male. Two of the men and one of the women have long narrow heads but short broad faces, thus approaching the Obercassel and two Barma Grande specimens in this respect, one of the men has strong supra-orbital brow ridges. The other two men have the maximum breadth of the skull 78·6–78·7 per cent. of the maximum length; and among the nine remaining women this percentage ranges up from 75·7 to 88·9. In all save one the cranial height is considerably less than the maximum breadth. Five of these nine women have broad faces. On the whole the Ofnet group may be compared with the specimens from Solutré.

Furfooz in Belgium, Nagy Sap in Hungary, Mugem in Portugal, Val de Areiro, Romanelli, and Olmo in Italy have yielded skulls which in general come near the Solutré group, save that one of the Mugem skulls (of a woman) is narrow with low orbits and projecting mouth, i.e. may be compared with the Combe Capelle group, most perhaps with the woman from the lower layer at the Grotte des Enfants. On the whole, therefore, the periphery of the Alpine area, apart from the Riviera, gives late Old Stone Age skulls with cranial indices in most cases high medium or indicating quite broad heads, whereas those from western France and the Riviera are for the most part long-headed, some suggesting parallels with the Cro Magnon and others with the Combe Capelle specimen.

There are several British skulls of the Upper Pleistocene or of the aftermath of the Old Stone Age, though most of these cannot be closely dated. A very narrow, long, high-ridged skull from Cheddar and one from Baker's Hole with strong brow ridges are considered Upper Pleistocene. A skull from Langwith, again long, narrow, high and with strong brow ridges, was long considered doubtful in date, but Leslie Armstrong has recently found a female skull of this general type in clearly Upper Pleistocene deposits at Cresswell, near by. This may reasonably be held to support the hypothesis of an Upper Pleistocene date for the Langwith specimen. The Halling skull, Upper Pleistocene, is, again, high, but not as narrow as the others just mentioned. A narrow, high skull (male) from Cissbury may be mentioned here; it may be Upper Pleistocene, or may date from the aftermath of the Old Stone Age. To the latter period belong two male skulls from Aveline's Hole in the Mendips; they are narrow and rather high. The same cave has also yielded one male and one female skull of broader type, with measurements more like those of the Solutré skulls. To the same period, broadly considered, also belong three skulls from the Macarthur Cave at Oban. Two of these are juvenile, one nearly full-grown. The third skull is of an adult male, very long, narrow, and high with strong brow ridges.

Broadly, therefore, finds in Britain tend to emphasize the importance of the Combe Capelle type in the physical heritage of Britain. Still, at the present day, long-headedness is very widespread in the British Isles, with some nests of extreme forms (cranial indices often below 73) in remote areas with old-established populations that export youth, and, to a considerable extent, inbreed.

But many other regions also have the extreme long-headed element with fairly marked brow ridges, rather broad noses and cheek bones, and prominent mouths. Claims have been made for its identification in the Dordogne, France, sixty years ago by Collignon, who also thought he found the Cro Magnon type there. In Tras os Montes, north-east Portugal, it was described by Costa da Ferreira, and in Sardinia Dr. Duckworth found it in numbers. It appears to be a feature of the people of some oases of North Africa and the Sahara, but satisfactory details are not available. Broom noted its importance among the Korana in South Africa. Mrs. Milward[1] made a special study of it from a sculptor's point of view among several forest peoples of India. The large collection of Australian skulls at Washington, U.S.A., catalogued by Dr. Hrdlička, shows a very large proportion of this extreme long-headed, high-headed type with brows well marked in the males and teeth large and mouth prominent. It is known among the Ainu, the non-Mongolian population of northern Japan. It is numerous among the Greenland Eskimo, and the Botocudo of east Brazil, and it occurs in the Fuegian remnants. There are a good many instances of it among collections of skulls from various parts of America, from pre-Columbian peoples.

That, in the various regions, it is combined with diverse types of skin colour and almost all varieties of hair suggests that inheritance of skull form does not necessarily go with inheritance of skin colour or hair type, and that therefore current race classifications among mankind have only very moderate genetic value.

The occurrence of the type in South Africa, Australia, parts of the New World at the far ends of lines of drift from the main entry, namely the Bering Sea and the Aleutians, and remote spots in west Europe suggests that it is an ancient type with characteristic discontinuous and peripheral distribution.

The skulls from Solutré, Ofnet, &c., including several with cranial indices over 78 and even well over 80, compare interestingly with the broad heads characteristic at the present day for most areas among and around the Alps.

The shovel-shaped incisor teeth of some of the *Sinanthropus* specimens from Chou Kou Tien are paralleled among modern Chinese here and there, and this suggests that the *Sinanthropus* hominids may have contributed something to the physical

[1] Milward, Marguerite, *Artist in unknown India*, London, 1948.

heritage of modern Orientals, much as the Neandertal hominids may have contributed to European man.

More data are much needed, but there is at least a probability that physical heritages of modern men can be traced from the Old Stone Age, at least in some regions.

3093 10

F

3

The Aftermath of the Old Stone Age

DURING the Old Stone Age hunting had been added to collecting as a mode of life; the great advance that was still to come was the evolution of cultivation. As some of the early students of ancient man inferred, the hey-day of the hunter-collectors, in Europe and Africa at any rate, was followed by a phase of decline in face of changed conditions; so, during what seem to have been thousands of years, there were groups lingering on in their old home regions or moving out to far-off places, while some learned to use the drier parts of the forests, and towards the latter part of this phase other groups were learning the art of cultivation, eventually to spread far and wide as the second great revolution in human affairs.

The retreat of the ice sheets in the Alps and northern Europe, and no doubt on some of the ranges of central Asia as well, brought a rise of summer temperatures and liberated vast amounts of water that had been locked up as ice; but, until the ice sheets had shrunk a great deal, winter cold still remained a dominant factor. Sea winds brought rain to western Europe, and cyclones spread inwards from the ocean, whereas they had previously been kept out by the mass of dense cold air overlying the ice. Those cyclones had previously penetrated farther south, into the Mediterranean and northern Africa with a little winter rain shed, on their southern flanks, over the western Sahara. The new conditions increased the aridity of the Sahara and North Africa and drove its peoples northwards or southwards or to the Nile; the same changes may have driven the population of north Arabia towards Syria on the one side and the Mesopotamian foothills on the other. The Nile and Euphrates and, probably, some neighbouring areas were, long afterwards, to become prime homes, perhaps the prime homes, of the arts of cereal cultivation, but for many a century they were utilized as hunting-collecting grounds of modest value. Swampy flood plains provided retreats for a certain number of animals that could be hunted, and plants gave some food; but, if we reflect upon the narrowness and the small areas of these riverine regions, we shall appreciate that neither could they support large herds of wild buck, nor could they have had more than small populations, probably a few thousands at most. Those hunter-collectors lived for the most part, it is thought, on the borders of the flood plains and we may speculate as to their women gradually learning to take care of plants which would yield them grain and so venturing on to the flood plain when the rivers had fallen. It was only later on, when men added to cultivation the art of managing the flood plain, that this great advance in mode of life gathered real momentum. That aspect of the story will be the subject of succeeding chapters; here we are considering mainly what is known concerning regions in which the change from hunting and collecting to main dependence on cultivation came only much later and as an introduction from one of its early homes.

In Europe the ice sheet may have begun its retreat from south Sweden about 12000 or 11000 B.C., but it had barely reached the stage at which it was reduced to two masses, on the northern and the south-western Scandinavian heights respectively, by 7000 B.C. according to calculations by Liden, following de Geer, based on observations of annual layers of mud, or varves, deposited from the water running out of the melting ice-edge in summer. This change of climate with the retreat of the ice sheets might seem to favour man, but at first that was not the case. The summers seem to have become fairly warm, reaching perhaps above 10° C. mean temperature for the warmest month in the south-west Baltic, but the winters were still cold and the typical vegetation was pines and firs, with birch and willow. Scandinavia was rising slowly after losing its load of ice, and this gradually converted the Baltic Sea of the Yoldia phase, during which it connected with the open ocean, into a fresh-water lake (Ancylus phase) for a time. Later on, with increased melting of ice, the sea gained on the land, the water connexion between the Baltic and North Seas was re-established and spread across the Swedish lake-belt, and we get the warm temperate Atlantic phase, including a number of *Litorina* phases of the Baltic, so called because they were warm enough for *Litorina* (the periwinkle) to prosper there. Summer temperatures must have been rather higher than those of modern times, as Praeger in Ireland first showed. It was the spread of forest that was at first unfriendly to man. He might find food along the sea-shores or from rivers and lakes; and cliffs might furnish him with cave-shelters, especially for the winter. He might, alternatively, use hill-brows above the forest and thence raid the forest edge for food. But, for a while, he seems to have been unable to do much with the forest itself; a pine forest can be a place of darkness and difficulty with very little undergrowth which might yield food. The vicinity of the ice would have abundant water in summer and might develop much herbage, thus attracting animals and their hunters, and we get hints here and there of seasonal movements. Schwantes found, at Duvensee in north Germany, a succession of floors, partly sanded over for use as hearths, partly lined with bark. This allows the inference that the place was visited again and again, probably in summer seasons.

Clark argues that, in the Late Palaeolithic period and its aftermath, light structures of a tent-like character must have been in use in summer; and either earth-houses, half subterranean no doubt, or caves were used in winter. Students of folk-lore will appreciate here a basis for the interpretation of disappearances of the fairies into a hole in the ground, and of fairyland as a land below the earth whence comes strange music. The souterrains of the Iron Age should also be remembered here. There are numerous modern instances in the north-east of Siberia and the north of North America of seasonal change of habitat from tents to earth or stone or snow houses. Timber-framed earth-houses may well have led their builders on to brick on the one hand, and to the precursors of our medieval timber with lath and plaster filling on the other.

In eastern and northern Spain, the hunters who used very small flints and made drawings in rock shelters apparently lived on, and people accumulating shell-mounds and using small flints occupied sites in Portugal. On the coast of the Asturias in northern Spain, and in some caves in southern France, is found a culture called the Azilian. The people concerned used very small flints and also scrapers. They also used antlers for implements, shaping them into barbed points sometimes called harpoons. Some of these implements have a hole bored through them. In certain French caves, especially the Mas d'Azil, whence the culture is named, are found pebbles with signs painted on them that even have been thought to be alphabetic; a few of these have been collected in northern Spain, and probably many have had the colouring washed away in the damp climate. The Azilian inhabitants of the Asturias coast collected and ate molluscs, among which the periwinkle, *Litorina litorea*, was very abundant, indicating cool conditions as compared with those of later times for this latitude. It should be carefully noted that the occurrence of *Litorina litorea* in the Baltic implies, on the other hand, a phase or rather phases of maritime conditions during a relatively warm period for that much higher latitude. Stations ascribed to the Azilian culture on the strength of so-called harpoons have been described from the Victoria cave at Settle in Yorkshire, and Macarthur's cave near Oban, as well as from Bobach in the department of Drôme in France and

FIG. 26. Azilian harpoons.

FIG. 27. Painted pebbles, Azilian.

Birseck near Basel in Switzerland, both the latter with painted pebbles. Harpoons and scrapers and minute flakes occur at several other places in central Europe, but cannot be too certainly assigned to the Azilian culture.

Before we deal with other regions, however, we must refer to a later cultural development in northern Spain known by the name of Asturian. Its remains in several places overlie those of the Azilian culture, so it is later, but it has been studied for the most part farther west. It probably spread over northern Spain and southern France. It does not seem to be a lineal descendant of the Azilian. The flint tools are poor, and none are of the very small type of most of those of the Azilian culture noted above or the Tardenoisian to be discussed below; but some pebbles were chipped to make coarse points, one end being left untouched for holding. Obermaier thinks these points were used in knocking limpets off the rocks. These molluscs formed a considerable part of the people's food, and another sea-snail, *Trochus lineatus*, was also collected. This indicates warmer conditions than does the *Litorina litorea* of the Azilian culture. A few implements of bone and antler are known. It is likely that the Azilian phase in Spain, with its cool conditions, corresponds broadly with the cold period of the Yoldia sea in north Europe and that the Asturian phase came considerably later, perhaps when the *Litorina* sea was being developed in the north. The earlier may date from even as far back as 8000 B.C., the later from even as far forward as 4000 B.C. Neither can really be dated; the only purpose in giving these possible limits is to show what a long period is covered by the aftermath of the Old Stone Age.

On various hill-brows in France and central Europe one finds numbers of worked flints, and, if these are all very small, the culture is called Tardenoisian from La-Fère-en-Tardenois, in France. If flattish horn weapons, so-called harpoons, occur, the culture is said to be Azilio-Tardenoisian. In Britain the little

Tardenoisian flints occur at many places near or over the 1,000 ft. limit on the Pennines, for which Buckley has described at Badgerslacks what seems to be a little group of shelters probably hollowed out, covered with branches and used in summer. At Cresswell, Tardenoisian men lived in the caves. This culture, characterized by its very small flints, is also widespread on sandy areas on the Continent, and it spread slowly northward. A curious fact is that, while there are many Tardenoisian sites on sandy moraines and the like in Poland, there are few on the loess, though it is often said that the latter had little dense wet forest. It is probable that, in a fairly early post-glacial phase, the loess zone had a good deal of woodland, but when, later on, this was cut by man, after the 'Atlantic' phase of climate was over, it did not regrow easily beyond a bushy stage.

It seems that the people concerned were hunters and that their occupation of sites which were useless for cultivation allowed them to persist even after that art had been introduced. The risk in dating finds from their type is therefore peculiarly great in this case. Pigmy flints are a feature of Indian archaeology and an indication to us that this culture, having its province for the most part to the south of the region of the Maglemose-Mullerup-Ertebölle cultures of north-west Europe, extended its influence eastward in warm countries. The 'Wilton' industries in Africa indicate another widespread extension, southward through the east of that continent.

Another culture, found widely on the European plain and described especially by Schwantes, also has flint flakes as its typical tools. The most distinctive form here is the tanged point, possibly inherited from the Font Robert point of the Upper Palaeolithic Age, perhaps a parallel development linked in both cases with methods of hafting. There are also small flakes of various kinds, and it is generally agreed that this culture mingled with and lost its identity in the Tardenoisian, save in

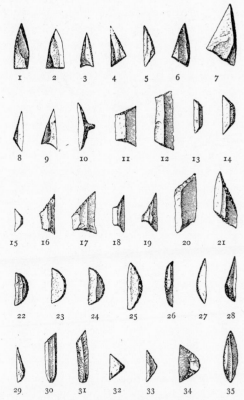

FIG. 28. Pigmy flints (½). North France (1–9), Vaucluse, south-east France (17), Meuse Valley, Belgium (11, 21, 26), Cabeço da Arruda, Portugal (18–19), Italy (10, 20), Tunis (23, 24, 35), Egypt (31), Kizil Koba, Crimea (12, 16, 30, 34), and India (13–15, 22, 25, 29, 33).

the Arctic north. The fact of this fusion suggests that the tanged point is more likely to be an inheritance than a separate invention, and it is possible that the people who made these tanged points had inherited a Palaeolithic tradition and mingled with the Tardenoisian culture in the course of time. The tanged point spread to the Arctic and was important in early culture there.

Bogs and other sites in Denmark, south Sweden, and northwest Germany have yielded reindeer antlers cut into the form of axes and adzes, which Schwantes has claimed as the oldest in the world and the forerunners of the flint axes and ultimately of the polished axes of the Neolithic period. This is to a considerable extent a speculation at present. These antler implements have been described as the Lyngby culture, but we know very little of associated work in flint.

A change supervened when the northern lands were invaded by the oak, elm, alder, and hazel, in other words when winters had mildened to a considerable extent and summers were becoming warmer, while the rise of sea-level was compensating for the rise of the northern lands, and when perhaps even a certain amount of sinking of the land was occurring around the southern periphery of Scandinavia. The borders of the forest developed a population of pigs, dogs, deer, and wild cattle, and hunting became more profitable for those who could attack the forest edges, though they would still live on dry spots in bog areas or mudflats near rivers and lakes or the sea-shore for at any rate a part of the year. The groups of people seem to have been quite small as befits the hunting life in such an environment. To deal with bushes, axes were necessary and the arming of a reindeer antler with a flint edge was a valuable device. It remains doubtful, however, whether at this early stage men could really penetrate the damp oak forest (*Quercus robur pedunculatus*). The flint edge could be sharpened from time to time by removal of a flake, and flakes seem to have been used as small cleavers,

(French: *tranchet*; German: *spalter*), but small flints, often blunted along one side as in the Tardenoisian culture, were the most numerous implements. The very small graver (micro-burin) is a feature at Duvensee. Mathiassen has described a fairly early variant of this culture from sites near various streams of Jutland, especially the Gudenaa; it developed a special form of triangular flint arrow-head. Schwantes has made ana-logous finds in Schleswig-Holstein. The Maglemose culture was generally distributed over Danish Zealand and Scania with some sites in Fünen (Fyen), Jutland, and north-west Germany and near the lower Vistula. It used small flints often blunted along one side, also axes, that is flints with the cutting edge at right angles to the main axis. Some of these last, usually fairly large, were made from cores, others, generally smaller and much less common, were made from flakes. The sites in Zealand (Den-mark) have yielded good specimens of minute flints showing most of the characters of the Tardenoisian pigmy implements and derived no doubt from the same source. Flints are known inset into bone slots; they were probably also hafted into wood, but we have no direct evidence of this. Scrapers, usually chipped on flakes, are a feature. Pebbles were sometimes used with hollows ground out of opposite faces to serve as holds for finger and thumb; and some axes have the surface ground smooth and may have a hole perforated in hour-glass fashion right through, apparently to hold a wooden handle. These are probably an adaptation, in stone, of an idea first worked out on antler. Wooden paddles have been found and it is likely that wood was extensively used.

A chipped flint core would be of little use for splitting timber as its irregularities would crush and tangle the wood fibres when it was hammered in, but an axe ground smooth could serve as a wedge. The art of grinding liberated men from dependence on the few kinds of stone (flint, chert, obsidian, rhyolite, some quartz) that could be shaped usefully by chipping, one also finds quartzite and gneiss utilized. It is still open to question whether this art of stone-grinding was not an introduction into north-west Europe from outside. It is, however, a fairly simple notion easily derivable from observation of the smoothing of a chipped implement used for digging, and its value for woodwork was so great that it might well spread from a forested region.

FIG. 29. Maglemose implements.

Antler and bone axes and other tools were often decorated with incised lines or tiny holes or pits made with a bow-drill. The decoration may give a conventionalized human body or animal form, and the whole antler may be shaped to look like an animal's head. At Mullerup and Svaerdborg and Holmgaard in Fünen a specialized late phase of this culture has yielded barbed points of bone.

The Maglemose culture extended its influence into northern France and part of the British Isles, where remains have been found at Thatcham in Berkshire, Broxbourne in Hertfordshire, Skipsea in east Yorkshire, and the Bann valley in Antrim.

Professor J. G. D. Clark has (1939) described some sites, mostly on the Lower Greensand in Surrey and Sussex and especially near the river Wey, but also on the sands of the Horsham and Ashdown areas. He uses the name 'Horsham Culture' and notes a statistical contrast between these sites and those of the more typical Maglemose culture as exemplified in England.

	Axes	Mierbliths	at
Horsham culture	22 or 2·22%	970 or 97·78%	Farnham and Selmeston
Maglemose culture	14 or 11·67%	106 or 88·33%	Broxbourne and Colne Valley

The south-eastern areas of Lower Greensand in England are just about where the Maglemose culture finds its limit over against the more southerly microlithic or Tardenoisian scheme, which, however, overlapped as far north as Cresswell and the Pennines. Horsham may well illustrate overlap.

In 1949 Clark began an examination of Star Carr, Seamer, Scarborough, Yorkshire, a Maglemosean Mesolithic site on which bog conditions gave hope of finding organic as well as stone artifacts. A flint workshop with abundant debris was found. It also yielded burins and their sharpening flakes, flakes with scraper ends, pigmy flints, a few awls, a couple of axes or adzes with transverse-sharpened edge, and one flint saw. Sandstone had been used, probably for rubbing, and various pebbles showed signs of wear. Red-deer antlers were much used, and many barbed points were made by detaching splinters with a burin. The points were probably fixed into a wooden haft. Other worked portions of antlers were also found, but bone, though abundantly present was apparently little used, a curious fact as on many sites of this culture-phase bone is found as material for many tools. Many rolls of birch bark were collected, and Clark thinks they were stored for use in making containers for water, &c., before the development of the potter's craft. Birch-wood floors were another feature.

By the time the connexion between the Baltic and the

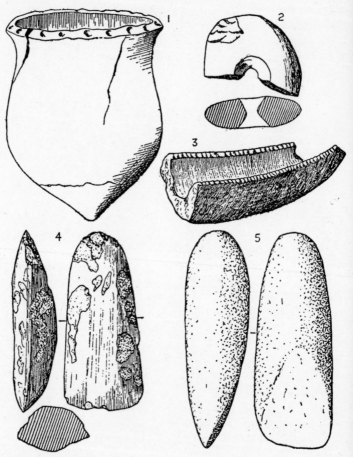

FIG. 30. Ertebölle (Mesolithic). Pottery and stone implements. 1 ($\frac{3}{16}$), 2 and 3 ($\frac{9}{32}$), 4 ($\frac{3}{8}$), 5 ($\frac{9}{16}$).

Skagerrak, across the Swedish lakes, had developed to its fullest extent the climate was apparently warm and wet, the pine-birch forests gave place to those of oak, elm, hazel, and alder, and even the beech began to appear. This was the 'Atlantic' phase and it may have had its best development about 4000 B.C. The culture of this phase obviously lingered on side by side with the more complex cultures involving agriculture that probably came into north-west Europe in the third millennium B.C. It is difficult in most cases to decide whether the finds that seem to belong to this Atlantic phase of climate may not indicate borrowings or imperfect adaptations from those more highly equipped cultures. The sites of this late, or Ertebölle (Fig. 30), phase of the Maglemose culture sequence are mostly near the shore and often have shell-middens. A pot with pointed bottom, from Ertebölle, is well known, and may illustrate the penetration of ideas from outside into the old modes of life, then still lingering on much as do lowly modes of life among aboriginal Australians and other people today; it may, however, be a purely local development.

It is indeed a notable fact that, while lowly peoples of the present day may have taken up items of equipment they have seen in use among groups with more complex cultures, they rarely seem able of themselves to step right over the gap between the hunting-collecting life and a life based on food production by cultivation. Aboriginal Australians will chip a European glass bottle into pointed implements; and on various ancient sites one finds an occasional fragment of a polished axe which has subsequently been chipped. Estyn Evans has shown, also, that megalith builders on the higher lands and hunting-fishing-collecting peoples on the coast were contemporary in Northern Ireland.

Mathiassen has shown that, while at Havnelev one gets querns, impressions of (probably) emmer, bread-wheat and barley, thin-butted axes, sherds of collared flasks, many beakers, bones of cattle, sheep, and pigs, &c., all indicating food production by cultivation and stock-farming, at Strandegaard there was no evidence of cultivation, though a few beaker fragments were found; yet there could be little doubt that Havnelev and Strandegaard, both in south Zealand (Denmark), were contemporary.

There are so many recent and modern instances of the disappearance of an introduced element of culture that we shall not be far wrong if we think of the ancient hunter-collectors side by side with the more advanced schemes of life, picking up a half-understood idea here and there, perhaps cherishing it for a while, but often forgetting it, and in most cases omitting to fit it into the scheme of life. Hunter-collectors lingering beside cultivators or commercial folk at the present day tend to forget what some among them may have learnt. But this is only a part of the story; some of the hunter-collectors become mixed up with the better-equipped folk as domestic drudges or concubines bearing half-caste children. We must not therefore picture the complete dying out of the hunter-collectors; there may be half-caste descendants of them among many societies of better-equipped peoples.

The aftermath of the Old Stone Age was a very long one. It was ultimately brought to an end by the spread of the idea of cultivation of cereals from south-west Asia and north-east Africa, followed by diverse features of agricultural civilization, some of which tended to travel faster, others more slowly. Somewhere in northern Eurasia the men of the aftermath of the Old Stone Age found a species of animal which died out as a wild beast but became man's first helper—the dog.

Finds giving clues to the early inhabitants of central and northern Asia have not yet been very adequately studied. Near Krasnoyarsk under a layer of loess was found a quantity of flakes, many with one edge blunted, a few pigmy flints, and numerous round scrapers, also objects in bone and ivory and one in deer antler with scratches made on it and a hole bored through it. So-called harpoons of reindeer antler are found and have barbs; there are also laurel-leaf implements recalling those of the Solutrean of the west. Many Siberian kitchen-middens have been described, especially on dunes; they show that their men had the domesticated dog. Axe types in quartzite, roughly chipped, are known from the Minussinsk area where they occur along with clumsy flakes. The Siberian finds generally may be a mixture of objects characteristic for the Middle and Late Palaeolithic period with the pigmy flints and points having blunted sides that we have seen are a notable feature of the aftermath of the Old Stone Age.

If Milankovitch has been right in ascribing climatic oscillations in a considerable measure to changes in potential solar irradiation in particular latitudes, i.e. if warmth in north-west Europe makes it probable that there was relative warmth at the same time in corresponding latitudes in north-east Asia and North America, a further argument is opened up. The way over to north-west America from north-east Asia may have been much less difficult in the phase of post-glacial warmth perhaps 5000 B.C. onwards for two or three millennia than it is now. And, as glaciers and ice sheets were melting fast, there was water in the rivers in many parts of inner Asia that are now barren, so man's movements to north-east Asia would be made easier. It is during this aftermath period as well as before it, during some late interlude in the glacial series, that we think some of the the early drifts of man to America occurred.

PART II

REGIONAL CULTURAL EVOLUTION

4

South-West Asia

OF beginnings of cultivation one can speak only in terms of possibilities. Seeds or fruits thrown on a heap of organic refuse or over a buried corpse, would be likely to grow well. Some peoples who do not cultivate have been known to clear a little space round about a plant that they knew would yield food later on. Plants may give food from enlarged storage roots, or from pith or leaves, seeds, fruits, or buds and shoots. Of all these the most important have been and are still the seeds of cereals, mostly of the grass family. The cereal plants include wheat, barley, the various millets, rye, oats, rice, and maize.

Maize is the New World cereal, the origin of which has been and is still under discussion. It could be effectively cultivated without the plough and the New World lacked plough animals.

Rice was cultivated in China north of the Yangtse early in the second millennium B.C. and it is thought to have been linked with the culture that made chisel-shaped stone axes with rectangular cross-section. This type of axe is very important in Further India and penetrated westwards to Assam, the Santal Parganas, and Chota Nagpur, probably in the second millennium B.C. Possibly, therefore, rice cultivation spread from Further India or even south China to India, but an Indian origin for rice cannot quite be ruled out. Rye and oats came into use in the early Iron Age in Europe, and seem late additions to cultivation. Millets were grown in early north China and are evidently old-established in central India and what used to be the United Provinces, also in the central Deccan, but we have at present no

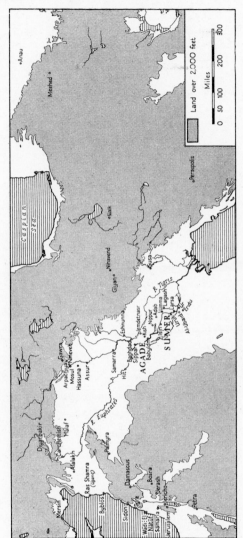

FIG. 31. South-west Asia in antiquity.

direct prehistoric evidence from India on this matter. They are
grown on considerable areas in Egypt and to some extent in
south Arabia and Syria but are quite secondary in these regions.
They are the traditional crop (mealies) of Africa south of the
Sahara and Abyssinia. On the whole, if one is to make a hypothesis about the original home and the spread of the millets, one
may suggest that they were brought into use in south-west Asia
or Egypt along with wheat and barley and that they spread
thence long ago, but remained a secondary crop in areas suitable
for wheat, barley, or rice. In the present state of knowledge,
however, one must bear in mind the possibility of two or more
independent origins. We do not know why they are older than
other cereals in north China. Millets are able to tolerate a considerable range of seasonal variation, especially in rainfall, but
they are inferior to wheat and barley as food.

Wheat and barley are known to have grown wild in south-west
Asia, probably chiefly in the Syrian hills and in favourable spots
in the zone from Cilicia to north Persia.

Barley can grow under a wider range of climatic conditions or
seasonal variation than wheat. Wheat in earliest antiquity was of
two main types: Spelt or *Triticum monococcum* with seven haploid
chromosomes and Emmer or *T. dicoccum* with fourteen. But, in
prehistoric times, a third group of wheats appeared: the bread-
wheats, *Triticum vulgare* with twenty-one haploid chromosomes,
the result of a cross between *T. dicoccum* and some related grass.
Afghanistan, Turkestan, and the regions between Mesopotamia
and the Caucasus have been suggested as the original home
of bread-wheat. Evidence is very slight and one cannot say
more than that bread-wheat was grown in the earliest known
Anau settlement and in the region of the Indus civilization.

Even with our still scanty knowledge we can therefore
appreciate the point of view put forward during the last thirty
years by the late Harold Peake that, somewhere in Syria, or along

the zone from Mersin (in Cilicia) to Meshed (in north Persia), the great step forward from mesolithic hunting and collecting to agricultural routine was taken, probably by several more or less adjacent groups. An attempt to locate one place of origin would be unsound, and we also have at the moment little evidence to date this great change. As organized states dependent on cereal cultivation had developed by 3000 B.C. or soon afterwards, and it is known that there was a long preliminary period, it has become customary to date the beginnings of cereal cultivation before 5000 B.C. This is useful for the present, provided it is not over-emphasized.

In caves at Wadi el Natuf, Mt. Carmel, Palestine, Professor Dorothy Garrod found evidence of people with a primarily hunting equipment. But they also had implements which were flint blades fixed by gum into grooved bone, with the blades notched to give a row of teeth. These implements had the edges of the flint blades polished by use, and it is an almost certain inference that they had been used as sickles to cut grass-stalks rich in silica (to give the polishing). Some sickle handles are decorated with carved animals. Stone mortars for pounding grain, and hollows in the ground, for the same purpose, were also found. So, though we cannot be quite certain that these people of Mt. Carmel did more than harvest wild grain, it is probable that they cultivated wheat. There is no evidence of cattle, sheep, or goats, though the sites have yielded a certain amount of bones of wild animals.

Dr. Kenyon has recently (1952–3) found at Jericho a settlement of early agriculturists still without pottery, but making finely modelled heads. Agriculture without pottery is also now known from other localities in south-west Asia. The remarkable finds at Jericho are thought by Miss Kenyon to suggest even germs of urbanism, and yet they seem to be very early, perhaps not long after 5000 B.C.

Hassuna, on the west side of the Tigris not far from the later Nineveh, shows some early phases of agricultural development. The bottom layer of the mound or tell has remains of hearths and of hollows in which grain was ground with stone pestles. Stone hoes have been found with remains of bitumen that had fastened them to hafts. The contrast between Hassuna and Wadi el Natuf is threefold. The hunting implements of the latter are not paralleled at Hassuna. Hassuna, on the other hand, had cattle, sheep, and goats; and the people made pots which they ornamented with incised lines.

Sialk in Persia, east of the Zagros ranges, is another very early site of occupation by cultivators, who also kept sheep. Here, again, hearths have been found, also stone hoes, as well as pottery, but here the pottery was painted with designs in black, showing that the pots were baked in an oven, protected from the direct flames. There have also been found bones with slots cut in them for mounting toothed flints for cutting grain, and the handles of these sickles are decorated with carvings in some cases.

Jericho, Hassuna, and Sialk yield evidence of early cultivation and of some, at any rate, of the concomitant advances in equipment. The stone axes, ground smooth and with transverse edges, are to some extent a heritage from an earlier time, but were in these circumstances often used as hoes.[1] Sialk has yielded traces of some kind of shelter even in its oldest phase. Of pottery we have no evidence of initial stages in the Middle East, but clay lining of a grass basket, subsequently hardened, whether deliberately or accidentally, by fire was found twenty years ago by Leakey in a cave-layer of Late Palaeolithic culture in Kenya. With

---

[1] The smooth grinding of stone tools gave men a far freer choice of materials—basalts, jadeites, diorites, syenites, &c., so they were no longer dependent on some degree of proximity to flint or chert. They could now make a stone wedge and this improved carpentering; a long straight edge became possible and they could hollow out grooves for a leather band, or bore a hole through the stone for insertion of a handle.

the beginnings of cultivation and even temporary settlement it became possible to store grain, and, on occasion, to soak it and probably to ferment it, if a vessel was available, and the use of hardened clay accordingly expanded into the potter's art, in the hands of women. The notion of sowing seed with a view to a harvest some months later meant not only a longer stay in one place than had been characteristic for at least most hunters, it further implied acceptance of a routine with responsibilities for seasonal activity and increased foreknowledge of expected harvests. Men were beginning to 'look before and after' in a more regular way than hitherto. It was henceforth a serious fault to omit part of the seasonal routine, and the lazy member of the group would incur blame. This is therefore the stage which has been dramatized in the legend of the Fall of Man. Little as we know of it, we can, however, glimpse the pioneering activity especially of food-questing women, breaking through old feeding habits and introducing new methods and new foods, perhaps against old-time taboos, as the story of Eve indicates.

Wadi el Natuf suggests that cultivation began before herding, and Hassuna and Sialk show that herding was added at an early stage as an accessory where there was grass-land available. The sheep is one of the most important animals concerned. Its varieties include the Mouflon of Mediterranean lands and south-west Asia, the Urial of the borders of the great steppe of interior western Asia, and the Argal of Mongolia. It is interesting in this connexion that the Soay sheep, named from the islet of Soay in the Hebrides, is thought to be in part a descendant from mouflon ancestors. Other breeds of modern sheep in Europe and the British Isles are descendants mainly of Urials, and it is in the European Bronze Age that steppe-land breeds of animals came to central and western Europe in numbers. Goats and cattle also lived wild on the hillsides of south-west Asia, so all three were available for domestication, which at first was apparently for milk and flesh, and only much later for work. It is quite probable that a baby of some animal would be captured and kept perhaps in the little courtyard around which the mud-walls of the habitation-rooms might be built. The mother of the calf, lamb, or kid would come to it with intent to give it milk, and she might be tamed with food and protection. Probably even after she had been more or less tamed she would be allowed to run wild at the appropriate times to be impregnated by a wild male. The domestication of the bull, at any rate, was a difficult matter.

At Jericho, Hassuna, and Sialk there is evidence of considerable later development beyond the crude beginnings. The great feature of this development is the building of durable houses of sun-dried and stamped mud at these places and at many others. Hassuna has yielded evidence of an oven and of storage jars, while at Sialk have been found a few very small bits of copper, no doubt softened in an oven.

The building of huts for long-continuing use by a family group is a hint of the more definite existence of the family or household within the group, as well as of the growth of the idea of property, and, no doubt, of the difference between the skilled, industrious, or lucky households and those with less in the way of resources. The mud walls crumbled after a time in most cases, and new ones were built over the debris of the old, so the site gradually became a mound. This came to be important in some cases, as a mound made possible settlement on the edge of a flood plain where annual floods of a river would bring down mud and so renew the fertility of the soil.

Permanent dwellings and polished stone axes used as wedges and chisels made possible considerable developments of car-pentering, so this as well as metallurgy came to give man more varied equipment. Cooking of food became a more regular feature when ovens had been added to household equipment, and the need for very powerful jaws to tear flesh food or chew tough roots was diminished. The diminution of the teeth and jaws was in progress, but we cannot in our present state of knowledge—perhaps one should rather say ignorance—give a picture of causal relationships between these two facts. There is no evidence for the passing on of the effects of use by an individual to his (her) offspring. On the other hand, we know very little at present about the influence of hormones on growth.

Other early settlements include Mersin, in Cilicia, Ras Shamra in the Syrian coastlands, one at Persepolis in south-west Persia, the oldest traces of habitation at Nineveh, Giyan towards the western border of Persia near Nihavend, and Gawra somewhat north of Nineveh. At Nineveh a pit has been sunk 70 feet below the floor of a temple built by Manishtusu about 450 B.C. and the remains of an old village were reached (Ninevite I). The people cultivated cereals and made pottery, usually decorated with incised lines or pressure-impressions. Above this layer is one with at first the same pottery (Ninevite IIa), but later on Ninevite IIb) designs painted on the pots in black or brown. In the course of time settlements along this zone (Mersin-Meshed) became more numerous and some still await discovery and excavation. Generally, the people concerned made painted pottery. It should be realized that to achieve any success in fixing clean paint on pottery the vessels must be baked in a closed oven, whereas rude pottery can be hardened in an open fire; but then it will naturally be smoke-stained. The development of an oven, a protected hot chamber, is therefore one of the many technical advances among the groups of early cereal cultivators. It led on to the development and the spread of painted pottery and metallurgy. As pottery was a woman's craft in the main, so long as it was hand-made, and without using a potter's wheel, the designs and colourings are characteristic for a group; women probably did not move about much or see much of ways of making things differing from their own.

At Nineveh, in the Ninevite layer II*b* mentioned above, the ornament on the pottery had become more elaborately painted; the people also made stone vessels and valued beads of cornelian, turquoise, and lapis-lazuli, materials brought in by trade, lapis-lazuli probably from the Pamirs or Badakshan (north-east Afghanistan).

Tell Halaf, near the frontiers of Iraq, Syria, and Turkey, is a site of special importance. The village had mud-dwellings (probably sun-baked brick) with walls set fairly square fronting cobbled streets. The people cultivated emmer wheat and barley and made fine pottery painted in red and black on a buff base. The pot often shows a shiny gloss, as though the silicates in the paint had been vitrified. The chequered patterns give the impression of derivation from woven mats or baskets, but the shapes of the pots do not suggest baskets. Some animal designs are found. Halaf may be of about the same period as Ninevite II*b*.

At Samarra, farther south, the painting on pots was in black only, and this pottery seems a little older than the more northerly Halaf type if we may judge from finding the Samarra style below the layers containing the Halaf style in the upper part of the mound at Hassuna.

Mention has been made above of the occurrence of small copper objects at Sialk after the initial stages of that settlement (Sialk II) and more metal has been found at Halaf. The earliest metal used was copper, though gold has almost as long a history. Native copper is found, or was found at one time, in many localities, sometimes in lumps, sometimes in veins, sometimes in gravels. But native copper is not easily malleable; it quickly becomes brittle when hammered. Coghlan has drawn attention to the importance of annealing (repeated heating followed by slow cooling) to reduce brittleness. Heating was effective once the oven came into use, and a temperature of 800° C. could thus be obtained, but annealing required experience. Some ores of copper such as the carbonate (malachite) came into use quite early. The sulphide was more difficult to treat. Utilization of the oven for metallurgy after its introduction for pot-making, finding of copper, understanding of annealing are all part of the process of early copper-working. On the whole, therefore, we may suppose that metallurgy had a very long introductory phase. As copper is found in the mountains in the neighbourhood of Diyarbakir, near the middle Euphrates before it leaves the highland, it is likely that evidence of early metallurgy will accumulate from the zone of early cereal growing in northern Mesopotamia and perhaps also Persia. To melt metal and run it into a mould for casting was a further and later invention, involving new problems so far as copper was concerned though perhaps not in the case of gold.

At present, therefore, it seems that the zone, largely of foothills and river banks, from Mersin in Cilicia to near Meshed in north-east Persia had been specially important for early cereal growing and durable settlement and, in parts, also for beginnings of metallurgy perhaps some centuries later. Whether irrigation canals are another development in this zone we cannot as yet say; but it seems possible as the region has rivers racing down from the highlands and tending to spread their waters in flood time as they reach the plain.

It used to be thought that lower Mesopotamia had been formed largely through recent sedimentation extending southwards from a supposed Pleistocene coast-line at Hit now between 350 and 400 miles north of the Persian Gulf. Recent research shows that the mountain ranges of the Persian border have risen from time to time and the axis of the trough between them and the block of Arabia has sunk. Subsidence has given scope for sedimentation. Rise of sea-level when Pleistocene ice sheets melted may be the real fact behind some of the supposed sinkings. Sedimentation and denudation have altered their balance from time to time and the coast-line may have varied but it has probably not been far from its present position within Pleistocene and recent times. River floods have been endemic in lower Mesopotamia since the Pleistocene, but general floods are not to be lightly postulated though sometimes rapid snow-melt in Armenia may have had disastrous results.

Floods have given rise to temporary shallow lagoons and marshes and to changes of river-courses, so Mesopotamia was difficult for early cultivators until they learned to dig drainage and irrigation canals. These were facilitated by the fact that the Euphrates runs in some places at a higher and in others at a lower level than the Tigris. The Noah legend is apparently that of a herdsman of the marshland border who was skilled in weather-forecasting; it is risky to try to date the flood concerned.

On the eastern border of the swampy land is the ancient settlement of Susa, and an early settlement there is broadly contemporary with early attempts to use and control the flood plain of which there is much evidence at Al-Ubaid a few miles north of the ancient Ur. The people who made these efforts came from north Mesopotamia with painted pottery, but apparently not metal tools, though the phase at Sialk (Sialk III) which is generally thought to be contemporary with Al-Ubaid and Susa not only has metal but was learning to cast it. Al-Ubaid was on a dry patch in what had been a large lagoon more and more obstructed by silt and growth of reeds. Its people had hand-made painted pots and stone hoes and grew barley which they harvested with pottery sickles. Perhaps they had a stand for making pots and rotated it by hand. They had a little copper. The huts or houses were either of sun-dried brick or of bundles of reeds probably covered with mud. Irrigation canals gave some control of floods. Town-like developments began and Al-Ubaid lasted two centuries or more and may have been brought to an end by a great flood which deposited silt, in some spots to a depth of 11 feet, but the thickness of this deposit decreases northwards. After this flood, sometimes dated about 4000 B.C., population returned and northerners immigrated. The next evolutionary stage is best known at Uruk or Erech.[1] The old culture of Al-Ubaid is basic here, but there are added to it pottery made on the potters' wheel, and also metalwork. The pottery fashion favoured plain red or grey ware. The Uruk culture sought stone for special purposes in making public buildings, and it developed architectural ideas. Sir Leonard Woolley thinks that bundles of reeds were set up in long lines with their upper ends bent over to meet one another and so form a kind of arch. Horizontal bundles were lashed to the vertical ones, and the structure was plastered with mud outside and covered with mats internally. Palm tree trunks were sometimes used in place of reed bundles. When sun-dried brick came into general use, columns made of it might be patterned to imitate frond-bases on a palm trunk. The Uruk culture used a pictographic system of writing by incisions in clay which was then baked. There may have been earlier pictographs on perishable material.

The value of cattle for farmwork was no doubt recognized fairly early among cultivators of cereals, but success in the matter necessitated solution of some problems. If the cow was used as a draught-animal her milk supply might be reduced and her calf-bearing interfered with. The bull was too fierce for work. Men solved this problem by cutting out the testes of male calves, and so they grew up strong and patient. This process of castration of males reduced previous waste that had been due to the killing of surplus male calves to minimize fighting in the

---

[1] Delougaz has recently divided off the early part of the Uruk phase and has given it the name Warka. He puts the later Uruk phase and the Jemdet-Nasr culture together and emphasizes the spread of irrigation, probably accompanied by elaboration of social organization.

Fig. 32. First Dynasty Temple, Al-Ubaid.

herd, and it allowed the use of the very powerful, if slow, animal for pulling. Carpenters could then fix a stone hoe, later an edged metal implement, to a wooden framework that the ox could pull, and so a small plough came into existence as an improved hoe.

Under Mesopotamian conditions what was desired or required was to prevent the surface soil from caking hard after the annual floods, which came with the snow-melt in spring and were followed by the heat and drought of summer. Oxen pulling a little plough criss-cross over the dried flood-land could be effective in limiting caking if the plough were used repeatedly, in some places four or even more times in the year. The silt laid down by floods gave fresh soil with organic content every year, so the same area could be used year after year indefinitely. An axe shaped more or less like our modern shoe-last was probably most useful for the work of surface ploughing.

We do not as yet know when the plough and castration of bull-calves began, they were among the great steps forward. They and irrigation on a large scale seem to account for the immense rise in status of the civilization at Tell Halaf in north Mesopotamia, and in Sumer, though we await more proof. It is difficult to imagine at any rate the Uruk culture without ploughs, and, if so, the plough goes back, at least, well into the fourth millennium B.C. but it may be older still. The Al-Ubaid culture had cattle, sheep, and swine so may have had the plough; its people cultivated the date-palm as well as cereals.

The Uruk culture shows so many special features that some students have emphasized the idea of its origin from a new immigrant population rather than its continuity with the earlier Al-Ubaid culture. There is probably a measure of truth in both ways of looking at the question. The grey pottery of Uruk type spread in Turkestan and Persia to the Indus, later even to north China.

A few observations may be added here concerning Anau in

Turkestan, east of the Caspian and north of the Persian border. The Anau people from an early stage grew bread-wheat, but the earliest stages yield no indication of domestic animals, though later on both long-horned and short-horned cattle as well as turbary pigs and both turbary and long-horned sheep appear. At a still later stage copper became abundant, hornless sheep, the dog, and apparently a domesticated camel become characteristic. In this late phase red and grey pottery were made as well as the older painted ware, which was painted in black on a rich red, the designs being conventional.

Developments in metallurgy occurred alongside of those in agriculture and pottery. The invention of the oven, which had made it possible to manufacture much finer pottery than could be hardened in an open fire, had also made possible the colouring of the pottery surface with patterns. It also provided a reducing condition for some copper ores. These were of variable character, with differing results. In the course of time it was realized that copper mixed with tin-sand (cassiterite) was better than copper alone. It did not become spongy when heated, and the product was harder than pure copper; it was bronze and could be hammered into shape with fairly sharp edges however quickly they might become blunt with use. A still greater development occurred when men learned to melt the copper-tin mixture in a very hot oven (about 1,100° C.) and to run the molten alloy into a mould. The general scheme, followed in most lands, was to model in wax the object it was desired to make in bronze and to place the model in a mould of fine clay. The clay was then heated to harden it and the melted wax ran out through a little hole left for the purpose. The clay mould was typically made in two parts that could be separated afterwards so as to take out the alloy which had been run in after the wax had melted. This process, called in modern times *cire perdue* (wax lost), was one in which much skill and refinement could be developed and, from the early part of the third millennium onwards, the bronze workers of south-west Asia so arranged a complex mould as to cast an instrument with a hollow socket for a wooden handle. The bronze-casting in the Indus civilization did not attain to this and the corresponding skill in Europe did not develop until many centuries later. The chapter on China refers to the very great skill of the bronze-workers there in casting elaborate objects during the last quarter of the second millennium B.C. If north China became the home of unique skill in bronze casting, south-west Asia and Egypt were its primary home and developed the main processes concerned. Egypt had malachite (copper carbonate) in Sinai, Mesopotamia had copper and tin in the east Anatolian hills near Diyarbakir, and perhaps also secured some metal from Magan, which Mr. Peake thought was in Oman, south-east Arabia. Whether both copper and tin were in reasonably constant supply for the Mesopotamian and Syrian centres is doubtful; indeed the probabilities are that people were forced back to using stone from time to time.

The search for copper and for tin-sand, the bringing of them to a centre for treatment, the development of skill in making wax models, and in shaping moulds all suggest that the art of bronze working was a major contribution to technical skill as well as to commercial organization and prospecting.

The civilization of Uruk had an abrupt end apparently due to invasion by conquerors whose work is best known from the site of Jemdet-Nasr. The pottery differs strikingly from that of Uruk and is painted in black or in buff on a deep red background. Woolley has suggested that the Jemdet-Nasr invaders may have come from the Persian Gulf. It would be too speculative to suggest a link with the red pottery used in north Baluchistan in the days just before the rise of the Indus cities, i.e. at a time probably not far removed from that indicated in the occupation of Jemdet-Nasr. The conquerors were skilled in work on large

H

shells and they made stone vessels, using chiefly limestone, trans-
lucent calcite and steatite and thus contrasting with the stone
vessels of igneous rock and alabaster, as well as limestone, made in
early dynastic Egypt. Another development is that of an incised
linear script on clay, the forerunner of
cuneiform writing. The conquerors
apparently subjugated a considerable
area, and so brought to an end the
phase in which most settlements had
probably been largely self-contained
and perhaps autonomous in some
measure. The dominion of the invaders
was overthrown after a short time and
the older Uruk culture reasserted itself.
Its pots are henceforth for a time
mostly plain red or grey. The linear
script of the invaders, however, survived, and from this time onwards there
was rivalry for power over considerable
areas, and one finds more evidence of
trade. We have reached a period of
wide expansion round about 3000 B.C.
Woolley's investigations at Ur have
given much information from the royal
tombs, apparently of local rulers not
yet supreme in the region. The facts
are widely known and are accessible in
several books so they need not be detailed here. Very fine work in gold and
in semi-precious stones is a great feature.
Among the latter is lapis-lazuli probably
brought from the Pamirs and thus evidence of long-distance trade-links. The

FIG. 33. The hilt of lapis-
lazuli is ornamented with
gold studs and pierced by
a gold-lined lanyard hole.
Blade and sheath are gold,
the latter with openwork
front patterned on plaited
and woven grass-sheaths in
common use.

very elaborate tomb of Queen Shu-bad is most remarkable. Ladies-in-waiting and servants were sent to the spirit world to continue to serve her there; a small cup, no doubt of a narcotic, was found near each body. The general impression is of a highly sophisticated hierarchical social system; and, following this phase, there came that of the Ist Dynasty of Ur (about 2800 B.C.) with the port-city in a position of regional leadership. Two-wheeled ass-drawn chariots were in use; the wheels were apparently solid disks of wood (two half-disks dowelled into the axle). It was thought until recently that the coast-line lay near Ur, but recent study suggests that Ur was approached up a creek or river.

Apparently the period 2800–2300 B.C., using approximate dating, was one of, in the main, prosperity and economic expansion, with Sargon of Agade as conqueror and organizer towards the end of this phase, probably, that is, in the vicinity of 2350 B.C. Sargon's rule seems to have extended northwards and westwards from Sumer and its northerly neighbour Akkad or Agade to the Mediterranean in the neighbourhood of the Gulf of Alexandretta. In that region there arose during the third millennium B.C. the port-cities of Ugarit (Ras Shamra) and Byblos, trading, *inter alia*, with the old kingdom of Egypt.

Recently, Sir Leonard Woolley has been digging at Alalakh in the ruins of the capital of a one-time buffer state near the Gulf of Alexandretta. This work has been specially important because Mesopotamia, Mitanni, Syria, Egypt, and Anatolia traded with Alalakh for timber. Finds of objects brought from these various regions may be found together in the same layer at Alalakh and this has helped to improve dating, though we must remember that possibly venerated cult-objects may upset facile dating. Alalakh seems to have traded with Sumer from the early years of the third millennium B.C. Later on, Alalakh craftsmen may have helped to develop Knossos soon after 2000 B.C.

FIG. 34. Pottery from Alalakh, with affinities to Cypriote types.

Influences on Cyprus are also suggested. Al Mina was the port for Alalakh.

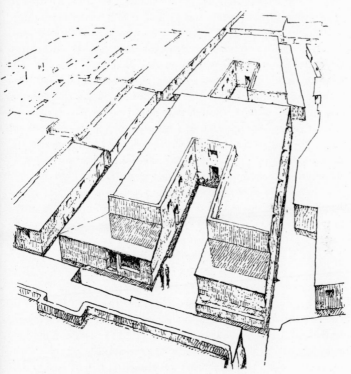

FIG. 35. Al Mina warehouses.

At some date not very far from 2300 B.C., after the death of Sargon and the decay of his empire, there was widespread disorder and destruction at Ugarit, Byblos, and Ur, and at Hissarlik in Asia Minor. The Old Kingdom of Egypt (VIth Dynasty) had also broken down into disorder, to the consternation of the people. What was the main factor of this widespread disaster is not known. It may be that the old authoritarian system and its religious sanctions were becoming inadequate to a situation in which long-distance trade was making communities more inter-dependent, and so more definite laws were becoming desirable. Interior Asia was waking up to larger-scale activity within and beyond its home-steppes, and on this something is said in the chapter on China. It may be, too, that finer metal tools were making spoked wheels possible and thus increasing the military efficiency of chariots, though that might rather have promoted a great effort of conquest and authority than a general disorder such as seems to have occurred. The death of Sargon and the breakdown of his empire may have been an important factor of disorder. A change of pottery-types in Syria and Palestine and the spread of a new style, with often a narrow base and broad rim, highly burnished, red inside and black outside, is most notable. Some think it came by invasion from what is now the eastern part of Trans-Caucasian U.S.S.R. It was identified at Khirbat Kerak in north Palestine and later at Tabara, west of Aleppo.

Whatever may be the truth in this matter it seems that the phase of general disorder passed away and the IIIrd Dynasty at Ur attained power for a time, while Ugarit and Byblos were active and had considerable relations with the Middle Kingdom of Egypt. Hissarlik in Asia Minor was also active, and this phase, formerly called the later part of Hissarlik II but now more usually named Hissarlik III, precedes a period of earthquakes, war, and the rise of Knossos in Crete to a dominant status in Aegean trade. Ur declined early in the second millennium B.C., and this decline was final. It was almost certainly connected with the silting of the approach from the sea; the port ceased to function. Another leading ancient city of the lower Euphrates, Kish, also died out, because of a change in the braided river channels. Babylon, on the other hand, developed into a leading centre, and, in the eighteenth century B.C., was ruled by Hammurabi, in whose reign the famous law-code was written down. After Hammurabi came another phase of destruction and disorder. At Hissarlik there is a long period, perhaps 1850–1550 B.C., with practically no evidence of any activity of importance, and at Ugarit there is the same lack of evidence for a period about 1750 or 1700 to 1550 B.C.; at Byblos there is the same rarity of finds for the period 1700–1500 B.C., and one might instance most other sites in south-west Asia here. This is more or less the period of the Hyksos or Shepherd Kings in Egypt, and, in its later years, it is also apparently the period of Indo-Aryan invasion of India. Barbarian warriors with horsed chariots were evidently spreading far and wide between Hissarlik and India and between Turkestan and the Nile. They had the aim of dominion as an aristocracy, and as such they seem to have had the typical fate of early aristocracies; they lost their distinctive traits and habits through intermarriage with girls of the conquered peoples. The horse spread to Egypt and probably in parts of south-west Asia, Persia, &c.; the smelting of iron soon began, apparently first in Asia Minor among the Chalybes. Ugarit and Byblos recovered about 1550 or 1500 B.C. and Egyptian objects found at Byblos are assignable to the reign of Thutmosis III now dated in the early half of the fifteenth century B.C.

Egypt had changed from its old rather self-contained condition and had become an imperial expansionist power conquering for a while in Palestine and beyond. But this phase passed, though an effort for its renewal was made under Ramses II (thirteenth century B.C.). The middle of the fourteenth century B.C. apparently witnessed great earthquakes which brought much disturbance and destruction to Asia Minor and Syria. Hissarlik, Ugarit, and Byblos all suffered and difficulties apparently spread in north Mesopotamia also.

During this period of 1500–1200 B.C. the Hittite power was dominating Anatolia and no doubt owed much of its might and prestige to its iron-works. The art of working iron is, however, a fairly simple one as far as the basal processes are concerned, and it spread to other peoples after a while. Egypt by about 1200 B.C. had come under the power of the priests of Amon-Ra after suppression of the ideas of the heretic Pharaoh, Ikhnaton, and the passing away of the phase of military effort made under Seti I and Ramses II. The priestly rule repressed thought and initiative, and Egypt henceforth was usually weak. Babylon was at a distance from sources of iron. On the other hand, colonists, apparently from Crete, were building up power in the fertile lands of the Gulf of Argos with their red soils yielding food crops sufficient for a considerable population, into which came rulers from farther north. Knossos in Crete, the dominant port for most of the period 2000–1400 B.C. was destroyed about the latter date, apparently through the attacks of its one-time colonists of Argos. Refugees from Knossos appear to have gone to the south coast of Anatolia, and some wandering still farther became the Philistines of the coastal plain west of the Judaean highland. The people of Argos, under the leadership of the royal city of Mycenae, attacked Hissarlik (formerly named Hissarlik VI but now Hissarlik VII) which seems to have grown rich and important as Knossos declined and disappeared. In the Aegean and eastern Mediterranean region there was thus widespread disturbance and the old ports of Ugarit and Byblos, weakened by earthquakes and fires, succumbed to 'peoples of the sea', as did Hissarlik to Agamemnon and his confederates in 1184 B.C. The Hittite power declined and, towards 1100 B.C., Assyria with its capital at Nineveh on the Tigris rose to imperial status. The power of Mycenae was destroyed about this time by Dorian invasions. The iron sword was replacing the bronze one and the custom of patrilineal was replacing that of matrilineal succession. Whether the disturbing activity of peoples of the sea round about 1200 B.C. was in some measure a result of bigger and better ships connected with the use of iron we do not know, but it is not impossible. New tools, new weapons, new customs were spreading in an area of already very ancient development. For the next 600 or more years there were changes in the relative power of Babylon, Nineveh, and Damascus in south-west Asia, but neither Anatolia nor Hissarlik attained to any great dominion during this time. Hissarlik indeed was superseded by Byzantium on the Golden Horn, where Greek ships could refit before venturing through the Bosporus into the Black Sea. And Greek colonies around that sea became more important than inland Anatolia. Athens, with its fine harbour at Piraeus, was enabled to overcome local limitations of relatively poor soil and steep slopes and to get food from the Black Sea coastlands.

During the same centuries the Philistines went through the usual cycle. Rising to power well before 1000 B.C. they hindered the Hebrew hill peoples behind them from having smiths to make iron weapons. A long struggle with the Hebrews, at first successful, eventually turned against the coastal people. They had come to a coastland that did not favour maritime activity and they would have needed a great metamorphosis to fit them into their new home. Moreover, the immigrants were no doubt largely men and the usual process of intermixture with more indigenous women led to the loss of their distinctive traits, probably without corresponding gain in other ways.

In the hill country behind, the Hebrews, at first largely herdsmen of Sawaqa type from the desert border, became more settled as cultivators, 'everyman under his own vine and his own fig tree', in a period in which rainfall seems to have been somewhat heavier than previously. This was accompanied by the development of magnificence under Solomon at Jerusalem and later under Omri at Samaria. It was also characterized by repeated departures from the worship of Jahweh, the god of flocks and herds, in favour of the rites of Baal, the god of cultivation, and Ashtoreth, the goddess of fertility, as well as other deities of the region. The subjugation of Samaria and later of Jerusalem by the Mesopotamian powers was to be fateful for subsequent developments of thought. Judaean Hebrew groups transported or living in Babylon, but clinging to their tradition, which had been cleansed of its more barbarous elements by a reform under King Josiah, came into contact with Zoroastrian ideas. These ideas pictured the world as the scene of a struggle between principles of good and of evil, between Ahura Mazda and Ahriman, between light and darkness. The concept of Jahweh took on a great deal from the new contacts; and also, in the course of time, Satan is developed in Hebrew thought as an impersonation of evil owing something to the idea of Ahriman. We do not know how far Egyptian ideas of Set may have contributed as well.

The ancient maritime activity along the Persian Gulf and the Makran coast, important in the third millennium B.C., diminished in the second, but the analogous activities in the Red Sea increased. They had apparently reached early importance about the time of the IIIrd Dynasty of Egypt, when frankincense, myrrh, balm, and other materials were brought to Egypt, and some of those new materials from the lands around what is now the Gulf of Aden were making the embalming and mummification of the great dead customary. With vicissitudes, the trade went on through the centuries and we have as evidence the famous fresco of the temple of Deir-el-Bahri near the Valley of the Kings in Upper Egypt. This depicts traders going to Punt and returning with frankincense and other products in the days of Queen Hatshepsut (early part of fifteenth century B.C.).

Decline in Egypt and general unrest about 1200 B.C. led to new routes and controls. Ugarit and Byblos drop out of the picture and Sidon, with Tyre later on, rises to prominence in trade; and Hiram, King of Tyre, makes use of Solomon in developing Red Sea trade. How far these Phoenicians (the name is used to mean merchants) were transplanted from Ugarit or Byblos, whether there were Aegean traders amongst them, and whether they were partly Mesopotamian, we do not know. It is widely agreed that we owe to the Phoenicians the basis of our alphabetic system of writing.

The rapid decline of Mycenean and Trojan maritime activities gave larger opportunities to the Phoenicians after 1000 B.C., and they developed in the succeeding centuries a habit of bold sailing across long sea-distances. Carthage, near the modern Tunis and Tarshish in the modern Andalusia, as well as Cartagena in south-east Spain and Ibiza in the Balearic Islands, bear witness to Phoenician activity.

The twenty-seventh chapter of the prophecies of Ezekiel in the Hebrew Scriptures gives a comprehensive picture of the trade of Tyre about the middle of the last millennium B.C.

In the Early Iron Age of Asia the invasion of Persia by Aryan-speaking people had paralleled the analogous changes in India and the assumption of power by the Chou Dynasty and its feudal schemes in north China, as well as the, rather later, rise of the Scythians in south Russia. All these changes exhibit pressure from the steppe-lands of interior Asia and south Russia upon the more cultivable areas and all are connected with warriors using horses and chariots. But the invasion of Persia led to the emergence of altered concepts of power. Previous conquerors had often killed or enslaved and deported the conquered people. Cyrus the Great, as a conqueror, set out to be rather the king of kings than the destroying master This meant that the Persian system hoped for the co-operation of the conquered rulers as the subordinates of the conqueror, and with this aim allowed them dignity, security of their traditional ritual, and some measure of autonomy. The gods of the different peoples were considered to be inter-identifiable and the king of kings was ready to sacrifice to Jahweh, Chemosh, or Amon Ra when he had occasion to visit the countries of these gods.

The Persian conquerors were also concerned to develop communications, and the royal road from Susa on the Persian border to Sardis in Asia Minor via central Anatolia was made and then supplemented by another road through the Cilician Taurus having a course through Anatolia farther south than the older road. Stations for refitting and change of horses were a part of the scheme. Persia was autocratic but sought to win over the conquered rather than to indulge in mere repression. It attempted, at its best, an extension of ideas of toleration and law, but all depended on the quality and the vision of the autocratic king of kings.

It is probable that the so-called tanks at Aden were made under Persian direction, and under Persian rule in Egypt reoccupation of the oasis of Kharga occurred after a gap of, apparently, thousands of years. The Persians were evidently leaders in civil engineering as well as, for a time, in land-warfare. The tanks at Aden suggest a period of more rain than falls there at present.

The oft-told story of the Persians' clash with classical Greece and their defeat at 'sea-born Salamis' by the Greek sailors need not be repeated. The way of autocracies leads to decline at the centre with breakdown as a consequence when someone with a larger vision and greater energy appears. It was Alexander of Macedon who, in his short life, overwhelmed not only the Persian Empire from Turkestan and India to Egypt, but also the remnants of classical Greece. Cities founded in Turkestan, Alexandria in Egypt, and many other new centres attest the vigour and vision of the new conqueror. He sought to link the Mediterranean with India and Asia generally and apparently in his day or soon afterwards Chinese silk was coming west in increased amounts. It is noteworthy that Alexander's efforts from Macedonia are not far removed in time from those of Asoka in India and from those of Chin Shih-hwang-ti followed by the rise of the Han Dynasty in China. The transient nature of the empires of Alexander and Asoka contrasts with the greater durability of that of Han China based on the far greater homogeneity of its people. But, however transient actual empires might be, the spread of a modified Greek culture had considerable and lasting effects in the Middle East, where it gave rise to a culture so steeped in Greek ideas that it is called Hellenistic.

The Roman effort which succeeded the Alexandrine was centred in the desire to protect the Mediterranean lands from invasion, and so it reached out to frontiers a good distance from the sea which it sought to make the centre of what was basically a land-power. Its strong organization allowed local cults to continue as the Persian had done, provided they did not claim exclusive allegiance and so nullify the idea of exchangeability. It sought to use Greek thought and Greek skill in maritime commerce. In the Middle East its effective frontier was the Euphrates or the Tigris rather than the Zagros range. Beyond the Euphrates the old Persian power redeveloped with the name of Parthia. In the vicinity of the Russian steppes the Roman Empire made a frontier across the Dobruja, and for a while controlled a frontier province called Dacia east of the Tisza and in the later Transylvania. When these frontiers became strategically the most important, the Roman capital was moved to Byzantium, renamed Constantinople, situated between the two danger zones and not too far from either. Civil engineering was developed far beyond Persian achievement by the Romans in the matter of bridges, aqueducts, and roads. Citizenship was extended very considerably and the administration of law made more regular and impersonal. Yet the growth of luxury, the exploitation of slaves, and much harsh cruelty stained the Roman system; and the size and internal diversities of the area it controlled made a military autocracy almost inevitable, with, in the end, disastrous results specially marked in contacts with the peoples of the desert border.

We must go back in time to consider some special features of human activity along some land-routes in south-west Asia. Trade between the Persian Gulf and Syria, the Levant, Anatolia, and the Aegean has apparently been going on from the third millennium B.C. onwards. At some period, perhaps about or after 2000 B.C., traders from lower Mesopotamia (Sumer) had a commercial agency at Kara Euyuk in Anatolia, an early example of a type of settlement that became very important with the growth of overland trade in Hellenistic and Roman times.

Among these trading cities or caravan stations of the interior, Damascus stands out as of perennial importance in spite of fluctuations of trade and of political power. Its unfailing water-supply by the Barada river, which is protected on its way by flowing through a gorge, gives pasture and waters crop-lands. And Damascus is situated at the south-west end of a long hill-foot way towards the Euphrates, a way that is not without grass at some seasons. Of Damascus we know little before the Iron Age, because the site has been occupied continuously, and to learn about earlier phases it would probably be necessary to destroy the monuments of later times. But there is little doubt about its importance at several periods. Its zenith of power came in the early phase of Islam under the Umayyad caliphs (about A.D. 660–750).

Some other cities, among which Petra, Bosra, Jerash, and Palmyra are specially well known, had their major periods in Hellenistic and Roman times after the more definite establishment of desert roads under the Persians. Overland trade had developed before this and had taken a step forward when in the latter part of the second millennium B.C. the two-humped Bactrian camel appears to have come into use as a carrier. In the early part of the last millennium B.C. it was superseded in the desert between the Persian Gulf and the Levant by the one-humped camel or dromedary, and the Assyrians are supposed by some to have improved desert tracks, but, as we have seen, it was the Persians who made the great step forward in this respect. Petra, almost half-way between the Gulf of Aqaba and the Transjordan area, is a highly defensible site in what are almost clefts in the rock. It was important under the Persians, and declined with them, to revive under Nabataean kings in the last century B.C. Its prosperity continued during the early part of the Roman domination but, under Trajan, Bosra in Transjordan became the important centre linked with the Roman road-system and Petra declined. Jerash, a city south of Bosra, in Transjordan, became another important caravan station in Roman times. These cities declined in the third century A.D., but revived with the renewal of imperial power in the early fourth century. They soon declined again with the decay of the Empire, but some, notably Jerash, revived for a time under the Byzantine Roman Empire organized under Justinian (sixth century A.D.).

Palmyra is a special case of an almost indefensible site which developed as a neutral exchange station near the (Euphrates) frontier between the Roman Empire and Parthia, and it was more or less recognized for this purpose by both. It therefore had little to fear except from occasional minor Badw (Bedouin) raids, and it became very rich. It is known to have dealt in lengths of Chinese silk. The quarrel between the Roman Empire and Queen Zenobia, leading on to her surrender and acceptance of a life as a Roman lady, was the end of Palmyra.

Nisibis may be mentioned here as a site of lasting importance.

It lies north-west of Mosul and has functioned in the past as a frontier fortress between the Roman Empire on the one hand and the Parthian-Persian monarchy on the other. It has revived in modern times.

In the cases of all the desert-border cities, except Damascus, water-supply depended on special constructions needing skilled maintenance. A period, therefore, of disorder was specially dangerous to such places, as a broken-down water-system may not be easy to rehabilitate. Most of the cities, except Palmyra, had a citadel or acropolis for defence and refuge. Arguments from decline of these cities to changes of climate are risky, beyond the general possibility that in Persian, Hellenistic, and early Roman times the rainfall may have been rather more copious and regular than it has been of late. At present an occasional good rainfall gives widespread tracts of grass perhaps one year in five or six.

Christianity, with its claim to exclusive allegiance, was one of the many factors undermining the Roman system. In course of time it stimulated a hostile and more strictly monotheistic reaction in the Arabian border lands; and the equally exclusive propaganda and military fervour of Islam spread into the decayed remains of the Roman Empire in south-west Asia and North Africa. That the Islamic power spread so rapidly to Persia and Turkestan is an indication of the effectiveness of Hellenization in and after Alexander's time.

This extension of Islam had a vastly important consequence. A new Mesopotamian capital, Baghdad, arose a little above the junction of the Diyala river with the Tigris and on the latter river. The way up the Diyala led towards Kermanshah, i.e. it was a way through the mountains to north Persia and onwards via Meshed to Turkestan, the golden road to Samarkand. The Abbasid Caliphs of Baghdad succeeded the Umayyad Caliphs of Damascus in the leadership of Islam. Characteristically they

developed Hellenizing tendencies. Greek science, Greek medicine, and Greek ideas in many fields were encouraged at Baghdad
and translations of Greek works were made; thus much classical
learning was saved for later generations and was passed on to
Europe, perhaps most of all through the medical school at
Salerno and the centre of learning at Cordoba in Islamic Spain.

One must also note that improvements in pottery spreading
west from T'ang China to Persia were adopted at Baghdad and
passed on thence to the west, mainly it seems via Spain. We
should further bear in mind that early Islam developed Indian
Ocean trade and may have been largely responsible for the
spread of citrus fruits to the Mediterranean lands.

If we think of Hejaz, Syria, Mesopotamia, Persia, and
Turkestan we realize at once the difficulty of achieving any lasting unity in such a region of diversities and difficult communications. Especially was this the case under despotic rule with the
ever-recurrent degeneration of families of despots. Struggles for
power and internal decay led to the decline of Bagdad and,
later, the great Mongol invasion of the twelfth and thirteenth
centuries brought south-west Asia very near to final ruin. Irrigation systems decayed and have been very difficult to rehabilitate
even with twentieth-century engineering skill.

5

North Africa

IN north-west Africa the last phase of the Old Stone Age seems to have had a microlithic industry that has long been called Final Capsian, from the station Capsa or Gafsa in Tunisia. The relation of north-west African to Iberian industries of the time has been debated a good deal and a tendency has emerged to think of a spread from Spain to Africa. The Neolithic industries in north-west Africa seem to be imposed, as introduced features, upon this culture of very small points and blades. It is now claimed that the story near the Nile is a different one. According to Huzayyin the late phases of the Old Stone Age in northern Egypt were characterized by the making of implements through the shaping of cores on all sides (usually called bifacial chipping) rather than the making of flakes, blades, and points shaped on one side and knocked off a flint core. Flakes and blades and points were made but, according to Huzayyin, remained very unspecialized; the making of core tools, on the other hand, developed. So the 'pre-Neolithic or proto-Neolithic' core tool or axe was, in northern Egypt, not an introduction from outside into a Capsian culture; it was rather a local evolution and some small flakes (often called Sabylian or Sébilien) are introductions at a fairly late stage. Huzayyin uses the term Fayumian for the industry that made these pre-Neolithic core tools. He thinks it was a feature of a time when men lived around the higher, northern, shores of the Qarun lake of the Fayum basin, when rainfall was considerable but declining, so that the lower Nile valley was becoming more distinct from its surroundings and people were settling on the dry borders of the flood plain of the river but not yet digging irrigation channels. The Nile floods were probably very extensive as a consequence of heavy rainfall in

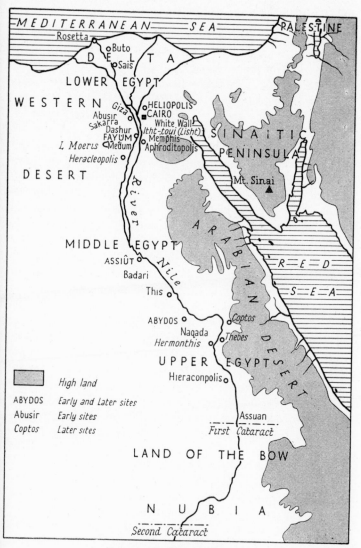

FIG. 36. Sites in Dynastic Egypt.

Abyssinia, and large quantities of fertile black mud were thus brought to Lower Egypt. Merimde, west of the Nile delta, and Deir Tasa in Upper Egypt are early settlements, and Badari, south of Assiut, is probably almost contemporary. Deir Tasa has yielded some beautifully formed pots shaped rather like a tulip, and some Deir Tasa pots have impressions of grain. Badari has also yielded pottery of fine workmanship with a polished black surface and also some buff ware. Figurines of women are another feature and they have been carved in ivory. There are hollow-based, barbed, arrow-heads, some flint blades shaped by pressure flaking, some slate palettes, and a vase carved in ivory. But there are also a copper pin and two or three copper beads made from a narrow copper ribbon. As these sites are supposed to antedate what it is customary to call the Predynastic period, very early dates have been conjectured for them. The length assigned to the Predynastic period has been estimated, or one may venture to say over-estimated, at 2,000 years. Perhaps 1,500 years or even a good deal less would be a more moderate figure, and we need not then suppose that Deir Tasa, Merimde, or Badari go back beyond 5000 B.C., if indeed they are as old as that. The pottery at Deir Tasa and Badari certainly suggests a long course of prior evolution, probably in south-west Asia rather than near the Nile.

The present trend of thought about origins of cereal-cultivation and irrigation is emphasizing the importance of a zone from Cilicia to north Persia in this connexion, and the finds from Deir Tasa and Badari in Egypt seem so clearly an intrusion from the Asiatic side that they at least do not create difficulties for this view. The Nile was bordered by a reed-swamp with, still, very heavy floods bringing down dark Abyssinian silt, and wadis with seasonal streams from the hills between the Nile and the Red Sea. The delta was very swampy. It is probable that a rise of land-levels, whether partly due to silting or not during Predynastic times, helped to reduce swampiness through deeper cutting by the river. Hippopotami and crocodiles abounded in the river and the swamps, while wild asses and sheep and antelopes ranged along the flanks of the valley.

At Diospolis parva Flinders Petrie, investigating cemeteries, found it possible to infer sequences in material, form, and ornament of grave-pottery. He therefore numbered the stages of his sequence and set out to use numbers from 1 to 100. Nos. 1–29 were left for future discoveries and the effective succession began with 30. 30–38 were named Early Predynastic, 39–62 Middle Predynastic, and 63–78 Late Predynastic. No. 79 corresponds with the beginning of the Dynastic phase. Some of the stages are characterized by impoverishment of the graves in question, and it is possible that in some cases we may have richer and poorer contemporary graves rather than a time sequence. As already hinted, the duration of the stages of the sequence, as well as their number, has probably been rather over-estimated. It was at one time thought that cultivation and domestic animals came into Egypt during the Predynastic, possibly the Middle Predynastic, period, but, if the people of Deir Tasa cultivated grain, and if Deir Tasa is really earlier than the Predynastic period, this opinion must be given up. There can, however, be no doubt about a wide increase of cultivation in the Middle Predynastic period. If this was really a period of down-cutting by the Nile, as suggested above, the arable land would increase as the swamps diminished.

Some of the Early Predynastic pottery is plain red or black, the latter being rather like what has been found at Badari, but there is also other fine ware ornamented by white-filled cross-lines in well-developed patterns suggesting basket-work models. This is not found towards Nubia and it has been suggested that it came up the river from the margins of the delta. Petrie thought it came from Libya, but whether Libya was too desertic is a question. Basket-work styles do not seem to suit a desert

environment. Some students of climatic history think there was
a fairly rainy period before 4000 B.C., and we know that wadis
from the Mokattam hills were still flowing, at least seasonally,
after that date.

Another style in black pottery based on basket-work, clearly
distinct from the cross-lined fashion, appeared a little before
that style suddenly came to an end. The newer decoration

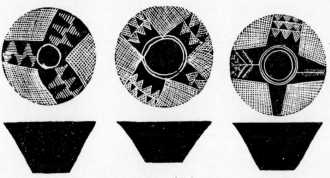

FIG. 37. Cross-lined pottery.

may also have come up southwards from the delta margin, but
the two fashions seem to have very little connexion with one
another. The new style lasted, or lingered, on through all Predynastic time. The Middle Predynastic period is thought to be
characterized by considerable advance in technique. Mention
has already been made of a possible down-cutting by the Nile
with consequent decrease of marsh and increase of arable land.
According to Frankfort, groups came into the Nile valley from
the Wadi Hammamat, near Qena in Upper Egypt, while Newberry thought others came up from the western margins of the
delta where the region of Mariout long remained and in a sense
still remains in doubt between desert and cultivated land, with
fig-trees planted in what seems almost pure sand and poor crops
of barley gathered by Badawi who now breed camels and are

still only partly settled. The Middle Predynastic phase yields plain pots with wavy horizontal ridges functioning as hand-holds and they are thought to be of Syrian, probably north Syrian, origin. It is thought that the people concerned brought in the cultivation of flax, if it was not already known in Egypt, and Newberry believed that after they came to Egypt they developed the idea of hieroglyphs or picture-writing. Metal, in the form of copper, became less rare in this phase and daggers and chisels are found. Pressure-flaking of flint implements also developed considerably, and luxury work in gold, silver, and semi-precious stones became a feature.

It is thought that the people of the hills between Upper Egypt and the Red Sea were the originators of the making of stone vessels, and it has already been mentioned that people from Wadi Hammamat, near Qena in Upper Egypt, came into the Nile valley in the Middle Predynastic phase. The art of making vessels of stone was remarkably developed in the Nile valley. Perhaps alabaster, with its beautiful veining and its trans-lucence, was the favourite material, but limestones, syenites, basalts, and even rock crystal were used. The artists learned to take advantage of veins in the stone, variations of colour, em-bedded crystals, and so on, and to work them into schemes of decoration. A bowl of rock crystal, probably belonging to the very beginning of the Dynastic period, rather than to the Pre-dynastic, is one of the major treasures recently found by the excavations at Helwan a few miles south of Cairo. The stone pots cost much labour and skill and were precious. Some were barrel-shaped and some were bellied, both these forms ordinarily having on the outside a pair of cylindrical horizontal swellings pierced by a hollow canal for holding a suspension cord. Still others were cylindrical, often with a flat base, and these do not so often have the canal for the suspension cord. It has been thought that the valuable stone vessels may often have been protected by a framework of spirally-coiled rushes. The Middle Predynastic period witnessed the introduction of painted pottery (and therefore probably ovens) into Egypt, presumably from south-west Asia, but many designs on Egyptian pots are very different from those used in Mesopotamia. It is often the case that a general idea is transmitted to a new region in which it finds detailed expression along fresh lines. One design on Predynastic Egyptian pots is a spiral that may be derived from the spirally-coiled rushes of the protecting framework around the stone vessel. Another design is that of a boat with rows of oars, a mast, upraised bow and stern, and other features. As the traditional Nile boat has not got the upraised ends, which are said to be Sumerian, this feature is of special interest. The Nile provides a great means of communication and, one may add, made road-development and land transport far less important than in south-west Asia.

The new peoples apparently coming into Egypt from the hills between Qena and the Red Sea, from the western margins of the delta, and probably from the Syrian direction, added considerably to the population of Egypt at the time. An ivory knife-handle from Jebel el Arak is carved to show a representation of fighting between two groups with different appearance. This suggests that the Middle Predynastic period saw invasions and conflicts connected with the contacts of the diverse peoples just mentioned.

The pots supposed to come from north Syria and having wavy handle-ridges were considered by Frankfort to have carried imports of olive oil, but Newberry and others have thought resin and spices more probable. It has been supposed that the olive tree is rather Libyan than Asiatic, but this inference is still speculative. The pots of this type ceased to be imported in the Late Predynastic period; indeed, the cessation of importation of these pots has been made the dividing line between the Middle and Late phases.

Inferences have been made concerning diminution of rainfall in the Late Predynastic phase. Pastoral peoples from the north-east came into the delta, and on the west the Libyan peoples, later called Tehennu and represented as of rather light colour-ing, also closed in on the delta. They appear to have tamed the wild ass; and the Egyptian donkey became and still remains a most intimate feature of Egyptian rural life. Cylindrical pots were used more than ever. Slate palettes, which had long been in use, were still made, but not so often shaped in the form of birds or beasts. Ivory combs were no longer made, but ivory was still used for pins. Perhaps the hippopotamus was less abundant, or the ivory was more used for other purposes. The recent excava-tions at Helwan show some finely carved ivory representing figures from Egyptian life at the beginning of the Dynastic period. Metal became commoner and flint work correspondingly declined in quality, but still remained in abundant use for knives.

Moustafa Amer has long been excavating on a site at Ma'adi between Cairo and Helwan on the border between the slope of the Mokattam hills and the Nile, and the report when it ulti-mately appears should bring forward a good deal of new know-ledge. For the present it is supposed that it was inhabited chiefly in rather late Predynastic times. Wadis from the Mokattams were at least seasonally active when Ma'adi was occupied. There were large store-pots, masses of flint chiefly as blades and scrapers, shells with edges shaped for cutting or sawing, malachite and copper, painted pottery, ochre, and so on. It seems that the equipment of the settlement relates it more to Palestine and south-west Asia than to Upper Egypt. In view of what will be said below about Heliopolis it is worth noting that the burials at Ma'adi are of short people. Polished stone does not seem to have been common for implements.

At Heliopolis again, on the transition between desert and cultivated land, another site has recently been opened up and will be reported upon some time in the future. The burials are of tall men, and apart from them and with no grave goods are the remains of small adult women. The settlement is thought to be Predynastic, though examination of the percentage of radioactive carbon has suggested a date after 3000 B.C. Living organic matter contains two varieties of carbon with atomic weights respectively 12 and 14. The latter is radioactive, and is very gradually transformed into the former after death. Analysis is thought to give an estimate of age with a considerable margin of error. At Heliopolis we may have a settlement on the desert edge without the full Egyptian equipment.

The recent excavations at Helwan, on a site first found by Moustafa Amer, are giving much promise of important results in the near future. Deep shaft-graves are often faced with stone roughly dressed and mortared, but sometimes they are walled in sun-dried brick, and some were roofed in wood. Fine stone vessels and the splendid bowl of rock crystal already mentioned are accompanied by finely carved ivory figures, one of Narmer's queen showing an inscription very finely executed in hieroglyphic. There are large store-pots, many flints, toys, boats broken in half, and a good deal of copper. Speaking generally, we seem to have a considerable advance in both building and equipment as compared with any Predynastic finds, yet a general condition below that which developed in the IIIrd and IVth Dynasties.

The beginning of the annual rise of the Nile at Memphis corresponds, very regularly, with the day on which Sothis (our Sirius) rises with the sun. This Solar or Sothic year does not quite fit the scheme of a year of 365 days because the revolution of the earth around the sun occupies just under 365¼ days. The beginning of the 365-day year and the Sothic year would thus coincide exactly only once in 1,461 years, and this period has been called the Sothic cycle. A writer of the third century A.D.

says that Sirius rose with the sun at the beginning of the year
which is A.D. 139 on our numeration. The same coincidence
would have occurred in 1321 B.C. and correspondingly further
back. It was formerly thought by some Egyptologists that the
Sothic reckoning must have begun on the date of such a coincidence and as 2781 B.C. was thought too late, a beginning in
4241–2 B.C. was surmised. It is now more generally thought
that the 365-day system is older than the Sothic system, and
that the latter, for the special purpose of foretelling the beginning of the inundation, came into use under the Old Kingdom in the third millennium B.C.

The famous stone now in Palermo, incised late in the time
of the Vth Dynasty, gives a summary chronicle with names and
durations of reigns of kings; and the Turin papyrus, written
late in the period of the New Kingdom or Empire, also gives
lists of kings. These have been used to compute dates for
Egyptian history. In volume 4 of this series, Breasted's dates,
making the beginning of the Ist Dynasty about 3400 B.C., were
used. Edward Meyer's dates are a little lower, 3315 B.C., or, in
a revised calculation, 3197 B.C. Burchardt has suggested 4186
B.C., but it seems that Meyer's figures are tending to be accepted
or further reduced.

At the end of Predynastic time a people who apparently worshipped Osiris lived in the north of the valley near the site of the
later Cairo, having spread from the delta. Some students credit
them with Syrian origins. Osiris, a god of the dead, was supposed
to revive once a year to make Isis, goddess of fertility, pregnant
and so to ensure the growth of the crops. Libyans, called on the
monuments Tehennu, were on the west of the delta, and their
king was or became king of Lower Egypt, with a red cap as his
sign of majesty. There were probably also semi-nomad herders
on the eastern border between the delta and the desert.

From Cairo southwards towards Assiut another early kingdom

had as its sign of majesty a high white crown. The people, who apparently had come into the Nile valley from the eastern hills and wadis of Upper Egypt and had made stone vessels, were another group and they worshipped Horus under the emblem of a falcon. A conquest spread from south to north, and apparently the King Narmer or Menes took the white crown of Middle Egypt and then the red crown of Lower Egypt, marrying a

FIG. 38 *a*. Red Crown, Lower Egypt. *b*. White Crown, Middle Egypt.

princess-daughter of the presumably defeated Tehennu king. So Egypt became one kingdom, with a double crown, and the first of the thirty historic dynasties began. The date is variously estimated, as already stated, between about 3400 and 3200 B.C., and dates of subsequent reigns and dynasties are subject to the view taken concerning these estimates. Apparently the kingdom met great difficulties during the IInd Dynasty, probably from resurgence of local princes against the unified rule, but attempts were made to observe and measure the Nile flood throughout the valley from the first cataract northward. There seems to have been a system of royal officials. Copper (from Sinai) and gold became more abundant, silver less so. Several of the early kings were buried at Abydos, but increasingly identified themselves with Memphis, near the border between the land of the white crown and that of the red, in other words near the later Cairo.

The king who was either the last of the IInd or the first of the IIIrd Dynasty achieved his position by marrying the daughter of his predecessor, and it may be queried whether this may not be evidence of matrilineal succession.

Under the IIIrd Dynasty building above ground with dressed stone became a highly developed art applied to tombs of kings, and, later, of nobles. The idea of preservation of the body in expectation of future life was accepted, and was no doubt helped by the introduction of resins, oils, honey, wax, &c., as preservatives, apparently through foreign trade including commerce with lands in the south of the Red Sea. As Aegean potsherds are found already in IInd, Dynasty tombs in Abydos, sea trade was expanding. One specimen of gold from the IInd Dynasty, found at Abydos, has given rise to some speculation. It has a red crust of a compound of antimony said to be formed only in the presence of tellurium. The only places known to yield gold and tellurium together are in the Carpathians, chiefly in Transylvania. So it is possible that gold from Transylvania may have got to Egypt about 3000 or 2800 B.C., but these inferences based on chemical analysis of present-day finds of metal are not too certain. Sea trade was considerable under the IVth, Vth, and VIth Dynasties. Sir Arthur Evans thought Libyans (Tehennu) migrated to Crete in the days of Menes, but it seems possible that this occurred in connexion with the great developments under the IIIrd Dynasty.

In the IIIrd Dynasty's time Memphis on the west bank of the Nile, a little to the south of the modern Cairo, became more important and the edge of the desert plateau to the west of it began its unique development as the greatest of Pharaonic cemeteries. Zoser, the son of the king mentioned as the last of the IInd Dynasty or the first of the IIIrd, built the step pyramid of Saqqara with a great stone temple, the earliest of which appreciable remains survive. It is, however, stated that Menes (Ist Dynasty) had a temple built at Memphis in honour of Ptah, the creator-god. The later history of the IIIrd Dynasty is confused and suggests revolts. Snefru, the last of the IIIrd or the first of the IVth Dynasty, seems to have reorganized the Egyptian kingdom; he is said to have built pyramids at Dashur and at Medum, and to have fetched cedar from Lebanon. His son and successor Khufu (also known as Cheops) built the Great Pyramid. Khafre (Chephren) built the second pyramid, and, in his day, some of the work of carving the Sphinx was carried out, utilizing rock left projecting when part of the quarrying for the Khafre (Chephren) pyramid had been completed. Menkaure (Mycerinus) built the smaller third pyramid at Gizeh.

His successor was the last effective ruler of this most remarkable of all dynasties of Egypt, from which we have not only the great pyramids, the Sphinx, and associated temples, but also magnificent statues and models of scenes from the life of the period. The statue of Khafre in black diorite, now in the Egyptian Museum at Cairo, can be claimed to be one of the two or three greatest statues in the world.

The families of the nobility built their tombs near the pyramids of the Pharaohs. Those tombs were either rock-cut chambers or buildings (mastabas) containing various rooms, or a combination of both. The tombs of the Pharaohs might have ceremonial pictures or ritual expressions; those of the nobles, especially under the Vth Dynasty, had rather scenes from life painted or carved in bas-relief, often with fine artistic feeling. In the Vth Dynasty the nobles were increasing their power at the expense of that of the Pharaohs. The art of the IVth and Vth Dynasties was unsurpassed, indeed hardly equalled, in any subsequent phase of the long history of Egypt.

Under the VIth Dynasty, its third sovereign, Pepi, apparently made Memphis the permanent capital, but the period of great building had passed, and at some time between 2500 and 2300 B.C. (according to the chronology chosen) the Egyptian kingdom

Fig. 39. Statue of Khafre (Chephren).

fell into prolonged disorder. The inscriptions make it clear that the old order was overwhelmed, and it seems that Egypt suffered invasions from Palestine and from Nubia, perhaps from Libya as well. The breakdown of civilization in south-west Asia appears to have been about contemporary; it occurred after the death of the conqueror Sargon of Agade (Akkad) and the dates now usually accepted for him suggest utilization of the lower dates for Egypt, i.e. towards 2300 rather than towards 2500 B.C. During the VIth Dynasty the noble families tended to make their family tombs in their districts of residence and rule rather than at Gizeh or to north and south of Gizeh along the desert border. Apparently the burial of the dead for some generations in the family's own area was held to strengthen their claim to authority there, a feature in which the Egyptian nobility have been paralleled among noble families of many lands and periods.

Following the downfall of the VIth Dynasty came a period of disunity with civil war between ruling families of various districts and little building or sculpting. It is, however, during this period that a family ruling at Herakleopolis (at the entrance to the Fayum) encouraged literature, the works then created being still accepted long afterwards as classic. After 150–200 years, reorganization began under what is called the XIth Dynasty based on Thebes in Upper Egypt, the god concerned being Amon, probably a result of amalgamation between a god of Thebes and Min (of Coptos), a figure of phallic worship. He in a sense supersedes Ra or Re, the god of the VIth Dynasty, whose special seat was Heliopolis north-east of modern Cairo; but in some measure the two personalities combine and Amon-Ra becomes recognized as the chief deity, with the creator Ptah in the background. Thebes began with the XIth Dynasty its great history as capital of the Egyptian kingdom for many centuries and Memphis took a lesser position. A part of the temple

of Karnak on the east bank of the Nile nearly opposite Thebes
was built under the XIth and XIIth Dynasties.

There were military and commercial relations with Syria and
up the Nile southwards into Nubia, as well as along the Red Sea
to 'Punt' (? Somaliland or Arabia felix), but Libya is not much

Fɪɢ. 40. A Cretan vase in Egypt.

mentioned. Trade with Crete, apparently in the hands of Cretan
merchants and sailors, was active for a good while. Sir Leonard
Woolley found an iron spearhead in a XIIth Dynasty grave at
Buhen just below the second cataract of the Nile and he wonders
whether it may not be an indication of iron-working and perhaps even commerce in lands south of Egypt before 1800 B.C.

The XIIth Dynasty was a period of engineering enterprise.
A canal was made along Wadi Tumilat to connect the head of
the Gulf of Suez with the Nile, and it henceforth carried the
products of mines and quarries in Sinai to Egypt. The Birket el
Qarun, the lake in the Fayum depression, was made into a
reservoir, fed by the Bahr Jusuf branch of the Nile and feeding

the Nile farther north in the season of the low water before the summer floods.

The end of the XIIth Dynasty brought confusion again in the early eighteenth century B.C. Civil war was followed about a century later by the invasions of the Hyksos or Shepherd Kings from south-west Asia or Anatolia, in a period of widespread disturbance about and after 1700 B.C., as is mentioned in the chapters on south-west Asia and on India. This disturbance was partly due to the fact that the horse had come into south-west Asia as the companion of the warrior adventurers who conquered in a period of relative drought. A god of these conquerors of Egypt became identified with Se't or Seth, later on in Egypt a personification of the principle of evil.

About 1600 B.C. a vassal of the Hyksos, ruling at Thebes, started an ultimately successful attempt to drive out these alien conquerors. The new rulers, that is Dynasty XVIII, have been thought by some students to be Egyptianized Hyksos. Certainly they stand out apart from and in contrast with most other Egyptian dynasties. Egypt was organized by them as a military state under the control of officials rather than of local aristocratic families. And henceforth the Egyptians had horses as part of their equipment for war. Previous periods of prosperity might bring trade by both land and sea, and some military expeditions might have been needed, but definitive conquest of an empire outside the Nile valley had not hitherto been an Egyptian ambition.

The XVIIIth Dynasty gave Egypt power and luxury under Pharaohs bearing the names Thutmosis (I–IV) and Amenhotep (I–IV) and the one female ruler in the Egyptian dynastic succession, Hatshepsut. It has been thought that she was married to her brothers Thutmosis II and III, and it may be that they were supposed to rule as her husbands under a scheme of matrilineal succession. But she evidently ruled, at least for a time, as herself, and she accordingly sometimes had herself depicted as a male. It appears that Thutmosis III eventually had many of the representations of Hatshepsut on temple walls chipped out. The beautiful temple of Deir el Bahri, at least in part built in her reign, depicts on its walls a trading expedition to Punt bringing back incense. Thutmosis III was a great warrior who won battles at Megiddo (Armageddon) and Kadesh in south-west Asia. His power extended to Mesopotamia and the borders of Anatolia, and in connexion with these wars the names of the Hittites and the Mitanni peoples appear. The XVIIIth Dynasty apparently ruled Libya as well as Egypt. At the end of this dynasty came Amenhotep IV, also known as Ikhnaton, who, with his wife Nefertiti, is thought to have attempted the replacement of the Theban god, Amon-Ra, by a more spiritual concept of a god whose symbol was the rays of light spreading from the sun. Woolley thinks Ikhnaton was a hedonist rather than a religious enthusiast. He nearly caused the breakdown of Egyptian power, but the priesthood of Amon-Ra and the army re-established the old order partly during the short reign of the youth Tutankhamon, whose tomb has yielded such masses of grave-furnishings. The old order restored itself under the XIXth Dynasty, the Pharaohs of which include a famous conqueror Seti I and the extravagant Ramses II, less successful in Asiatic wars but bent on self-glorification through colossal statues. He also had built much of the great temple of Amon-Ra at Karnak on the east bank of the Nile opposite Thebes. The luxury and the scale of building of this period are without parallel in the Egyptian record, and often the craftsmanship is of high quality, but designs are typically very inferior to those of the VIth, Vth, and IVth Dynasties above-mentioned. For the period from the XVIIIth Dynasty onwards it is customary to speak of the New Empire as contrasted with the Middle Kingdom (XIth and XIIth Dynasties) and the Old Kingdom (Ist–VIth Dynasties).

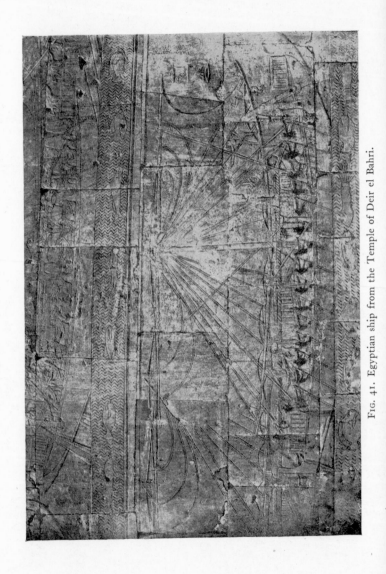

Fig. 41. Egyptian ship from the Temple of Deir el Bahri.

Under the New Empire mercenaries from Libya and perhaps Asia were largely used in the armies of Egypt, and those armies had to drive out invaders of the delta.

Fig. 42. Weighing precious metals.

About 1200 B.C. there was another period of general dis-turbance but apparently Egypt held its power for a while under Ramses III of the XXth Dynasty, the last great Pharaoh. Under Ramses IV–XII the central power declined. The high priest of Amon-Ra at Thebes became the chief power in Upper Egypt, and local families ruled in different parts of the delta. Egyptian influence in south-west Asia declined to nothing, and Assyria became powerful there. Judah and Israel apparently sought

Egyptian connexions for a time as a protection against Assyria. The Assyrians in the seventh century B.C. (XXVth Egyptian Dynasty) conquered Memphis and Thebes, but Nubians also held the country for a time. Under the XXVIth Dynasty, about the beginning of the sixth century B.C., Egypt became independent again for some years with the help of Ionian and other mercenaries, and even extended its power over Palestine. Ionian and other Greek merchant groups were settled in towns of their own in Egypt and carried on most of the country's trade. In the latter part of the sixth century B.C. Egypt was incorporated in the Persian Empire under which even the oases were revived, Kharga, for example, having had very little evidence of activity since Predynastic times, when it was of some importance. It is possible that this Persian period, especially 500–400 B.C., was a time of more rainfall; it seems to have been a time of cold wet summers in north-western Europe (see Chap. 7). After 400 B.C. Egypt again ruled itself for a time under the XXVIIIth, XXIXth, and XXXth Dynasties until the conquest by Alexander the Great, 332 B.C. Several writers take a very unfavourable view of the Persian domination.

North Africa west of Egypt has been studied much less than Egypt. Caves have been examined in which people lived who used very small blades and points, apparently lingering on from the Old Stone Age, as has happened in several other areas. In some cases strata with these implements have been thought to be followed without a break by later ones in which more or less ground-stone axes of fairly cylindrical section were used. Some of the latter show very little smoothing of the surface so have a superficial resemblance to the hand-axes of the Early Palaeolithic, but typically have some approach at least to a transverse rectilinear (*tranchet*) cutting edge. Flint arrow-heads are widespread; some are concave-based, some have a tang. There are also some flat-surfaced ground-stone axes. The use of minute flints declined in the course of time. Ostrich eggshells, often decorated, were used in some, but not all, areas. Metal was rare in prehistoric times in Libya and Mauretania. Oric Bates found five graves at Mersa Matruh, in one of which was a stone vessel that he thought akin to those of Late Predynastic Egypt. The date tentatively given was 3500 B.C.

Rough stone monuments or Megalithic graves are widely distributed in Africa from Tunis to Morocco. In the north-west they often occur singly and are scattered. Elsewhere they are often gathered into cemeteries. Some are cairns heaped over a body enclosed beforehand in a central space. Others have the dolmen form; that is, there are several upright blocks supporting one or two covering blocks; sometimes these may have a special opening that has often been called a port-hole and has been supposed to be a means of exit of the spirit of the dead for purposes of rebirth. North Africa has multiple dolmens side by side, some of which are more strictly stone boxes or cists. These constructions, as in parts of western Europe, may be placed in an enclosure bounded by a circle or ellipse of stones. There are also what one may call stone tumuli, the stones of which may be heaped up to the level of the roof of the stone chamber, and there may be niches in the tumulus unconnected with the chamber. Some, apparently late, monuments here have corbelled roofs. A low vessel with a snout is one type of pot found in these monuments; it was also made in the time of the Old Kingdom in Egypt, but it need not be so old in Tunisia, &c. Some iron has been found in North African Megaliths, suggesting that they were made or remained in use in the last centuries B.C. or later. One should note the occurrence of ancient Megaliths in the Sudan and in parts of Ethiopia as well as in Transjordan, &c. Some students of the subject doubt whether there is much relationship between the dolmens of North Africa, Transjordan, &c., and those of western Europe which it is customary to date

2500–1500 B.C. These doubts have considerable foundation. One must, however, remember the continuation or redevelopment of ritual importance of west European dolmens long after the construction of the early ones.

Under the last dynasty of the Old Kingdom in Egypt (i.e. towards 2300 B.C.) men from Libya are pictured with light skins, fair hair, and blue eyes, and this convention was sometimes used for Libyans in later periods. It is interesting that there are still men with light colouring among the modern Berbers. Apparently, early Sidonian sailors, and this means men between 1500 and perhaps 1100 B.C., came to the coast of North Africa west of Egypt. The great event here, however, was the founding of Carthage in the second half of the ninth century B.C. According to tradition, Elissa, later called Dido—that is the fugitive—led a group escaping from the oppression of her brother, the ruler of Tyre. Her wandering, in the growth of legend, became associated with that of Aeneas leaving Troy after its destruction by the Mycenaean Greeks. Carthage was favourably placed for Mediterranean maritime trade, which included importation of olive oil from the north side of the sea off her coast; and the Phoenicians of that period occupied Malta.

Before Carthage had been founded Tyre had traded with Tartessos (Tarshish), which in modern terms is the coastal region of Andalusia, especially near the ancient port which has become modern Cadiz. Carthage was the main agent in trade in this direction after the seventh century B.C., and the rivalry of the Greeks led to the enforcing of a western limit for Greek shipping at what later became Carthago nova (Cartagena). But Carthage none the less maintained activities in the Mediterranean north and east of that limit, and sometimes tried to banish Greek ships from seas west of Sardinia. A notable station was at Ibiza in the Balearic Islands, and Port Mahon in Minorca was founded by Mago of Carthage. There were other stations on Sardinia and west and north-west Sicily. Herodotus tells of Carthaginian efforts on African coasts beyond the Pillars of Hercules and of their pursuance of 'silent trade' with African peoples. In silent trade one party sets out the goods it offers, and retires a certain distance. The other party then comes and sets out what it is willing to give in exchange and, afterwards, also retires. The parties may adjust their offers and may ultimately effect the exchange or depart without reaching a bargain.

History tells of the long rivalry between Carthage and Rome in Spain and in the western Mediterranean generally and of the destruction of Carthage by the Romans in 140 B.C., after which Numidian kings tried to rule in North Africa.

During, and before, this period of Roman-Carthaginian wars Alexander's general Ptolemy, and the dynasty he founded, were reigning in Egypt, into which, as into North Africa generally, Roman influence penetrated in the last two centuries B.C. The district of Mariout, west of the Nile delta, became specially important as a seat of royalty and was apparently rather better watered than in recent centuries. Alexander the Great in 332–331 B.C. came to Egypt and founded the port-city of Alexandria, which became one of the greatest centres of both trade and culture in the world and maintained its high rank for several centuries. It was a Hellenistic rather than an Egyptian centre, but Egyptian ritual and custom maintained itself to some, diminishing, extent during about four centuries of Roman rule. For Rome, Egypt and North Africa generally were sources of wheat for the Roman people. Cities were built in North Africa, but apparently the Roman building in Egypt was relatively limited, though a great aqueduct still testifies at Cairo to Roman power and energy. Late in the Roman period Christian teaching spread among a population that had partly lost its Egyptian heritage and partly acquired some Greek ideas. The period of Roman rule was followed by some measure of Byzantine control, never very efficient. A population thus cut off from its indigenous cultural roots was easily conquered by Islam in A.D. 640. A succession of cities more or less within the area of modern Cairo can be traced archaeologically, and under Islam, with Mediterranean trade reduced through hostility between Muslim and Christian, Alexandria began a long process of decline, to be reversed only when Mehemet Ali reorganized the country in the early years of the nineteenth century. Its then population, mainly poor fishermen before Mehemet Ali came into power, is variously estimated at figures ranging from 4,000 to 20,000. It must be nearly a million now.

The vast majority of modern Egyptians consider the Islamic tradition to be their own and tend to look upon the older Egyptian heritage as something almost alien. There is an interesting analogy with the English people, who so often identify the Anglo-Saxon heritage as their own and look upon the pre-Roman heritage as alien. In both cases the ancient heritage had been profoundly disturbed in Roman (and in Egypt in Hellenistic) times, and it was too weak to withstand a new onset which brought with it more than the idea of mere conquest. The Islamization of the Berbers of North Africa shows the same factors operating less successfully. Islam spread quickly in North Africa west of Egypt, attaining the coast of Spain in A.D. 711. The sacred city of Qairwan was founded by the Islamic conquerors in A.D. 671, and became the centre of government of North Africa for some centuries. The Islamic armies, called Arab, faced long-continued hostility from indigenous hill peoples who came to be called Berber, from the unintelligibility of their language to the conquerors. The social contrasts between Arab and Berber outlasted the conversion of the latter to Islam; and, when southern Spain was settled by the Muslim, the Arab element tended to gather on the good soil in the valleys and on the lowlands, while the Berber groups rather inhabited the dry plateau of what became New Castile and lived as herdsmen with seasonal movement for change of pasture (transhumance). Islam spread its conquests into the Sahara and the 'Veiled Men' (now called Tuareg) became Muslim. In the eleventh century A.D., a 'reform' of Islam, largely concerned with simplicity of belief and with military ambition, arose in North Africa and was strongly supported by the Veiled Men. It secured power for a time in Spain by quelling disputes between different Islamic rulers, and founded the short-lived dynasty of the Almoravides. But another group of reformers grew quickly among the Berbers of the Atlas, who had long been heretical Muslim. These founded the Dynasty of the Almohades, at first very fanatical against Jews and Christians in Spain, but later becoming more scholarly and tolerant. Their power lasted about a century and a half, and delayed the decline of Islam in Spain.

On the whole, with fluctuations, the population of Egypt was probably lower after Roman times and onwards until the nineteenth century, since when it has increased at a terrifying rate with the spread of cash-cropping for export, of dams and perennial irrigation, and of beginnings of medical treatment on modern lines. Egypt, India, China and Japan, and Java all show this feature of a huge increase since 1800 or later, but, though cash-cropping for export and some medical efforts have operated widely, it would be wrong to think of all these cases as similar. This is a world problem that needs more analysis than has as yet been given to it by psychologists. It is noteworthy that North Africa west of Egypt has been far less affected by this increase; while parts of south-west Asia are probably still underpopulated, and could grow much more food, if irrigation were fully rehabilitated and government made more efficient in encouragement of raised standards of life and reduced reproduction among the peasantries.

6

The European Mediterranean Lands

IT is one of the best-attested inferences that Europe owes the beginnings of its development towards civilization to the region we now usually call the Middle East. Current opinion inclines to suggest that our debt is mainly one to south-west Asia, where, probably, the cultivation of cereals, the main steps in early pot-making and painting, and the beginnings of metallurgy occurred, as well as several early experiments in irrigation.

The silting of a flood plain allowed men to cultivate the same area year after year, and near the flood plain there was not likely to be a long shortage of water, while, on the fringe of the arable land, there was, in south-west Asia, grass for sheep, goats, or cattle. There might be even difficulties of wood-supplies for implements or fuel, and stone might be scarce on the plains.

The spread of the idea of food-production to Europe involved some new problems. It occurred first in the Aegean region, adjacent to south-west Asia, and here, alongside of new problems, there were new opportunities for those who were able to use them.

The islands of the Aegean, and the coasts of Greece and Asia Minor, have hill sites near the sea allowing habitation above flood-level, and fishing as one source of food. The slopes were, in early times, more or less tree-covered, allowing material for fuel and for boat-building. The regularity of the Etesian wind in summer was sufficient to allow boats, even small ones, to navigate among the Aegean Islands keeping in sight of land, so exchange could develop and members of one community could make contact with members of other groups without necessarily hostile intent. The rocks of the Aegean region are typically either calcareous or volcanic, and the former at any rate, being pervious, allow the winter rains to soak in. This water typically emerges from rock-joints or faults, that is, the water-supply is highly localized and concentrated. This has long tended, in the European Mediterranean lands, to encourage the agglomeration of population near the springs. It has been, naturally, springs near defensible hill-sites above useful inlets of the sea that have most commonly attracted settlement.

The long drought and heat of summer entails strong evaporation, so water with dissolved plant-food is drawn up to the surface, but that surface is very liable to form a hard crust in summer because of deposition of lime and iron brought up in solution and left on the surface as the water evaporates. Repeated and criss-cross surface-ploughing is therefore necessary in many areas, so the small plough of south-west Asia is a suitable implement. Usually however, there is not, as there is near the Euphrates and Nile and other rivers, the laying down of fresh silt by a far-spreading annual flood, so the same patch cannot be cultivated every year unless special measures are taken. Cultivation in alternate years is the European Mediterranean rule; but, in a few places with a small water circulation, one crop every third year is the limit. The small cultivator in the European Mediterranean lands is thus apt to be poor, and the restoration of a neglected arable patch may involve heavy work with a pick-axe to break the crust and reach the soil beneath. The hard crust, furthermore, may have a considerable proportion of the soil's plant-food in it, and this will not easily become available again.

On the other hand, the winter rains and mildness encourage evergreen trees with deep roots, especially if they are fond of limy soils, and have tough or hairy leaves as a protection against summer drought. The olive, introduced at some very early period probably from North Africa west of the Nile, does well in European Mediterranean conditions. The fig-tree, with its ability to grow in sandy soils, is another early introduction, if it was not indigenous in or near the Aegean. Most of all the vine, favouring well-drained soils of hill-slopes, has been at home in the Aegean for ages, whencesoever in Mediterranean lands it may have originated. It has encouraged the terracing of hill-sides to preserve the soil, and thus has been a contributor to agricultural progress. The keeping of some wines is a problem, especially in Greece, and resin may be put into the wine, which is then called Rendzina; the wines of the islands of Samos and Santorin and some others are not resined and have become widely famed. The Mediterranean cultivator, who has enough land for olive, vine, and fig-tree, and who can afford to wait while they grow, can get a considerable return from land. More-over, the sheltered soil under spreading figs or vines can grow delicate vegetables in the shade. The apricot and peach and the citrus fruits have been added to the Mediterranean assets in historic times, but olive, fig, and vine seem much older-estab-lished.

The keeping of animals in European Mediterranean lands has had problems to solve. In many parts the sward on the cliffs is burned brown by the dry heat of summer, and the arable areas must not be trampled while crops are growing; further, they may yield little aftermath during the dry summer following the spring harvest. It is therefore often necessary to take animals to a considerable height as soon as winter snows disappear, so that they may eat the grass rich in proteins that grows quickly after the melt-water soaks into the soil, while the sun warms up the surface and gives a plentiful supply of violet and ultra-violet rays. The small cultivator may have little land for animals; the advantage here, again, is with the larger proprietor. In some areas in Macedonia the valley bottoms are so deep and narrow that they are almost sunless in the snowy winter, and settlements have long been at a certain height along the valley sides, as in many other regions of sunless valley bottoms. The farmers may send animals down to the valley bottom when the bitter cold is over and grass is growing, but will often move them up again in summer.

Among plants, heaths are able to survive the dry hot summer and they and other plants, several scented ones, bloom in spring when the rains are over and gone. This gives an opportunity to the bees, which belong to the background of Mediterranean life. The supply of honey, added to that of sugar from grapes and figs and that of hydrocarbons from the olive, makes a great addition to nutrition, while the drying of grapes and figs has allowed the sugar-supply to continue throughout the year. The fact that the tunny and bonito, with solid, highly nutritious flesh, are characteristic fishes is also of importance.

We must note the volcanic rocks such as the obsidian of Melos, as well as the emery of Naxos, also probably copper from Paros and Crete and, most notably, from Cyprus, which gives, or owes, its name to the metal. Obsidian was invaluable for giving sharp-edged flakes, emery was a valued abrasive for rubbing down stone to make bowls or fine implements, and copper was an important asset, especially after the finding of tin at Crissa near the Gulf of Corinth below Delphi.

How far back in time the beginnings of cultivation of the soil in the European Mediterranean may go we do not know. Thick deposits containing potsherds found under the site of the later Knossos were formerly taken as evidence for a high antiquity, but more recently the thickness of deposits from settlements has been found too variable to be used for trustworthy chronological estimates. With these potsherds are found smooth-ground stone axes usually with oval cross-section and transverse edge, a form which is the initial type accompanying the truly Neolithic culture in many lands. It has been claimed that decoration of pots with patterns of incised lines came only after a long phase of undecorated but often burnished ware, with flat bottoms and wide mouths. Female figurines modelled in clay are thought to be associated with fertility rituals. The fact that obsidian tools have been found in very early strata in Crete suggests some sort of maritime communication with the island of Melos in the Aegean, and the female figurines are fairly widely distributed and point to Aegean connexions, especially as some figurines found in Crete are in marble, found on Aegean islands but not in Crete itself.

A bivalve mollusc called *Pectunculus* seems to have had some ritual significance, and its shells are found in early strata in Crete. They, and pottery rather like the early Cretan, are found also in Sicily, Sardinia, and on the Italian coast; so, on the whole, one is tempted to think of an early spread of the beginnings of cultivation over the coastlands of the European Mediterranean, western as well as eastern. Further development was far earlier around the Aegean than around the western Mediterranean. The Aegean was in touch with south-west Asia, advancing rapidly from about 3500–3000 B.C.; and the Aegean early acquired the olive, which apparently did not spread in the west until after 1000 B.C.

Mouflon sheep and more than one species of goat are indigenous wild animals of the Aegean and may have been domesticated at an early stage in Aegean cultural development, but we have no direct evidence. Nevertheless it is difficult to imagine that people who had communications by boat between Crete and Melos and probably elsewhere did not have domestic animals. Models of cattle have been found. The early strata do not show signs of agriculture, but we have smooth-ground stone axes, used as hoes in cultivation in many lands, and stones have been found which have been interpreted as pestles, so the hypothesis of cultivation, probably by hand, is permissible.

It must not be assumed that the early Aegean had only one type of culture and equipment. Crete, with its island-to-island links towards Asia Minor, and its own relatively fertile plains, is in some ways distinct. In addition to its links with Asia Minor it had early connexions with Egypt. Stone bowls apparently related to those of the IIIrd Egyptian Dynasty (*c*. 2900–2800 B.C.) have been found in eastern Crete. The Cyclades had more individual burials and less collective tombs than early Crete, and this implies a difference of tradition. The mainland of Greece seems at first to have lagged behind the islands. Hissarlik on the south side of the Dardanelles is a site that, in a late phase, gave rise to the Troy destroyed by the forces of Agamemnon of Mycenae at the date usually given as 1184 B.C. This late Troy was formerly described as Hissarlik VI, but now, often, as Hissarlik VII. VI seems to have been destroyed by earthquake about 1300 B.C. after lasting nearly five centuries. V and IV were less important. Before them there was an important settlement on this site and this is now usually called Hissarlik III (formerly it was considered a late phase of Hissarlik II). Hissarlik III may have lasted from about 2300 to 2100 B.C. It arose after the destruction of Hissarlik II, which occurred as part of widespread disaster in Egypt and south-west Asia near 2300 B.C. Hissarlik II may have had a life of two or three centuries. Its predecessor Hissarlik I was apparently not of great consequence. Some have dated its beginnings even earlier than 3000 B.C.

It seems likely that during the major stages of Hissarlik's long history the place was of maritime importance. The main current in the Dardanelles sets perpetually towards the Aegean, and the counter-current towards the Marmara is mainly underneath, but reaches the surface under the shadow of Gallipoli. Hissarlik could be a station for crossing the Dardanelles; it could also be a transhipment station, so that ships might land their cargoes without battling up the straits against the Dardanelles current, and those cargoes might, if necessary, be re-embarked on boats in Marmara. When larger ships came into use in the Iron Age they could apparently go up the Dardanelles to Marmara, and the site of Hissarlik lost its old significance; while, later on, Byzantium grew as a harbour for Greek ships to and from the Euxine.

Sir Arthur Evans, the excavator of ancient Knossos (Crete), thought the island was awakened from its early Neolithic state by the advent of North Africans, the surmise being that they were Tehennu from the coastlands west of the Nile delta who had been disturbed when the Egyptian kingdom's organization was spreading. That organization is often given a date about 3400 B.C. or, in some chronologies, a couple of centuries later. But it is evident in Egypt that the organization developed considerably under the IIIrd and IVth Dynasties with extension of trade and development of buildings; these dynasties are dated 2900–2600 B.C. It may have been at any time during this period that Crete and Egypt developed commercial relations. These involved considerable open-sea journeys, though regularity of winds was presumably a help in summer. The islet of Mochlos (north-east Crete) and the plain of the Mesara in south Crete were the most important sites in the island during the third millennium B.C. This phase was called by Evans the Early Minoan and was subdivided into three periods. Copper occurs in Crete and the use of this metal became important during this phase, but bronze was not known. Very thin gold objects were placed in tombs on the Mesara and in Mochlos, but the origin of the gold is unknown. Vessels of stone were made to some extent on the basis of Egyptian styles. It used to be thought that many of the Mesara tombs had been corbelled chambers, but it has more recently been shown that this inference was wrong. Some of the early pottery shows an unusual decoration imitating the graining of wood. The double axe was already of ritual symbolic importance in this early phase; it retained this importance during many later centuries.

Evans supposed his next major phase, the Middle Minoan

(again with three subdivisions) to be datable from 2100 to the sixteenth century B.C., but the last 200 or 250 years (Evans's Middle Minoan III) were a period of decline in Crete; they were a 'Dark Age' in south-west Asia, while Egypt was under the Hyksos or Shepherd Kings and the Indus cities were suffering from barbarian attacks, perhaps of early Indo-Aryans.

FIG. 43. Ritual with priestesses and double axes, Hagia Triada, Crete.

Before this Crete was in touch with Egypt rather than with Europe. It was in this phase that Knossos, just inland from the mid-north coast, became very important, the usual date given for this being about 2000 B.C. A great palace was built at Knossos, and in it were enormous stone jars for grain, wine, and olive oil, which formed a large part of the ruler's wealth. Another palace was built at Phaistos, and it should not be supposed that Crete was wholly under one prince, but the fact of internal peace suggests that one, at Knossos, was supreme. Pottery, at first still hand-made as in the Early Minoan phase, soon came to be shaped on the potter's wheel. Bronze was made, but implements and weapons of bronze from this stage are not very numerous. It may be noticed in this connexion that evidence of defence and of war is slight.

Seals are a great Cretan feature, and on them one finds pictographs, forerunners of the later linear script. The decline above-mentioned seems to have reached its deepest point in Crete with destruction of the palaces at Knossos and Phaistos, but redevelopment, more or less on the old lines, soon occurred. The sixteenth century saw a Cretan revival (the late Minoan phase). In its second stage (L.M. II) resemblances to mainland Greek culture appear at Knossos but not at other Cretan sites. Ventris has recently deciphered a script, known to students as linear B, at Knossos and it is in an ancient form of Greek.

The other Aegean islands were exploited in very early times. Obsidian, occurring only in Melos, was taken to Crete, where it is found at levels that seem to antedate the use of copper. It was taken also to Thessaly. Phylakopi on Melos seems to have developed as a port about the end of the third millennium. The emery of Naxos was also used, and marble from several islands was valued for making figurines of women, probably in association with fertility rites. These figurines became highly stylized and abstract in the course of time. It is thought that the earliest traces of habitation on the lesser Aegean islands are dwellings, and that, subsequently, walled and fortified settlements were developed, thus strongly contrasting with Crete. The importance of the islands (except Crete) diminished early in the second millennium B.C., though the obsidian of Melos remained important until after sharp-edged iron came into use.

On the mainland of Greece there is nothing that can, with any confidence, be dated before the third millennium, and there is no evidence of use of metals at first. Important early settlements are at Orchomenos, near Lake Copais, and at Dimini near the Gulf of Volo, perhaps a little later in beginning than Orchomenos. Dimini has yielded a little bronze and gold from its early phase. Orchomenos had a marked development in the later Bronze Age. Figurines of women are a feature here, as in the islands, and here, also, they become stylized and abstract. The great hill above Corinth (Akrokorinth) has also yielded pottery and other evidences of early settlement.

Before proceeding to the west we must think of Cyprus, a link between south-west Asia and the Mediterranean. In Cyprus, Khirokitia has yielded stone objects, including stone bowls found in tholoi. A tholos is a more or less round chamber with a domed roof which is usually built by corbelling, i.e. by arranging the stones so that the upper ones project inwards above the lower ones. The tholoi of Khirokitia are said to recall those of Arpachiyah in northern Mesopotamia, thought to be the oldest examples of this type of building. At Khirokitia the lower part of the tholos wall is of stone, the upper part of sun-dried brick. A date near the middle of the fourth millennium B.C. has been ventured for this settlement, though the stone bowls suggest a period a few centuries later. Well-made red pottery appears fairly late in the sequence at Khirokitia as an introduction from elsewhere.

Erimi has yielded pottery from modified tholoi, the upper parts of which are of reeds and brushwood daubed with clay. The process of corbelling needs skill and a rough dome of reeds and clay is a substitute. Other substitutes for a corbel are found in the western Mediterranean and western Europe. At Erimi and at most other sites of importance in Cyprus, except Khirokitia, there is evidence of the use of metal, but Erimi yields this only from upper layers. The site, though of early occupation, may have begun its life later than Khirokitia.

Specialists who have studied Cyprus think copper was obtained from and used in the island from the middle of the third millennium onwards. In the Early Bronze Age the intercourse of Cyprus was especially with Anatolia, but local styles in pottery resurge after a more Anatolian phase. Thus far Cyprus has not shown much evidence of the revolutionary disorders that so deeply affected south-west Asia and Egypt about 2300 B.C.

Fig. 44. Ancient models of scenes from early Cyprus.

(after the VIth Dynasty in Egypt and the death of Sargon of Akkad in Mesopotamia). A local Early Bronze Age feature in Cyprus, usually dated near the end of the third millennium, is the modelling of scenes from life. One shows yoked oxen drawing the small plough or aratrum. Another shows a ritual enclosure with three figures in relief on the walls; they have bulls' heads and hold hands, the hands having snakes suspended from them. A priest or prince sits, naked, on a throne and there are several other figures, including a mother with a baby, also a man peeping over the wall near the entrance. This model appears to illustrate some ritual and was found in a tomb. It is a unique specimen and a useful hint to us not to limit too closely the possibilities of play of fancy. About this time or somewhat later, intercourse with the Syrian coast greatly increased, and much white pottery was brought to Cyprus. The early part of the second millennium B.C. was a period of great activity at Ugarit, Byblos, and other ports of the Syrian coast during the XIIth Dynasty in Egypt and while Babylonian commerce was active, especially under Hammurabi. Those ports had a phase of decline, as did Egypt, from about 1750 to 1550 or 1500 B.C., but, as in the case of the troubles round about 2300 B.C., the evidence of decline in Cyprus is not marked.

Looking westwards in the Mediterranean instead of eastwards, the scene is very different. Early use of metal in Cyprus contrasts with long persistence of occupation of Malta by people who have left no metal. Malta is one of the great mysteries of antiquity. The earliest remains known are at Dalam cave, with pottery dated by Sicilian parallels to the last centuries of the third millennium B.C. The Dalam people have left no evidence of building with great stones. At Mgarr a long stratified sequence of later pottery-types has been found and a Megalithic construction has chambers in a tre-foil pattern. Ggantiji in Gozo has an oval chamber added to a large-scale tre-foil plan. The typical later Maltese Megalith, Hal Tarxien being the supreme example, has an entry which may be recessed in a forecourt and which leads into a long oval chamber and opposite the entry of this passage into the inner chamber is a large niche or apse in the wall of the latter. The lower parts of the walls of these spaces are of vertically-set great rectangular stone blocks, above which are evidences of corbelling of horizontally-laid stone blocks, often also very large. It is held to be at least doubtful whether the ovals were roofed, but the apse or niche, and subsidiary niches, may have been corbelled over. A large complex underground system of chambers at Hal Saflieni seems to have served for burials, and, later, as an ossuary.

Carved figures of women, probably linked with a mother goddess ritual, as well as other features, including pottery, suggest Aegean connexions of 2000–1500 B.C., the period of Cretan and early Mycenean expansion; but local characteristics predominate in figures and architecture. As 1750–1600 B.C. was a time of disturbance in Egypt and Asia, Aegean traders may have turned their attention westwards and it is to the years about 1600 that most of the greater Maltese Megaliths, notably much of Hal Tarxien, are now ascribed. Several of these great structures were, or became, temples rather than tombs, and they have pillars and altars as foci of rituals. Their fore courts suggest a link with some rough stone monuments of Atlantic Europe and there are resemblances in pottery to Sicily and Spain, also in Jadeite implements to the west generally. Spiral ornament and corbelling may be links with both the Aegean and the west. Recent work is likely to amplify and improve interpretations, and evidence of Mycenean connexions with the west is accumulating.

This early civilization of Malta ended suddenly about 1500 B.C. An invasion of bronze-users who cremated their dead may have caused, or followed, this end. Some have thought the invaders came from Sardinia. Malta regained importance only

Fig. 45. One of the chambers in Hal Tarxien, Malta.

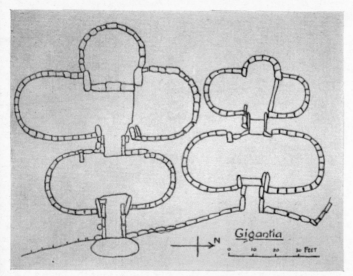

Fig. 46. Ground plan of the elliptical chambers of the
Ggantiji, Gozo Island, near Malta.

with the coming of Phoenician traders in the last millennium B.C. It has been suggested that Megaliths generally are, in one sense, a 'colonial' style of building spread by sailor merchants from the eastern Mediterranean. Whereas in Crete, for example, dressed stone is widely used, it becomes far from general in Megaliths west of Malta, and some regions have almost none.

Over 130 miles west-north-west of the Maltese islands lies the island of Pantelleria, within sight of the African coast and less than 50 miles from it. Pantelleria is volcanic in origin with an extinct crater rising to 2,743 feet above sea-level. It has an area of ancient habitation enclosed by a wall carefully made of un-hewn stone and over 30 feet broad at the base. Obsidian is found on the island and was used for implements, mostly rough. The pottery is plain, but of fairly good quality suggesting links with Sicily and south-east Spain. Near the habitation site, on a rough lava surface, are Sesi, which may be described as carefully built up elliptical heaps of unhewn stone into which lead several separate passages each ending internally in a small domed chamber. The largest Sesi are over 20 feet high and have as many as eleven entrances or passages. No trace of metal seems to have been found. The Sesi have resemblances to monuments on the Tunisian coast, and it has been thought that people came to the island from Tunis, probably for the sake of its obsidian. There is not the wealth of achievement that characterizes Malta, though, in its position, Pantelleria is to an almost higher degree than Malta a junction of the eastern and western Mediterranean basins.

Italy and the Iberian peninsula, as suggested at the beginning of this chapter, may have felt a very early stimulus which started the art of food-production by cultivation almost as early as was the case in the eastern Mediterranean. But subsequent develop-ment around the western Mediterranean long lagged behind that which happened around the eastern basins of the Great

Sea of History. In Spain the art of painting on rock surfaces is claimed to have continued onwards from the last phases of the Old Stone Age into the early days of the New Stone Age, identi-fied with food-production by cultivation, and this has been held to imply a larger continuity than occurs in most other parts of Europe. Spain was obviously relatively important in several phases of the Old Stone Age, but there is not a suggestion that cultivation of food crops had an independent origin in that country. Stimuli from the eastern Mediterranean are generally credited with the awakening of the west; but, for Italy, sunward migration of peoples from the Danube basin accounted for a good deal of early development.

We may perhaps describe in terms of a 'colonial' style the building of monuments with great stone blocks in an unhewn state. These monuments are thence called Megaliths. It is note-worthy that, a little way beyond the east of the Mediterranean, Megaliths occur in Palestine and the Caucasus, as well as in regions as remote as south India, parts of Indonesia, Japan, and some Pacific islands. South of Egypt, again, they occur in the Sudan and Ethiopia. Whether all belong to the same cultural heritage is a question that can hardly yet be answered satis-factorily. The distribution of Megaliths and of other burial customs in western Mediterranean lands shows interestingly that the people who built them were not the only immigrants stimulating the west.

In Italy, Megaliths are found in the heel as it is called, that is in Apulia, particularly in the Terre d'Otranto. The absence of what are Megaliths in the stricter sense from Sicily, which is characterized by early rock-cut tombs, is highly characteristic, while the occurrence on Sardinia of differing types of Mega-lith, including one strikingly contrasted with those of the Terre d'Otranto, is another fact of great interest. In Sardinia the tombs of the giants, as they are called, show a more or less semicircular forecourt marked out by walling on its curved side, but having the straight side open. At the head of the forecourt is a long stone-built 'gallery', and this type of tomb has been called

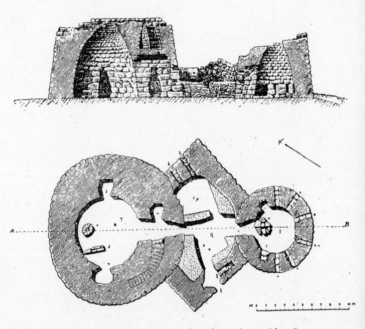

Fig. 47. Vertical and horizontal sections of nuraghi at Santa Barbara, Sardinia.

a gallery-grave. Something like it, but with the long gallery divided by partitions, occurs in Antrim, south-west Scotland, the Isle of Man, west Wales, and north-west England. How far these share a common cultural heritage with the Sardinian monuments remains very doubtful. The Sardinian tombs of the giants seem to be the cemeteries attached to fortified

enclosures guarded by a series of what are called nuraghi. These
are elliptical or circular stone buildings with very thick walls
and they are shaped like a truncated cone. What still stands may
be more than 30 feet high and may have alcove-passages in the
thick walls. Any intruder could either be dealt with by a defender
stationed in one of these passages or could be forced by the
narrowness of the entry to come in sideways and so expose himself to easy attack. The external entry into these nuraghi might
be at a considerable height above the ground, and could be
closed from within. The arrangement of series of nuraghi around
fortified areas suggests organization on a considerable scale
unusual for the early time to which, from their contents, or
the absence of objects of later periods, these monuments are
tentatively referred. Whether the nuraghi have any link with
the Sesi of Pantelleria is an open question.

Sardinia lacks painted pottery which south Italy and Sicily
have yielded. In Sardinia, however, some pots, with ornament
in incised lines, have the incisions filled with coloured material.
The occurrence of megaliths in the Terre d'Otranto is under-
standable when one realizes that they are on the west side of the
Adriatic at its narrowest. The Gulf of Corinth, with the islands
of Ithaca and Leukas near its mouth, was a westward route from
the region of Aegean civilizations, and boats aiming at crossing
the narrow mouth of the Adriatic had a sheltered course from the
Gulf past Corfu northwards. But it is probable that this route was
not in use very early, and the megaliths of this region may be late.

The case of Sardinia is probably to be interpreted as connected with the importance of copper and lead in the island;
and, again here, the megaliths and nuraghi may not all be quite
as early as has sometimes been supposed. Their use may have
continued for a long time. At Anghelu Ruju in north-west
Sardinia and elsewhere in the island are shaft graves, in earth,
very different from the megalithic tombs. Piggott thinks they

may be a spread eastwards from Spain and notes the shaft graves at Mycenae. It is one of the puzzles of antiquity that, though Malta, Otranto, and Sardinia have megalithic monuments, Sicily lacks the kinds found in these areas. The dominance, in a small area, of one tomb-type is a general feature in western Europe. Sicily has late tholoi on its east coast, and there are some graves which are stone boxes or cists made of large slabs, but the great majority of Sicilian graves have been hollowed out in rock, usually limestone, and have a window-like entry closed by a stone slab. There are also shafts in earth. One of the best-known early sites in east Sicily is Stentinello, with fine pottery but relatively poor stone implements, though some are made of imported obsidian. Origins and dates of various phases of early Sicilian culture have been much discussed and are probably not yet definitely interpreted. One must be careful to bear in mind that men were inventive in the days of transition from stone to metal and of expanding intercourse and consequent growth of the need of defence against aggressors. Some influence from the eastern Mediterranean is usually credited with stimulating painted decoration of pottery and perhaps the building of the tholos type of chamber. Immigrations from Africa have also been suggested, and the trend of opinion has been against the idea of the main dependence of Sicily on continental Italy for its early culture. Classical writers have numerous references to the Sicani and Siculi as among the pre-Greek peoples of the island, but their closer identification with archaeological relations is not yet satisfactory.

At Casteluccio in Sicily have been found two bone ornaments with round bosses in relief, and Sicily has yielded pottery of hour-glass form. Both these items suggest Aegean connexions, perhaps with Hissarlik III, at any rate with the northern as well as, in respect of other details, with the southern Aegean. The same affinities can be inferred for the high-spouted jug type of pottery found in the Aegean and in Sardinia. There are a few indications also of connexions between the Aegean and Portugal (see p. 163). The impression at present is that the communications between the northern Aegean and the west may have been via the Gulf of Corinth and the Ionian islands. When, probably about the middle of the second millennium B.C., metal became more abundant, Sicily and the west were related by exchanges to the Mycenean principalities.

In western Sicily, towards the north, bell-beaker pots have been found at Villafrati, and at Gerace and Puleri a little farther north. In Sardinia they have been found at S. Bartolomeo, near Cagliari, and at Anghelu Ruju. It seems probable that these beakers may represent a spread from Spain at or before the beginning of the metal era; beakers are very important in Andalusia.

In the early days of metal, Italy was stimulated by immigrations from the continental north-east as well as from the eastern Mediterranean. Prior to the coming of those stimuli there had been a good deal of cave-dwelling and settlement near caves, apparently on a small scale; and this type of life is thought to have continued in a few spots into historic times. Some peoples, also, moved over from the east side of the Adriatic. The east coast north of the heel or Otranto was not very encouraging to early settlers; harbours are few, metal is rare, soils are poor. The west side of the peninsular Apennines was more attractive, as it yielded some copper, and even tin, in its northern half; and later it was to be also a source of some iron from Elba. Moreover, the soil was better, water-supply richer, and sites for defensible settlements with cropland and water more numerous. The Po basin, near the river and its chief Alpine feeders, must have been subject to severe floods, and early communities lived rather on the moraines south of or between the Italian lakes and on the plains of Emilia well away from the Po.

The major immigration from the north-east, perhaps partly from eastern Switzerland, brought in the idea of building a village on piles and the rite of cremation. Probably the incomers who built what are called the *terramare* villages already knew something about metal. They liked to dig a ditch and to build an earth rampart on its inner side as a protection of their village as already discussed in volume 7 of this series. The *terramare* may have continued in some places until the Iron Age, but various writers have thought that they declined probably about the middle of the second millennium B.C., though one is quite uncertain whether such a decline, if it occurred, had any connexion with the period of eclipse through which so much of south-west Asia, and apparently parts of the eastern Mediterranean, passed about and before that time. While speaking of north Italy, mention should be made of bell-beaker pottery found at Remedello and a few other sites in the Brescia district of Lombardy. These are rather isolated finds, like the few beakers of Sardinia and Sicily, and the suggestion is that they are a result of some contact and exchange with Spain, probably with the Almeria district of that country, to which province the fashion of making bell-beakers spread from Andalusia farther west.

Spain and Portugal have yielded masses of evidence from Megaliths and other remains concerning early settlement and intercourse which it is customary to date to the latter part of the third and the major part of the second millennium B.C. This dating is quite provisional. Scholars have been a little too much inclined to argue that a site which has yielded stone implements but no metal must date back to a time before metal was known in the region concerned. The study of cultures of Neolithic and early metal-using types in the Iberian peninsula has also been influenced, perhaps rather too much, by the hypothesis of local origins as against importations from, for example, the eastern Mediterranean. Corbelled chamber-tombs are found in Andalusia and near the Tagus entry in Portugal and may represent a cultural intrusion from the eastern Mediterranean. If not, we have a remarkable case of convergence of ideas. One must, however, not suppose that these western corbelled tombs are the results of influences from the great monuments of Mycene and Orchomenos. These latter may represent the end-term of a great development. Khirokitia in Cyprus and Arpachiya in Mesopotamia give hints of earlier stages. Piggott, however, wonders whether the great corbel at Mycenae may not express an idea imported from the west.

In Spain and Portugal, instead of the corbel, we often find slab-roofing with great blocks often weighing several tons. It may be that this is a result of the difficulty of the art of cor-belling, or of the presence of the great slab-blocks, which in any case roof the passage from the exterior into the chamber. If the length of the passage were reduced, the ultimate result might be a monument formed by a number of standing stones support-ing one capstone or perhaps two or three, i.e. a chamber without a passage, a dolmen, to use a Breton term. The Leisners think Iberian corbelled tombs are an intrusion into an older slab-roofed tomb scheme.

Dr. and Mrs. Leisner have published inventories from south Spanish Megaliths, and they think the tombs with circular chambers are more south-eastern and those with quadrangular chambers rather south-western in distribution. The latter often have longer entrance passages. The Leisners think the Megalithic idea entered both south-east Spain (Almeria) and west Portugal probably 2200–1800 B.C. They think corbelled chambers come relatively late in the Iberian sequence and that any burial with beaker pottery in a megalith is intrusive.

Spain in its early metal phase made bell-shaped beaker pots of fine quality. These have been looked upon as results of an

a

b

FIG. 48. Spanish bell-beakers. *a*. Ecija, Province
of Sevilla; *b*. Los Millares, Province of Almeria.

evolution from early rough pottery of southern Spain, but may be an introduction from outside. The form known as the beaker is known from the eastern Mediterranean region. In Andalusia this pottery has been found at Carmona and Coronil, also at Ciempozuelos and neighbouring sites north of the Tagus in New Castile. It spread to the Portuguese coast in the west and to Almeria in the east, and from this latter it may have gone to Sardinia, Sicily, and Italy. On the Portuguese coast it was made only for a short time, but in Spain it had a longer history and a wider spread, to the two slopes of the Pyrenees. From either the Portuguese coast or the Pyrenees the idea of the bell-beaker spread to Brittany. Beaker pottery is further discussed in Chapter 7.

Almeria in south-east Spain is thought to have used copper very early. The people at Los Millares and some other places built Megaliths, but also, at some places, buried their dead in a hole in a rock, in a cave, or in a shaft grave, covered by a stone slab. When the shaft is partly or wholly lined with stone we get virtually a stone box or cist. Whereas, in the rest of Spain of the days when metal was coming into use, arrow-heads of finely chipped flint were typically made with concave bases, i.e. may be said to have had barbs but no tang, those used in Almeria usually had a tang as well as barbs. The tang in some cases is so wide as to give the whole arrow-head a lozenge shape. The Almeria culture spread along eastern Spain to Catalonia and the Pyrenean region generally.

Here one may mention that a decorated ivory knob found at Nora in Portugal is very much like one found in what is now often called Hissarlik III, that Portuguese monuments have yielded about 1,100 beads of callais, a semi-precious stone, and 27 beads of this material have been found at Kadi Keui near the Bosporus as well as about 800 in Morbihan, Brittany, and that a segmented stone bead, much like some from the Cyclades, has been found at Palmella, Portugal.

Apparently the fashions of Almeria, notably the use of bronze, spread in the course of time over the rest of Spain, but there is general agreement that the prosperity of the Iberian peninsula declined very markedly late in the second millennium B.C.

The attempt has been made to show that, about or before the middle of the second millennium B.C., there was much disturbance and change in south-west Asia, North Africa, and the Mediterranean. The quest for copper and tin had been widespread before this for some centuries, but supplies in many areas were not yet very large, nor was there as yet any general use of furnaces hot enough for actual complete melting of bronze. There was still a great deal of hammering of softened bronze to make weapons, which, in the next phase, would be cast, but casting was already old-established in south-west Asia and had begun to spread at least in the eastern Mediterranean.

We can hardly claim that there were what could be called fully developed cities in the Mediterranean in the phases reviewed so far in this chapter, but there were agglomerations of population sometimes around palaces, sometimes for defence on a fortress site. In the west only Almeria shows evidence of this at the period under consideration.

In the period 1750–1600 B.C. troubles around the eastern Mediterranean, as also in the Indus basin, were due in considerable part to the spread of horsed warriors, probably from the Turkestan area in the first instance. They spoke Aryan languages, but these may already have been in use rather earlier in Greece and Crete as Mr. Ventris's work suggests. This period of disorder passed away, and, after 1500 B.C. came an increase of bronze tools made by casting in clay-moulds. This implies the more general spread of better furnaces to melt the bronze, towards 1100 B.C. It also made possible the remelting of old bronzes and this reduced difficulties about supplies of copper and tin. One should add that Malta seems to have lost its importance rather earlier, perhaps soon after 2000 B.C. Cyprus, on the other hand gained increased importance as a source of copper.

At some time, probably in the seventeenth and sixteenth centuries B.C., colonists, including a Cretan element, but also some, perhaps later, who came through northern Greece, settled at and near the head of the Gulf of Argos in Greece. There they found patches of fertile red soil to grow food crops, while there was also a reasonable approach from the sea, as well as the possibility of reaching the head of the Gulf of Corinth, and so using a way to the west without risking storms around Cape Matapan. It is quite probable that the westward way along the Gulf of Corinth had already been used for a long time, as is mentioned above (see p. 157). On the great hill, Akrokorinth, above the Roman and modern town of Corinth, one finds evidence of early classical and earlier (Mycenean) activity.

Mycenae and Tiryns are the two chief centres, the former being of special importance with the citadel overlooking the lowland but difficult of access for an enemy. It may have been a seat of authority from the sixteenth to the twelfth century B.C. It is more strictly a citadel than a city, a fortified palace with its subsidiary buildings and shaft-graves included within the circuit of a wall. Its famous Lion Gate has been reproduced in many publications. There has long been discussion as to relative dates of various erections and notably of the famous Treasury of Atreus some distance outside the citadel. Here a façade which once had over the doorway a relieving triangle with rampant lions leads into a great corbelled dome with a side-chamber on the right. It was thought by the early investigators that the monument, as we see it, was built in two phases, the passage and façade and then the corbelled dome and, in this view, one of these might be a new or a rebuilt feature. Later detailed study has ascribed the whole erection to the fourteenth century B.C. Professor Wace has recently found some inscribed tablets probably datable to the thirteenth century B.C., and apparently giving details of commerce, showing that literacy was well developed at this time. There is abundant evidence of general aggrandizement at Mycenae in the fourteenth century B.C., after the domination of Knossos had been brought to an end by the destruction of that city. At Mycenae power was in the hands of Achaean Greeks. Patrilineal succession was soon to emerge, and male gods of Olympus were to some extent to replace older female deities whose prototype was the Mother Goddess, the supposed source of fertility. But still in Mycenae the ideas of a goddess, Hera, and of matrilineal succession held sway. Matrilineal succession, in practice, meant that he who possessed the women of royal descent was widely acknowledged to have a strong claim to the throne concerned. David's use of Saul's daughter Michal for his political ends is a well-known feature of the Hebrew story (2 Samuel iii. 13).

The unique story of the Trojan war gives the last triumph of Mycenae and the destruction of Troy (Hissarlik VII) in 1184 B.C., according to recent dating.

About and after 1200 B.C. there was a widespread breakdown. Ras Shamra (Ugarit) and Byblos come to the end of their power. Egypt goes on in a weakened condition. The Hittite power in Anatolia breaks down. The destruction of Troy is followed by the decline of Mycenae. Decline in Cyprus is much less marked, as was the case also in earlier crises, but the precious metals become less abundant.

One factor of the general disturbance was the movement of warriors from the continental south-east of Europe into the area of more developed Mediterranean civilization and probably other immigrations occurred in south-west Asia; we note the rise of a new military autocracy at Nineveh, fighting Aramaean tribes in the early part of the eleventh century B.C. The camel was coming into general use in south-west Asia.

Another factor in the situation was the spread of iron-smelting from Anatolia and the consequent increase of iron weapons. It is now thought doubtful whether the Dorian invaders of the twelfth and eleventh centuries B.C. came into Greece with iron weapons; it is fairly certain that they had such

FIG. 49.   Urn in grave of a Dipylon Necropolis.

weapons not long after their arrival in Greece. With the coming of iron, commerce in copper, tin, obsidian, and emery would be subject to fluctuation. Iron tools must have been beginning to affect carpentering, and soon ships were to become larger and stronger. All this ferment of change was affecting an area of old-established cultivation, in parts of which the soil was probably getting poorer, as so often happens under rudimentary techniques of cultivation. In Greece the old Achaean-Mycenean aristocracy was overwhelmed by a military group of northern tradition that, for a time at least, recked little of the older Mycenean and pre-Greek heritages.

Thucydides reminds us that early Attica was still largely dependent on home-grown cereals, but the 'Dipylon' pottery of the ninth-century Athens indicates rising skill and wealth. Probably the native, closely related to Mycenean-Greek, tradition, gathering around the worship of the local goddess Athena, with the sign of the owl, was becoming self-consciously important again. But the later dramatists give us an interesting glimpse of a change in Athena, a change associated with the substitution of patrilineal for matrilineal succession.

During Agamemnon's long absence from Mycenae, Clytemnestra was taken possession of by his cousin and enemy Aegisthus. When Agamemnon eventually came back, a solution of the marital problem was sought through killing him and Cassandra, who had been allocated to him after the fall of Troy. Aegisthus thus became king, as now Clytemnestra's husband. But Orestes, the son, and Electra, the daughter of Agamemnon, disputed the succession and sought vengeance for the murder. Orestes was the patrilineal successor, and murdered Clytemnestra and Aegisthus. The Greek dramatists work up the subject and bring the gods and goddesses into the dispute. Apollo naturally favours the patrilineal succession. Athena, however, also claims to support the male; no female bore her, she sprang from the head of Zeus. The Eumenides or Furies seek the death of Orestes as a punishment for his murder of his mother. They are defeated by the gods and disappear for ever, but Orestes is committed to expiatory wanderings. Among many interesting points one may note that Athena, most probably an early Mycenean-Greek goddess, is given a new lineage, linking her with Zeus and the Olympian Pantheon. There is thence evident the long struggle between matrilineal and patrilineal schemes.

The Achaean and Dorian warriors were great meat-eaters as descendants of herdsmen coming into Greece from farther north. The older stocks, indigenously Aegean, ate more fish and little meat. As the generations passed, and herding played a smaller and smaller part in Greek life, the ration even of the wealthier people came to include very little meat and a good deal of fish; the indigenous influences forced themselves on the people. The olive-tree was increasingly cultivated, often on the lower hill-slopes, in Attica from Solon's time (beginning of the sixth century B.C.) onwards; and this gave a possibility of an export with which to pay for imports. These were apparently largely carried by Phoenicians during the early stages of the rise of Athens, but, later on, Athens developed her own shipping, greatly helped therein by her harbour of the Piraeus, and increased her wealth also from the silver of Sunium. So Athens emerged from her old rather simple life and self-contained economy into a centre of long-distance trade, with colonial foundations at many a distant harbour. It is one of the most important facts in the story of humanity that Athens strove to maintain as a seat of authority the general assembly of heads of, at any rate, a considerable number of leading families—a direct democracy or oligarchy in some measure, though slaves were kept as a source of labour.

During the period of the growth of Athens the great majority of her households practised cultivation whatever special occupation might also be carried on in addition, but in later days specialization had increased and made the old universality of food-growing impracticable; and the increased numbers of families made the old direct democracy, partial as it had been, impossible.

The typical scheme in classical Greece was that of the polis for which we use the English term city-state, and the rivalries and wars between the different city-states of Greece make up a large part of their story and largely account for their eventual subjugation by Philip of Macedon. Yet the polis fostered individuality and genius as perhaps no other system has ever been able to do.

The idea of the city spread far and wide in the Mediterranean and Euxine regions in the last seven or eight centuries B.C. Port-cities were established at many places on the coasts of Anatolia, in eastern Sicily, southern Italy, Mediterranean France, and north-east Spain. And first Italy and then the other regions of south-west Europe were thereby brought into what is called the domain of civilization. At the same time the Phoenicians, increasingly ousted from trade with Greek cities, developed Tyre, and then Carthage, Malta, Motya in west Sicily, Tarshish (Andalusia), and Cartagena (Carthago Nova).

In Italy, Greeks and Etruscans, spreading from the Aegean, developed the growing of the olive and built port- and hill-cities, meeting, and in places combining with, Latins and Umbrians who had come into Italy from the Danubian region. Whereas in Greece the classical civilization had developed through a large measure of absorption of rough conquerors by the indigenous tradition, in Italy one finds rather the clashes and combinations of diverse immigrants, some of them rather commercial, some more military. The heritage from indigenous folk of long standing seems much less definite in the cities of Italy, though no doubt the plebeian elements of their population had large proportions of descendants of indigneous peoples. The Adriatic coasts north of Corfu and Otranto were less affected for a while. In the eastern Mediterranean, too, Egypt stood to some extent aside from Mediterranean developments at this time, being under Persian dominion along with several parts of south-west Asia.

Among the newly developed Mediterranean cities of classical times the most significant was Rome, founded in 753 B.C. according to tradition. A number of fragments of a dissected table of lava on the banks of the lower Tiber formed adjacent hills on which groups settled bringing in Etruscan, Latin, and Umbrian traditions. Their meeting-place for discussion was a space between the hills, and it became the *Forum romanum*, the focus of the Roman Empire. A code of law was written out for the complex group and it claimed general validity and was not tied to any particular group of family traditions or cults. The city came to give hospitality to many cults, provided they did not claim exclusive allegiance; its law and administration were increasingly secularized or laicized. At the same time the Romans were impelled by their environment to develop civil engineering by building causeys (*causeways* is a corrupted rendering in English) across the marshes near their city, and by making bridges both across the Tiber and, as time went on, at many places along the roads. And the law was held to apply along the roads as well as, progressively, in the cities on those roads. The law was a codified *modus vivendi* between peoples of diverse traditions and not, as in the Greek city, a creative influence affecting the expression and development of the local tradition. Order and peace rather than creative expression were its primary aims, and wealth of equipment increased markedly as Roman rule first spread. As time passed, the growth of luxury and idleness at the centre, the long distances involved in the control and defence of the whole Mediterranean area and the approaches to it, the difficulty of succession to the imperial power, financial mistakes bringing depreciation of currency and decline of trade and towns, all contributed to weaken the system. After about the middle of the third century A.D. Roman towns in Britain were declining, though apparently villa-owners in the country had some prosperity. The wealth and display within the Roman Empire was a perpetual temptation to warriors from beyond its borders, who no doubt also felt that the Empire might attempt to conquer them and force them into the system. So defence came to play a larger part in the scheme, economic problems of standards of living became acute and the unity of the Empire was increasingly threatened. As two of the chief threats were from south Russia and Parthia (Persia), Byzantium was rebuilt on a large scale as Constantinople in the early fourth century A.D., a new capital between and not too far from the two most serious danger-points. And an attempt was made to establish a new unity by adopting Christianity as the exclusive official cult and discarding the moribund rituals of an older time. Byzantium, a Greek port-colony of the eighth century B.C., had had a varied story, some-times under Sparta and sometimes under Athens. It became more or less independent, and then came under Rome, was twice partially destroyed by Roman armies, but eventually attained imperial rank. Its splendid harbour, for the shipping of classical times, was in a position to make it a centre for refitting grain ships on their ways to and from the Black Sea.

The attempted unity of the Mediterranean lands under Rome, or Rome and Constantinople, collapsed after a last attempt to make it more effective under Justinian in the middle of the sixth century A.D. Currency and commerce declined and cities lost heavily in population. Local sovereignties multiplied and men were driven to seek protection under one or other lord, lay or ecclesiastical. The persecutions organized to enforce uniformity of religious belief at the same time led to disaffection, particu-larly in parts of south-west Asia where the tradition of religious thought was so old and so complex. All this gave a special opportunity in the seventh century A.D. to the followers of Muhammad to propagate the strictly monotheistic doctrine of Islam enforced by military power of men of the desert border.

A fundamental environmental contrast within the Mediter-ranean region was made dramatically evident. The lands south of a line from Armenia or Aleppo to Qairwan in Tunisia are dry and depend mainly on irrigation, with Tunisia and Palestine-Syria as transition zones. These regions of irrigation and desert borders became the basis of the Islamic scheme of life, and from them the scheme extended itself to Turkestan on the one hand, whither Hellenization had penetrated previously, and to North Africa and Spain on the other. There thus came about a division of the Mediterranean into mutually hostile areas with Italy no longer a centre of attempts at unity but rather a dangerous projection of Europe into a hostile unknown. This was a further disaster for trade and town life as well as for drainage schemes in rural areas. Land went out of cultivation, malaria and other troubles increased in areas now ill-drained, and poverty became a general characteristic on the European side, while early Islamic enthusiasm carried the ideas of Muhammad and some heritages from the Hellenistic civilizations of south-west Asia to Sicily, Italy, and Spain (see p. 113).

A revival began with a resumption of some little intercourse between European and Islamic Mediterranean lands in the tenth century A.D. Ravenna in Adriatic Italy had retained some importance during the Dark Age, and Venice and Torcello began to be important, the latter being rapidly eclipsed by the former; Salerno received elements of medical lore from Greek tradition transmitted via Islam. In this way the European Mediterranean lands began a third phase of blossoming of urban life and wealth. The first phase may be said to have lasted from about 3000 B.C. to perhaps 1200 or 1150 B.C., the second one was the classical phase from about 800 B.C. to about A.D. 500. The third one was preceded by extensions of forest clearing and plough cultivation in western Europe beyond the Mediterranean region, so that by the eleventh and still more by the twelfth century A.D. a demand for goods brought by Mediterranean commerce appeared in the west, and so the trading cities of Mediterranean Europe were beginning to have distant markets for their goods. In addition to this, Cordoba, the then capital of Islamic Spain, became a centre of learning and the arts, and to it came young noblemen from Christian Europe. It is probably through Cordoba, or at any rate through Islamic Spain, that the art of making glazed pottery reached post-Roman Europe (see also p. 113).

The hostility between Christian and Islamic Spain and the phase of decline into which the latter entered in the twelfth century limited the development of Cordoba as a culture-centre and it soon lost importance in that sphere of activity. In the Adriatic, Venice and Ragusa, both somewhat apart from ecclesiastical domination, seem to have been ready to trade with Islam. Ragusa has given its name (modified) to the English language as Argosy, with the meaning of a cargo fleet. The high mountain lines of the Balkan peninsula behind it limited its growth as contrasted with that of Venice. The latter on its islets was well protected from land invasion in the Middle Ages, and it had serviceable ways into Lombardy and up the Trentino to the Brenner Pass and so to the Germanic lands. The growing populations of the latter consumed salted flesh in winter; and, as salt was often scarce, salting was imperfect. This gave the pepper and other spices of the east, bought by Venice from Arab traders, an important market, and Venice became the chief of the early medieval trading cities. Her rival, Genoa, was under the Apennines, liable to interference from local potentates, and subject to the difficulty of the mountain ridge to be crossed on the way to Lombardy, with another great climb to pass the Alps. Genoa was thus usually weaker than medieval Venice, and another factor played an important part in their rivalry.

Venice's islet-site gave her a feeling of a separate individuality, and a consequence of this was a great growth of civic patriotism, and, for a long time, a disinclination to acquire territory on the mainland, though the fifteenth century saw a change here. Genoese merchants, on the other hand, might be drawn into alliance with some local lord or the city might seek to secure its safety by drawing a local lord into its system.

Pisa was an important, though lesser, rival of Genoa, and another early one was Amalfi. But both Salerno and Amalfi were limited by the choice of Naples as a capital city of the kingdom of the Two Sicilies in the twelfth century. Whereas Naples was a coast city with a resident dynasty, Venice and Genoa were oligarchies under merchant rulers. Milan grew as a trading city, a focus below Alpine passes. Florence developed as a merchant-oligarchy, inland, a focus south of the most useful pass through the Apennines. But before saying more about the inland trading cities, reference must be made to another great factor of urban development.

During the Dark Ages following the fall of the Roman Empire the memory of Roman Law became gilded, and this added to the prestige of the bishops of the Roman Church, who, more than anyone else, represented the imperial heritage. When revival came in the late eleventh and the twelfth centuries, Roman law and theology were objects of studious interest, and it was necessary to learn Latin in order to discuss them. On the way to Rome students from many directions would have to pass through northern Italy, and Bologna, at the northern entry to the chief southward pass through the Apennines, became a gathering-place for students who employed teachers of Latin and law. So began there the mother of western universities. 1110 is sometimes given as a date round about which there was a great growth of its organization. It added other faculties as it grew, and other universities developed on fairly similar lines elsewhere in north Italy. Pavia has claimed a foundation of some kind in the tenth century, but it became formally a university only in 1361. It grew at a gathering of roads from north and west near the Ticino river before that stream joins the Po and this river begins to spread its flood plain. Padua, on the way from Venice up the Brenta and into the Trentino, the route northward to the Brenner Pass, is another early university that has persisted. It is highly characteristic that these universities, originally student-democracies, grew more strongly north of the Apennines than to the south-west of those mountains.

Among the trading cities, Florence gained a very high position in the later Middle Ages, largely under the leadership of the merchant family of Medici. Fine cloth, dyed scarlet in quantities, became a main product and some of it was bought in England to be dyed and finished at Florence. The Pope at the time was receiving tribute from England, and Florence made an agreement with Rome whereby moneys collected for the Papacy in England were used by the Florentines to buy wool and cloth to be imported to Florence. Payment was made by Florence from its sales of finished cloth, and in this way complications of currency transfers were reduced. The wealth of Florence and of Rome both increased in the late Middle Ages for this and other reasons, and the latter city acquired many great buildings, notably the Church of St. Peter.

In the Balkan peninsula, struggle with the Turks not only held back city development but made for serious regression, from which only parts of the region have as yet emerged.

Spain was intensely occupied with the struggles between Romanism and Islam during the Middle Ages and from the twelfth century onwards for a time the latter, under the Almoravides and the Almohades, lost a good deal of the cultural tradition which, in earlier centuries, had been developing in Islamic Cordoba (see p. 173). Jewish learning sought for a while to mediate between the two religions of Spain, but growth of prejudice on both sides led to the attempted expulsion of the Jews from Spain after the final defeat of Spanish Islam in the days of Ferdinand and Isabella in the fifteenth century. Salamanca, however, at the northern (or Christian) end of a pass through the middle sierras of Spain, developed a university in the thirteenth century with a considerable interest in mathematics, a hint of some link between Christian and Islamic Spain. In the Christian north cathedral cities grew at stations such as Burgos and Leon on the road to the shrine of St. James (Santiago da Compostella), the base of the resistance to Islam. Toledo, at one time a Muslim advance-post facing Christian Spain, became the ecclesiastical metropolis of the latter, for a while facing the declining power of Islam in that country. Barcelona had the good fortune to remain more or less apart from at least some phases of the struggle between the two religions, and it grew considerably, in trade with Marseille, developing the Catalan language, which has Spanish and southern French elements in its make-up. Spain thus had some urban development in the Middle Ages, but nothing comparable with what occurred in Italy, and much the same might be said of Portugal. In Spain a good deal of the Islamic heritage, on the social and economic side, persisted among the transhumant herdsmen of the regions of New Castile and Estremadura who included numbers of Berbers from North Africa distinct in many ways from the irrigating Islamic cultivators of the huertas of Valencia.

The opening up of ocean commerce by the voyages of discovery from the mid-fifteenth century onwards led after a while to the decline of the commercial cities of Italy, but gave wealth for a time to Portugal and Spain. Lisbon became important, and Madrid was created as a new, centrally-placed capital. Lack of commercial skill combined with bitter persecution to frustrate the Spanish effort, and Portugal was very isolated from the rest of the continent and also hampered by persecution. The primacy in ocean trade passed to France, Holland, and Britain, with the first of these also suffering gravely from expulsion and other ill-treatment of an intellectual and spiritual *élite* for heresy.

Portugal maintained intercourse with Africa and also with the East Indies, and some people of partly African descent have since remained in the south of the country.

In Spain the early energy declined rapidly, and trade and cities were almost stagnant. Madrid had a long struggle with the chief towns of various sub-regions and was hardly a true capital until the railway came to its help in the nineteenth century. Even then, Barcelona remained something more than a rival.

On the whole the Mediterranean lands had a period of decline from the early seventeenth to the nineteenth century, partly because of the new importance of ocean voyages, partly because of the increasing inefficiency of the Turkish Sultanate and the Mamelukes in Egypt. One should note, however, at least one feature of a different kind. The invention of cannon had made the medieval castle useless, and the increase of commerce had led to the development of the mansion with new comfort in furniture and consequently new skill in woodcraft. One result was a growth of ideas concerning musical instruments, and northern Italy, especially at Brescia and Cremona, led in the improvement of the violin from the older viol. The names of several generations of the Amati family and still more of their pupil Stradivarius are universally acclaimed. But the major development of music following this improvement of instruments must be assigned to lands north of the Alps and especially to the German development culminating in J. S. Bach, and the Vienna tradition with Glück, Haydn, Mozart, Beethoven, Weber, Schubert, Brahms, and Strauss. On the other hand, decline showed itself markedly among the painters in Mediterranean lands. The leadership in this art passed to France, and especially Holland, with emphasis on secular and contemporary subjects and, gradually, on the life of the common people from the time of Pieter Brueghel the elder, as well as on landscape, no longer a mere background for a religious picture, but a subject treated in its own right.

The early nineteenth century saw the Mediterranean at a disadvantage, lacking coal and iron, and retaining a number of petty states in Italy, as well as an out-of-date system of government, education, and agriculture in Spain, and exhibiting more than ever the results of decadence of the Turkish Sultanate. Among the factors of subsequent recovery pride of place must probably be given to the cutting of the Suez Canal by the French engineer de Lesseps (1869). This was a most important item in the general economic development initiated earlier in the century under Mohammed Ali el Kebir in Egypt. Marseille, Barcelona, Genoa, Naples, and Alexandria grew remarkably, but grew chiefly as port-cities destined to live within regional governmental entities rather than as individual sovereignties on the lines of the medieval Italian city-republics.

At the close of the nineteenth century came the second Industrial Revolution introducing electric power and the oil-using internal combustion engine, as well as enlarged plans for the building of irrigation-dams. Cairo now has over 1·5 million people and the effective agglomeration at Barcelona is of this same magnitude with Milan, Rome, and (especially since the evacuation of Greeks from Asia Minor) Athens nearly as large. Naples and Alexandria are near the million mark; Marseille, Istanbul, Genoa, Turin, and Palermo overtop the half-million level.

The prehistoric, classical, and medieval blossomings of Mediterranean life may thus be in process of being followed by a new development concerning which one had better not attempt to prognosticate to any extent. Perhaps the polis or city-state is definitely out of date, and some regional sovereignties may need to combine. The absence of coal may be compensated by the presence of oil. The disjuncture between the poor peasant and the townsman remains as a serious handicap.

7

Europe North of Mediterranean Lands

THE development of social life in Europe north of the Mediterranean lands contrasts dramatically with what has been noted for the European shores of that sea. Whereas 'cities' began in the Aegean about 3000 B.C., in Europe north of the Mediterranean city development was in an embryonic stage until the conquests of the Roman legions. Roman power spread northwards to the Rhine and Danube and, as time went on, during peaceful interludes, barbarians from the wilds of central Europe might sometimes cross these rivers and find themselves in centres with streets laid out and public buildings in stone. Another contrast is dependent upon the above. Whereas, in the European Mediterranean, the city, and especially the port-city, stood rather apart from the rural folk, some of whom were typically extremely poor, in the lands north of the Mediterranean life developed mainly on a rural foundation, and, where towns and cities grew, they often functioned as foci for their rural surroundings. The territorial unit has often gathered around its common speech a wealth of associations; and these were enormously strengthened when, in the sixteenth century A.D., the prestige of imperial Rome, continued under the papacy, gave way over large areas, and vernacular languages increasingly replaced Latin, while freer-ranging Greek thought increasingly influenced men's minds.

The contrast between city-state in the European Mediterranean and territorial state in the lands farther north is naturally not absolute, the case of Lübeck in the late twelfth and the following centuries A.D. at once comes to mind. It is rather a difference of emphasis.

Another contrast between the two regions concerns their mineral resources, in this case apart from those of Spain. Italy

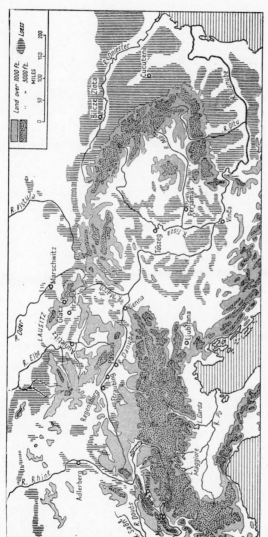

FIG. 50. Map of distribution of loess in central Europe.

and the Greek region were and are not well supplied with minerals, whereas Bohemia and Ireland were notable for copper in early times and the former and Cornwall were famed for their tin, while, with the utilization of iron smelted by wood fires, the forested north gained a great advantage, immensely increased in modern times through the use of coal.

We may subdivide our region of Europe north of Mediterranean lands, in various ways that are supplementary, and to some extent corrective, to one another.

Europe is the continent into which coastal seas penetrate most deeply, and the Baltic Sea has at times played a part analogous to that of the Mediterranean, though usually on a poorer level. Coasts and interiors are thus one scheme of division.

Europe, again, is a continent with a very varied assortment of rocks in its structure. Some are porous, others impervious, in some cases the hard rock is covered, at most, by a fairly thin soil, in others it is mantled in loose material which often is boulder clay transported by former glaciers and ice sheets. Hard porous rock may not have more than thin bush growing on it, while the impervious surfaces may often have better developed woodland. But both these statements are subject to reserves. The scarp-side of porous rocks may have water pouring out, and this gives an opportunity to trees, as, for example, in the hanger woods of the beech-tree on the scarp slopes of the Chalk in southern England. And many areas of hard impervious rock with very little soil-cover cannot grow much wood. These considerations help to interpret some data of distribution of settlements and lines of communication of early times.

But still more important in connexion with social evolution is the broad classification on the basis of soils.

From the ice sheets of the Pleistocene period winds blew out and picked up fine-grained material as they passed over the moraines at the edges of the ice sheets. They carried this material until forced to drop it, either after spreading a very long distance as in south Russia, or on meeting a high obstacle such as the Carpathian range. This dropped material allowed grass to grow on it, but this grass was progressively buried as the accumulation continued. If, as generally happened, there was a little lime or iron or both in the wind-borne material, it tended to form a crust around grass-stalks or leaves as they became buried. As they decomposed, therefore, a tube was left in the deposit, and the tube might be nearly vertical. So the deposit is typically fine-grained and yet porous because of these tubes. It is called loess and differs in character according to circumstances. The Russian loess, brought by winds from Scandinavia and Finland, was and still is frozen in winter and arid in summer, and there was no high obstacle on the way. So, in the first place, the loess is laid down over a very wide southwards-extending belt with its northern edge along a line from the Carpathians and the Dniester right away beyond Kazan into Asia and, in the second place, freezing in winter and aridity in summer have retarded decomposition of the grasses and draining off of the products of decomposition, so the loess is rich in organic matter in its upper layers and is called Chernoziom or black earth.

Farther west the winter freeze has not been so long and the summer aridity does not exist; in fact the summer has the maximum rain, in many cases largely thunderstorm rain. Therefore one does not often find black earth. North of the Carpathians the loess is in a belt of quite moderate width. Hungary is largely floored by loess, that between the Danube and Tisza being subsequently re-sorted by water and thus having fewer aeration tubes. The Hungarian loess, and also that of parts of south Germany, has been carried from the moraines of the Alpine and Tatra ice sheets. Towards the west the loess shows more and more effects of rain and grades into what is called *Limon des plateaux* in northern France and brick earth in south-east England.

The friability of the loess, its organic content, its aeration, and its very general iron and lime content all make it useful arable land. It was fairly easy to clear of bushes and small trees and often it does not grow trees to any large extent again when once cleared, so it was available for early settlement. Its friability made it workable with the small plough of probably Middle or Late Bronze Age times, and it shows traces of settlement from the early part of the third millennium B.C. onwards. But, as regards the part of the loess east of the Dnieper, its bitter winter and arid summer and its dangerous proximity to the great steppe, the region of nomad raiders, limited its utilization on a large scale until modern times.

In western Europe, at least south of latitude 60° N., large areas of lowland are covered with loam containing a good deal of clay and therefore not very permeable, often, in fact, practically impervious. Here there may be rain in all seasons, and, because evaporation is not often very rapid, dissolved salts are distributed throughout the whole depth of the soil instead of being drawn up to the surface as in the case of the red soils of many Mediterranean lands. A good deal of organic matter remains in the soil, which is therefore generally brown, a richer brown when there is more aeration and porosity, a greyer surface colour when there is less. These brown earths in the climate of western Europe mostly became forested after the ice sheets and glaciers passed away; and, after a phase of pinewoods, there spread oak and ash and elm and, in some places, beech. These were mostly large trees difficult for man to cut down on a large scale until he had iron axes. The lowland brown earths of western Europe were therefore not greatly cleared or used by man before the Iron Age, though no doubt river gravels gave more open surface and sometimes allowed river-bank settlement and movement. This paucity of woodland-clearance before the Iron Age kept back social evolution in western Europe far behind the early achievements of Mediterranean and Middle-Eastern peoples. In Britain, Stonehenge and Avebury show what could be achieved in a region without forest of a dense kind. Even if clearing was achieved here and there, another difficulty presented itself. In the brown earths the plant-food is distributed, as the colouring shows, throughout the thickness of the soil and not concentrated in the top layers as in the red earths of the Mediterranean. The little plough, which keeps the surface from caking under the hot summer sun of the south, is of only very moderate value in the case of the brown earths, and even it may not go back, in mid-Europe, beyond the Late, or Middle, Bronze Age. Here one really needs a plough making a deeper furrow and bringing up the deeper layers of soil to the surface, and such ploughs could not be very effective until they had iron ploughshares and were of considerable size, to be drawn by a team of animals. Here and there larger ploughs may have been made before the Iron Age, as Ligurian rock-drawings suggest, but it is in the Iron Age that plough-lands were increased by woodland clearance on the lowland clays with iron axes. This increase brought greater concentrations of population, and barbarian fortress-towns were developing as Roman conquests began to spread in Gaul and Britain. But, though towns began, and soon had widespread development within the Roman Empire, the large plough and its agricultural and social consequences have been fundamental factors of the further development of life in western and northwestern Europe, a development basically rural and territorial, though in recent centuries characterized by the mammoth cities, London, Paris, and Berlin.

In northern Europe, north of latitude 60° N. but still south of the Arctic Circle, the ground is often snow-covered for months and, when the snow is melting, the water drains down into the soil and carries down soluble plant-food. Evaporation is nearly always slow, so comparatively little dissolved material is drawn up. The soil is often grey at the surface, especially after rain, and any lime and iron is likely to be near the bottom. A big plough is more than ever needed in these circumstances, but the climate is too chill for wheat. It was when oats in the cool rainy north-west, and rye, especially in the north-east, came to be widely cultivated that the more elaborate social development spread to some extent in these regions, and that was not until well into the Iron Age. In more modern times lumbering and skilled mining have caused further changes. And, ever since men made boats able to venture into the stormy sea, that is chiefly from the Iron Age and the clinker-built boats, though these last were rather earlier efforts, fishing has been at least an auxiliary in the economic struggle. The boat has played a great part socially also. The leader in the boat is a *primus inter pares* rather than an autocrat, he must be obeyed but he relies on initiative among his companions. The boat may also be a means of escape from a local despot. Further, while the men are out fishing, their women have to exercise their minds and make decisions. All in all, therefore, we find among the fisher-farmers a large amount of initiative and revolt against, or escape from, despotic schemes. The spread of Norsemen to Shetland and Orkney is a classic instance here. In Norway the small arable patches cannot be subdivided *ad infinitum* after the unhappy fashion of the loess lands; and this is the home of primogeniture, made practicable by the boat which could give a chance to the younger sons to fish, or to adventure far away, as colonists in Britain, Iceland, and Greenland or as Vikings southwards along the coasts of Europe.

Arctic Europe, with its long duration of snow cover and its perpetually frozen depths of the soil in many places, is for these reasons unable to produce crops without highly skilled scientific effort. Mosses and lichens and, in the short summer, shallow-rooted herbaceous flowering plants give food to the reindeer. The European Arctic is, for these reasons, probably less of a fringing region of Europe than an extension of northern Asia, though there is not unanimity about the origins of its Lapp peoples; they are almost certainly a mixed breed, like most other peoples.

It will be seen from the above short introduction that the loess areas west of the Dnieper played a large part in the early stages of evolution of European rural society, but one must emphasize that it was a case of rural society, with only small concentrations of population. Towns on the European loess, apart from a few Roman stations, did not develop until the eleventh and twelfth centuries of our era. The contrast over against the Aegean with its cities beginning in the third millennium B.C. is a dramatic one.

Several coastlands of western Europe attracted relatively early attention largely because they had mineral products that were valued. There were many hard stones which lent themselves to grinding and polishing, there was often flint suitable for fine chipping, notably in Denmark; and the Danish and some other Baltic shores yield amber, which was probably considered magical because of its possibilities of electrification. Copper and tin and gold were found in several places, and the British Isles gained thence a considerable prehistoric importance, with Ireland's copper and gold as specially important products.

So, in considering social evolution in Europe after the beginning of food-production, we must pay special attention, for the early phases, to the loess and the sea-coasts, remembering, at the same time, that gravel banks of rivers were often utilized as stations from very early times, and some bare hill-brows may long have retained some of the importance they had had in the late stages of the old hunting-and-gathering societies.

It was round about 3000 B.C. that the old-established cereal-cultivating groups of the south-west of Asia had acquired enough consciousness of their social organization to be able to spread, and, as we have already seen in chapter 6, they spread to the Mediterranean, and also to the loess lands of Europe as just mentioned. From the Mediterranean, within perhaps five centuries, coastwise navigation was spread to the European Atlantic shores, and at about the same time subsistence-cultivation was creeping westwards along the loess belt of central Europe. It seems at first to have been shifting-cultivation, the use of a patch for a few years until it needed a rest, and then a move on. The spread along the loess westwards was apparently a humbler affair at first than the spread along the Iberian and western European coasts.

The latter is marked by the building of monuments of rough stone, generally, that is, in stone that has not been dressed. An individual block may often weigh fifteen or more tons, so this bespeaks considerable skill and organization, and probably a labour-force; and Estyn Evans has shown, in north-eastern Ireland, that near these builders of monuments there were humbler folk without that skill. Perhaps in some cases they were the labourers for the immigrants, and the latter had come probably as boat-loads of men more often than as families on the move. The monuments have already been discussed in volume 6 of this series and it is not necessary to repeat what was there explained. Here we are concerned with matters of general significance.

It is a very widespread feature of ritual among many peoples that they practise rites to secure the birth of offspring. It may be suggested that fertility rituals were associated with at least some rough stone monuments of western Europe. Most of these constructions are probably datable between 2300 and 1300 B.C., but there is evidence of veneration of these monuments in the pre-Roman Iron Age and in Christian times; it would therefore not be surprising if evidence were obtained of the building of some of them at dates long after the third millennium B.C. It

is known that fertility rites have gone on at some of the monuments in quite recent times. We are therefore dealing with
something that is not restricted to a remote and almost forgotten
past, but with something that began very long ago and has
either retained or revived its interest for western Europeans. A
supplementary hypothesis would suggest that Bronze Age customs
of cremation may have altered beliefs for a time, but a return to
inhumation came in the Early Iron Age. When we speak of
cremation and inhumation it is well to remember that there may
be partial cremation along with preservation by inhumation or
otherwise of some part of the body to which special value is
attached, probably because it is supposed to contain the vital
essence. In several cases in medieval and even later Europe the
heart of a great personage has received special treatment in the
hope of specially ensuring its preservation.

We have little evidence that mariners from any particular
part of the Mediterranean reached north-western Europe in the
third or the second millennium B.C., but there are Portuguese
schist-plaque idols in Ireland, Isle of Man, &c., in relation with
Megaliths. The coastwise intercourse in the west apparently
went on in relays. Baltic amber beads are found in connexion
with the ancient intercourse as far south as Finistère in Brittany,
but no amber has been collected from the monuments in the
adjacent department of Morbihan, probably the greatest focus
of early intercourse in western Europe. Morbihan has yielded
some 800 beads of a material called callaïs, said to be allied to
turquoise, and no bead of this material has been collected from
Finistère or the Channel Islands, the British Isles or the west
Baltic. This sharply marked distribution indicates a contrast of
ideas that seems to imply a difference of people. Callaïs occurs
also in Portugal (about 1,100 beads), in south Spain with some
amber of doubtful origin, in south France (over 100 beads)
without amber, and, again without amber, in a monument in the

Marne. Twenty-seven beads of callaïs have been collected from Prinkipo Island in the Sea of Marmara near the Bosporus. The origin of this material and its ritual or other significance are still quite unknown.

The route of the early coastwise intercourse used at first the coasts of the Iberian peninsula and western France, probably with transpeninsular land-routes across Brittany to avoid the special danger of the Ushant area with its fogs, storms, and tide races. The Channel Islands must have played a considerable part in the next section of the northward journeys, on the way to Cornwall, St. George's Channel, and the Irish Sea. Along this route were found rocks lending themselves to the making of polished stone implements, and, more valuable still, there were copper and gold to be collected from gravel of Irish rivers. The route continued northwards through the North Channel, the Firth of Clyde (with probable transpeninsular ways across Cantire), the Minch, Orkney, and Shetland as well as Caithness, also along the Great Glen. So it went on to Denmark. The west Baltic was, however, not a mere remote extremity; the richness in monuments and finds makes one certain that it was a goal of considerable attraction. We shall not go far wrong if we associate that attraction with the magical substance, amber, found on Danish and Baltic beaches.

It is probable that one type of rough stone monument spread by coastwise maritime intercourse was the corbelled chamber with a slab-roofed passage leading to it. The chamber might alternatively be slab-roofed and sometimes the passage was reduced or absent. In Antrim, south-west Scotland, the Isle of Man and Cheshire, &c., another type of monument occurs having a forecourt partly bounded by standing stones and leading to a series of stone cists or boxes in a straight line. In both types there may be varied elaborations or, on the other hand, simplifications. The corbelled tomb was important in early Spain; the forecourt type or something like it is known in Sardinia but we must not make too much of resemblances between Sardinian and British monuments.

Pottery-making, so long as it was done by hand, was in many cases a female craft. In view of the lack of communication between the women of different communities divided by difference of speech and probably of ritual, there were many local variants among the products of the female crafts. Among these crafts that of pottery-making gives specially valuable evidence, because pot fragments have so often persisted for thousands of years and a fair number of complete pots of early prehistoric date in Europe are known.

As Europe north of the Mediterranean was at first merely a barbaric fringe of the Middle East and the Aegean civilizations, it is natural that the painted pottery of the Near East should have been made, in the course of time, during the third millennium B.C., on the loess lands in Hungary and west of the Dnieper. But though skill in pottery did spread westwards, the idea of a coloured slip did not penetrate far. Instead, the surface, while still soft, was marked with incised lines, finger impressions and, later on, with incrustations. The lines might be traced with an edged or pointed stick or might be impressed by pressing a string. There are also pots in the Danish Museums ornamented by pressing a cockle-shell on to the surface before baking, and one of these pots, in particular, is considered quite a masterpiece, or perhaps one should rather say mistresspiece, of craftsmanship. Archaeologists trace the spread and the replacement of pottery styles in Europe as their best line of evidence for interpreting movements of peoples and of cultural elements.

It is a fact of some importance that about 2000 B.C. or soon afterwards there appeared in Spain and in central Europe pottery of finer quality than had for the most part been made hitherto in these regions. The vessels made were drinking cups or beakers;

the paste of which they were made was usually fine and the baking well done. The style is of interest partly because, though it, and its variants, last only a few generations, they can be traced over wide areas, both in Spain and on the loess of middle Europe as well as, in quantity, in Britain. One may infer from this that the Beaker people were highly mobile and probably their spread was largely a rapid spread of men with fewer women, and therefore intermarriage with women of conquered peoples and consequent decay of the beaker-making pottery technique. The reversion to a coarser paste is very marked in Britain.

The question of the origin and direction of spread of beakers has been discussed for a good many years. It seems agreed that the basic type is a bell-shaped vessel, fairly broad and, relatively, not very high; the sides show an S shape in vertical section. This type has been found in some Megalithic tombs in Portugal, Spain, and Brittany. It is also known from the loess of central Europe. It is, further, known from inland Spain, where beakers are found accompanied by poor equipment, as far as can be judged from the non-perishable objects remaining. A number of writers think the bell-beaker pottery spread from an origin in inland Spain. This raises difficulties. It is hard to imagine a highly skilled technique arising in an area of poor equipment, and there is little evidence of the spread from inland Spain to central Europe. The possibility of an origin in east-central Europe and a spread to Spain also raises the difficulty about the route by which it might have spread, but not so much difficulty about origins, as the bell-beakers of central Europe are found with considerable accompaniments, including metal weapons of Bohemian affinities. A third hypothesis is that both central Europe and the coasts of Spain and Portugal got the idea of a finer paste for pottery and the form of the bell-beaker from the eastern Mediterranean. The similarity between the bell-beakers of central Europe and Spain does suggest a common origin, but the maintenance of that similarity over such distant spreads is not very easy to imagine.

We may surmise from the archaeological evidence that the beaker-makers were a very mobile people, probably warrior-herdsmen and traders, very likely with a ritual of their own in central Europe. It is possible that the bell-beaker spread as a culture-object and that the beaker-making peoples, as a distinctive social element, were those who in central Europe, the Netherlands, and Britain developed, from the bell-beaker, the beakers with a long neck so characteristic in east Britain.

Whereas the coastal peoples used their rough stone monuments as collective tombs, the Beaker people made round mounds which were single graves, apparently for chiefs, though there came to be secondary interments in the mounds in some cases. This implies a difference of ideas between the two groups. Were the chiefs buried in single graves looked upon as in some measure sacred or divine personages, perhaps alone possessed of spiritual immortality? It seems at any rate that the idea of communal burial was superseded. Timber-post circles related to burial mounds with beakers are characteristic in parts of the Netherlands.

In Britain, perhaps because it was on the way to Ireland's copper and gold, and in the west and south Baltic probably because of amber, there was culture-contact and exchange between the coastwise mariners and the people who had moved along the loess, especially the makers of beakers or of pottery derived from beakers. This transfusion no doubt accounts in part for the remarkable cultural developments of the time in these two areas. In Britain we have Avebury and Stonehenge, the latter certainly based upon the idea of a timber-post circle but executed in stone. It used stones from Pembrokeshire as well as sarsen stones found on the Wiltshire downs. Whether Avebury was preceded by a circle of wooden posts we do not know, but a long avenue of standing stones linked the Avebury stone circles with what is called the Sanctuary on Overton Hill some distance away. Stuart Piggott has recently reinterpreted the pattern of post-holes at the Sanctuary as representing a timber-frame building several times reconstructed, and partly modified by the use of stone.

In Denmark one finds objects in some rough stone monuments that belong to a single-grave culture and vice versa, but we do not recognize any such outstanding combination of ideas as that exhibited at Stonehenge. The Aubrey holes with bank and external ditch are datable within three centuries either way from 1850 B.C., itself a likely date. Importation of blue stones and other volcanic blocks from Preseli, Pembrokeshire, also a sandstone slab from Cosheston, Pem., resulted in the building of a double circle with these stones. This seems associated with the Beaker people. Later still the sarsen stones of local origin were erected, and the sacred stones from Pembrokeshire were rearranged. Representations of bronze axes incised on the sarsens suggest a date about 1500 B.C. and so would a supposed representation of a Mycenaean hafted dagger if confirmed. Two rings of holes, called the Y and Z series, were made in the process of this late arrangement. Much new detail is being worked out (1954). Stonehenge is thus a unique combination of ideas associated with the west coast maritime peoples and those who had come westwards along the loess zone. Its astronomical significance hints at a growing importance of the calendar.

The partial fusion of two cultures of diverse history is thus a feature of early Britain. It was no doubt accompanied by marriage between immigrant men and more indigenous girls and consequent melting of the newly arrived ideas to some extent into the old. One notes that there was as yet no such establishment of elaborate settlements as there was along Mediterranean shores.

The utilization of metal involved experiments with new processes. Often the material used had impurities not at first recognized as such. Some of these, such as tin and arsenic, were valuable in that they obviated the tendency of melted copper in a confined space to form oxygen bubbles that made the metallic mass spongy. Tin and nickel harden copper and so allow better sharpening. But the using of metal also brought new social experience once it was realized that tin sand should be mixed with copper—i.e. once bronze was known. Tin sand was found in Spanish Galicia and on the banks of the Vilaine in Brittany; copper was found quite early in south Spain and in Ireland. The two products had to be brought together and processed to make bronze and this involved communications and organization of exchange. When copper and tin were found near one another in the Erzgebirge, Bohemia, that region became important in metallurgy, and it seems to have developed exchanges with the west Baltic, so famous for its amber. The Baltic thereupon began a great development of bronze craftsmanship that at first used Bohemian models. Beads are so easily carried that they are often of interest as evidence of communications. Thirty-six graves in Wessex have yielded blue faïence beads probably derived from Mycenaean trade and usually dated about 1350 B.C. Some are known from Brittany and from south-east Spain. Segmented beads are known from Sutton Veney, Wilts., and a necklace from Odoorn, Drenthe, Holland, has four segmented beads of faïence and twenty-five of tin; also some segmented faïence beads have been found at Tara, Ireland. Childe has identified a dagger found at Pelynt in 1845 as of Mycenaean type datable to the fourteenth century B.C.

When man had learned to keep the furnace hot enough to melt the metal completely and had acquired skill in mixing copper and tin in the proper proportions (approximately 9 : 1) and so avoided bubbling of oxygen in the molten metal, technique had remarkable further developments with important social consequences. Hitherto such implements had been made as could be shaped from softened hot metal by hammering. Henceforth casting was possible and the lost-wax (*cire perdue*) method came into widespread use. A wax model of the object to be made was first prepared. This was put into a wet clay mould made in two parts. The mould with the wax model in it was then baked, the clay hardened, and the wax melted and poured itself away through a hole left for the purpose. The hard clay mould was then filled with molten metal and in this way a metal replica of the wax model was obtained. The development of casting made it possible to have a hole through a bronze axe for the handle, and to have a socket for the wooden handle of a spear, a much better scheme than the old ones which depended entirely on some kind of tie.

The art of casting also facilitated the remelting of old implements. There was thus developed a greater continuity in the use of bronze which had apparently often been in short supply in earlier times. Pedlars henceforth gathered hoards of old bronze and finds of these hoards have helped the reconstruction of the story of the Bronze Age. The late Harold Peake organized a catalogue of bronze finds in Britain and it is now available for study with 17,000 or more entries.

In course of time the spear and the sword were evolved as war-weapons, probably from the dagger. They, and especially the sword, are weapons for men in chariots or on horseback, and there are indications of an increased use of the horse for riding, as well as for pulling a two-wheeled chariot with an archer in it. Britain, a backward area, has no evidence thus far of the use of the horse, or of the harnessing of any animals or of wheeled vehicles until the very late Bronze Age. In the early, pre-Roman, Iron Age we have evidence of the wheelwright's craft at Glastonbury and vehicle wheels were mounted at what has become the standard distance of $4\frac{1}{2}$–5 feet from one another. This standard distance (4 ft. $8\frac{1}{2}$ in. for most railway trains) was settled by consideration of the width an animal needed when harnessed. On the European continent the horse of Inner Asia (Prze-walski's horse) replaced the older European or western horse called the Tarpan (used in earlier times for pulling a load). In the Bronze Age also, sheep became far commoner in Europe and it was again the west Asiatic variety, called the Urial, that spread. This is thought by some to have replaced the domesti-cated North African Moufflon, and a few examples that may be partly of this old type have survived at Soay, in the Hebrides. Asiatic cattle breeds also spread in Europe. These facts indicate the important relations of Europe with the great Eurasiatic steppe in the Middle Bronze Age. It was in this period that the Hyksos or Shepherd Kings conquered Egypt and intro-duced the horse there, that there was much disturbance in Meso-potamia, and, apparently, that some Aryan-speaking barbarians invaded the old civilization of the Indus valley. These last in-vaders, at least, were equipped with horses and war chariots. It seems legitimate to suggest that, at some time before this, the power to ride and to harness the horse had developed in Asia north, or perhaps north-west, of the Indus basin.

The fact that invasions of China about this time did not bring in the Aryan languages there may hint that these languages belong rather to the low steppe-lands than to the high Mongolian plateau. As steppe-landers brought languages of the Aryan family to India and Iran, they very likely spread Aryan speech in Europe. The use of Aryan speech in Late Neolithic Europe has been suggested by some writers, but the evidence is not convincing.

Nineteenth-century scholars thought that successive Celtic, Teutonic, and Slavonic waves had come westwards one after another in Europe, the later waves pressing the earlier peoples and languages westwards. It now seems more likely that early Aryan, perhaps with some diversities, became regionally differentiated in Europe partly through isolation of one group from another by intervening forests, mountains, or waters, partly through contacts and intermarriage with older European populations. Sir John Morris Jones argued for pre-Aryan elements in Welsh syntax, and, nearly 300 years ago, Edward Lhuyd claimed that pre-Celtic words survived in some Welsh place-names.

Celtic was in use in south Germany and some precursor of Latin in parts of Italy not long after 1000 B.C. The case of Celtic was much discussed fifty years ago, on the basis of a hypothesis of the spread of two westward waves. The earlier one was supposed to have emphasized the sounds *q* and *k* (hard *c*) and the later ones the *p*, *b*, and *v* (*f*) sounds. More recently, it has been thought that a fundamental Celtic, probably nearer Welsh than Irish, spread westwards and was modified in Ireland by contacts with older tongues. *q*, *k*, and hard *c* are features in Irish and in Scottish Gaelic. *p*, *b*, and *f* (*v*) are features in Welsh and Breton. Manx belonged to the *q* group and Cornish to the *p*. *p*, *b*, and *f* are more easily pronounced by people with long upper lips. One notes that south Brittany, very important in pre-Celtic times, also keeps several 'Q' place-names—Quimper, Quimperlé, Quiberon, Questembert, Quéven, Locmariaquer, Quinipily. North Brittany, which apparently revived Celtic speech when post-Roman immigrants from Britain came to its shores, has specially numerous place-names in Plou, Lan, Pol, Tre, Pen (Welsh: Plwyf, Llan, Pwll, Tre, Pen), which also occur in south Brittany. Tre, Pol, Pen are well known in Cornwall and it was from Cornwall that much post-Roman emigration to Brittany occurred. But in discussing post-Roman changes we are anticipating and we must return to review earlier times.

Reference has already been made to early cultivation of wheat and barley on the loess of central Europe, chiefly Hungary, by villagers who moved on to new clearings from time to time. Their villages may have had a dozen or two dozen houses, but the sizes of these suggest a large and composite household. The village seems to have had grain stores, and cattle and pigs, but at first only a few sheep and goats. Later, both hunting and stock-raising became more important and fortification suggests war. Figurines of women are common in these early villages, and *spondylus* shells from the Mediterranean are found in Danubian lands. In a further development sheep became more numerous (perhaps wool had come into wider use), and perhaps the little plough came into use, but some think this came later, in the Late or Middle Bronze Age. Horses (probably Tarpans) were used, probably for traction. Figurines of women were no longer made. In the next stage metal tools were in use and there was trade with the amber coasts of the Baltic and the developing Mediterranean civilizations. When bronze-casting had spread there came to be real mining of copper, making of swords, fortifications, large farm-houses and urnfields with some hundreds of graves, but no hint of temples. We lack direct evidence for horse-riding in central or western Europe before the Early Iron Age.

The mobile peoples who brought the sheep to central and western Europe about the dawn of the Metal Age seem to have spread the idea of cremation. Monumental burial to await reincarnation was not an idea that suited mobile groups. In the west Baltic old cults remained strong, and Thor's battle-axe long kept its mythological importance in spite of the rise of the Odin cult with spear and sword and horse. In central Europe there seems indication of conflict between upland herdsmen and lowland cultivators.

Early populations and languages probably changed more than was likely later when writing and more settled life had spread. The book of Numbers tells us that early conquest often involved

slaughter of men and married women, while girls were appro-
priated by the victors. Behind this barbarous custom is the idea
of telegony, a superstition that the male animal or human who
first made a female pregnant influenced all offspring she might
subsequently bear to other males. The slaughter was thus imagined to be a means of keeping the victor's stock from con-
tamination, the idea being that the male supplied the seed which
the female germinated. Girls kept by the victors were probably
to some extent isolated in the houses of their masters, and must
learn their masters' language, but no doubt taught their children
a language modified by older usages of their own, and a mythology
that led to resurgence of old rituals, often with altered meanings.

The change from bronze to iron involved difficulties which
long delayed its accomplishment, though fragments of meteoritic
iron and probably of magnetite from river sands had been used
from the early part of the third millennium in Egypt and
south-west Asia. The larger-scale use of iron depended on the
finding of haematite (perhaps first used in ground form as a
pigment) or some other oxide of iron. The furnaces used for
good pottery in south-west Asia were hot enough for smelting
iron, but the spongy mass must be taken out of the furnace and
hammered hot, preferably in contact with carbon, this last an
easy matter with wood fuel. The necessary hammer and tongs
appear to have been one difficulty, and the maintenance of the
high temperature of the furnace for a sufficient time may have
been another. Iron oxides were abundant in Anatolia and by
about 1400 B.C. iron-smelting was a regular process there. The
downfall of the power of the Hittites about 200 years later
spread their knowledge of iron among surrounding peoples.
This knowledge reached the Aegean and Greece and, according
to present-day opinions, was there acquired by the Dorian
invaders. Older views thought the Dorians came to Greece with
iron from farther north, but the evidence for this is not forth-

coming. Knowledge of iron passed on to Italy and thence about the seventh century B.C. to Halstatt in Austria, which was already important as a centre for salt.

Iron axes could not only cut down wood fuel but were useful for felling large trees, even oaks. So the area of possible arable could increase, probably not much at first, but more rapidly after Roman times when smelting became commoner. Pasturing of pigs in forest glades among the oaks was another possibility and it may have given more salt pork as winter food. Whether this is one reason for the importance of sources of salt in the Late Bronze and Early Iron Ages is a matter of speculation. With oak timbers and iron chisels and other improved edged tools carpentering improved, and it is probably in the Early Iron Age that the later idea of the timber-frame house germinated. Boats could be made larger and tougher, so that voyages such as that of Pytheas became possible, and also Greek settlements spread in the Euxine and the loess region of south-western Russia. Iron for swords and spears replaced the much feebler bronze, which was bent out of shape after use; and we may be confident that quite soon the hammering of hot iron in contact with a little carbon gave rise to steel. In this connexion we note the growth of folk-lore of the magic sword, folk-lore revived in the Dark Ages after the fall of the Roman Empire. But almost more important still was the development of the plough.

Reference has already been made to the fact that plant-food is distributed throughout the whole thickness of the soil in the brown earths of Europe north of the Mediterranean. The surface weeds may have extracted the food from the upper layers and the last crop will certainly have done so. Evaporation is typically not strong enough in the brown-earth region to bring a great deal of dissolved plant-food up from below, so deep ploughing of a type that will bring up the lower layers of the soil is desirable. It is still more important in the cold lands where the surface soil is apt to be greyish because so much of the plant-food has been washed down into its lower layers where rainfall is often greater than evaporation.

With iron and better timber the plough could be made larger and the ploughshare could be shod with iron to dig more deeply in. A knife-like coulter fixed vertically just in front of the ploughshare to cut the sod for the ploughshare to dig was an important addition of the Early Iron Age. Whether wheels were given to the plough at this time is a question not yet decided. The plough might dig up the deeper soil but that earth must be laid down again at the side of the furrow. To secure this various additions to the plough were tried. The one which has been most successful has been the mould-board, a more or less horizontal projection against the underside of which the upturned soil would hit itself and be turned down again on to the earth. Larger ploughs and forest clearing gave more arable land, but usually land with less pervious soil, so that evaporation was insufficient to bring plant-food in solution up to the surface. The field needed periodical rest, or fallowing as it is called. Farming routine had to become elaborate, especially for lands growing exhausting crops such as wheat. The very important social consequences of all this will be discussed in a later paragraph. In Britain ploughs improved and we have evidences of coulters in Belgic times, that is, in the last century B.C., but this was part of a long process which began much earlier and was to continue to much later centuries, as F. G. Payne has convincingly argued. It has sometimes been said, for example, that the mould-board was an improvement of the plough due to the Cistercian monks of the twelfth century A.D., who did so much for agriculture and rural life, but it seems clear that this and allied devices for laying the upheaved soil are much older. Benedictine and Cistercian monks may, however, have made this and other improvements more widespread.

An instrument that seems to have been invented in the Early Iron Age is the scythe for reaping on a larger scale than was possible with the sickle; and it was used especially for hay cut for fodder, one of the many schemes for trying to keep farm animals alive through the winter. Counterbalancing improvements of boats, houses, ploughs, scythes, and so on, there was in the Early Iron Age a temporary worsening of climate in our region, a phase of cool wet summers variously dated about 700 or towards 500 B.C. Bogs invaded forest in Scandinavia, Britain, and France, the beech became far commoner in Denmark and the oak less general, lakeside villages of the Late Bronze Age in Switzerland, usually built on piles, were drowned by the rise of lake levels. Some Alpine passes previously in use seem to have become ice-blocked. Transylvanian prosperity and trade with north Italy of the Late Bronze Age gave place to poverty and invasion from the great steppe, now reinvigorated by the damper climate and become subject to Scythian invaders, whom Herodotus so dramatically describes. Southward movement of peoples became a feature in Europe, and in the cold north we have the period known in legend as the Fimbulwinter, when winters followed one another with no summer between, and also as the Twilight of the Gods, the decline of the old culture.

Continuation of southward pressure of peoples led to development of earthwork fortifications, sometimes remaking old earth ramparts of the Late Neolithic or Early Bronze time. With better timber and carpentering stony earth ramparts were sometimes given a strong timber frame (*murus gallicus*) helping to hold the stones together. Territorial lordships centring on fortresses became important, and sometimes the fortresses became centres of population, a germ of towns, while in favourable cases, as apparently at Rouen in Normandy, the population might leave the exposed height (St. Catherine's hill) and come down to the lowland (the future Rouen, which the Romans enlarged). Lutetia was a pre-Roman settlement on one of the islands in the Seine at Paris. Chartres was apparently a pre-Roman centre of sanctity on a hill overlooking the Eure river.

The cooler wetter climate favoured Mediterranean lands. Already in the Late Bronze Age, Celtic-speaking people had spread from south Germany to north-east Spain, but a much more important extension of Celtic speech occurred after the seventh century when conquerors spread across France to Spain, particularly north-western Spain. Here later on there grew great earthwork fortresses, Citanias, and, from north-western Spain in the third and second centuries B.C., military groups went to Brittany, Cornwall, and the coastlands of the Irish Sea and so northwards.

Memories of this have somehow found a place in the medieval *Histories of the Kings of Britain* by Geoffrey of Monmouth. In British archaeology these conquerors are spoken of as the invaders of Iron Age B, and are supposed to be the builders or rebuilders of many great earthworks of which Maiden Castle, Dorset, and Maiden Castle, Eddisbury (Bickerton), Cheshire, are notable examples which have been examined. At Eddisbury Varley found indications of timber forming something of the general type of the *murus gallicus*, but less developed. Apparently the Iron Age B men made or remade some ridge roads and perhaps other tracks as well, including timber-floored causeways in the Fens and in the wet lands near Glastonbury. Communication by water was apparently by coracle (circular basket-boat) or by curragh (skin stretched on a frame) worked by paddling. A few coins and parts of Mediterranean wine-jars have been found at Chun Castle (Early Iron Age), Cornwall, a good indication of trade which probably crossed France from the Mediterranean coast to Brittany on its way.

The relation of this movement to the problems of the distribution of the Celtic languages awaits further research. The

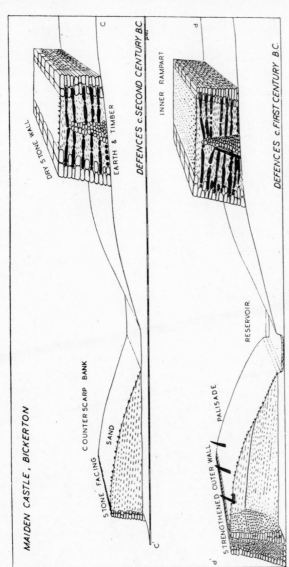

FIG. 51. Rampart sections, Maiden Castle, Bickerton, Cheshire

sound indicated by *th* in English and the related sound indicated by *dd* in Welsh are much used in Jersey and in Spain. In Britain the *th* belongs to the Irish Sea coastlands and the Midlands and North. In London it grades into *v* and in west Ireland into *d*, so that in extreme cases we get *muvver* and *muder* in place of *mother*. Danish uses a sound very like the English *th*.

The cool wet summers no doubt made wheat harvests poor, but they also had another effect charged with large consequences. Oats and rye spread probably first as weeds in barley fields. The wet summers favoured oats; and rye can grow with much less sun than wheat. These two plants became established crops in the Early Iron Age and made possible a spread of grain cultivation and ploughing into the cold north where hitherto only barley had been much worth while; the spread of colonization from the loess of Polish Galicia into what has become Russia as well as its spread into hitherto forest land on boulder clay in Poland, Lithuania, &c. This increased population promoted the spread of Slavonic speech.

During the Early Iron Age bronze remained in use especially for ornaments, notably safety-pin brooches or fibulae, which, from about 400 B.C. onwards, show in their decoration the influence of ideas spreading from the Mediterranean lands of classical times. The flowing curve is an important feature which, as time went on, so affected Irish work that it came to be a leading element in Irish Celtic art of post-Roman times. The styles of the brooches or fibulae of the pre-Roman period changed fairly often; so these objects have been used for closer dating of finds than is possible for those of earlier periods.

In the Early Iron Age, then, southward movement of peoples and, to some extent, northward spread of ideas were making the west and even parts of the north-west of Europe a twilight fringe of the classical civilizations of Mediterranean lands. A priestly order, the Druids, arose in the west, and apparently had a special seat of its learning and authority in Gaul at the future Chartres. Here, tradition says, a cave in the hillside was dedicated in pre-Christian times to a virgin who should bear a son. This cave is reached from the crypt of the later cathedral dedicated to the Virgin Mary. Sir Cyril Fox has given an account of Llyn Cerrig bach, Anglesey, an island which was a Druidic centre, receiving gifts from some distant parts of Britain. It seems, in fact, that a priestly order was trying to develop a system that would be more than local.

A unique statue of 'La Grand'mere' (The Great Mother or Grandmother) has been preserved at S. Martin, Guernsey. It probably dates from the Early Iron Age and the illustration is from a photograph taken by the late Mrs. Ayscough on a dark night with special illumination from below (Fig. 52, p. 208).

In considering very briefly a few essentials concerning Roman times we should remember that Gaul was Romanized far more than Britain, and that in Britain the country north of Hadrian's Wall as well as parts of Wales were less affected than was the south-east, while Ireland was practically untouched. So, in the west and north, post-Roman times are in some measure a continuation of the pre-Roman Iron Age. Roman organization was concerned to defend a frontier mainly along the Rhine and Danube against wild men moving westwards and southwards to better lands and ready to take advantage of any weakness in the Roman schemes. Roman cities spread to south Gaul and Spain where vine, and in parts olive, could be grown. With the progress of conquest in Gaul, camps in the Paris basin became cities such as Rouen, Paris, Sens, Tours, &c. Some, like Rouen and Paris, had probably already been Gaulish settlements before the Romans came. When the Rhine and Danube were reached, Köln, Bonn, Koblenz, Bingen, Mainz, Worms, Speyer, Strasbourg, Basel, Regensburg, Passau, Wien (Vienna), became important camps, and in due course cities. The cities with public buildings set in

Fig. 52. Statue of 'La Grand'mere', S. Martin, Guernsey.

regular lines and built with dressed stone, the laid-out streets, the courts of law and the maintenance of public order must have impressed very deeply barbarians who, for whatever reason, came across the frontier river in intervals of peace. We have here one of the foundations of Roman prestige which was to survive the fall of the Empire for so many centuries.

Before the Roman Empire fell a Christian ritual had become official and many a city had an archbishop or bishop (*episcopus* = overseer), and cities thus provided often strove to maintain what they could of the Roman tradition after the Empire had broken down.

The eastern Roman Empire, with Constantinople as its capital only from the fourth century A.D., by which time the Roman system was breaking down, was unable to rival the prestige of Rome in the field of ideas. Latin language so influenced Italy, Spain, and France as to become the mother of their modern languages. Beyond this, Latin was imposed for ritual purposes, however little it might be understood. Roman Law was revived to some extent in southern France in the Early Middle Ages and was later on received in parts of Germany as a substitute for petty local systems. From Constantinople the Greek language spread in only a very minor degree, and ritual and law adapted themselves to various peoples and languages.

Even in the west, however, weakness of the control of order made trade and towns decline very seriously, and this decline was made worse by the Islamic invasions of the Mediterranean and later by the ravages of the Norsemen. The towns and cities of Gaul, the Rhine, and the Danube were much reduced, building with dressed stone ceased for some centuries. Brick was no longer made for perhaps 500 or more years in western Europe. No roads were built. Roman roads were not repaired; law was largely neglected and the arts and crafts often declined except in the matter of making ornaments for chiefs.

The treasure recently found at Sutton Hoo, Suffolk, in the memorial mound of an Anglian king of the mid-seventh century A.D. is of remarkable craftsmanship and beauty. Some specialists think it may be the work of a Celtic, perhaps Irish, craftsman. Gold, silver, and red enamel are among the materials used and some designs are at any rate analogous with some used in Ireland.

In Britain the Roman town had not taken strong root, and the system of bishops was lost in the Anglo-Saxon turmoil. The British Celtic speech had been overlaid by Latin, and both were weak and were weakened by the flight of Romanized Britons to Gaul in the fifth century. So the Anglo-Saxons imposed their language. It is also important to note that they came as families, i.e. men, women, and children in boatloads. In west Britain and especially in Ireland the Celtic tradition remained strong and some of the arts, notably that of maunscripts, developed considerably. The Book of Kells is one of the finest of the world's illuminated manuscripts. The Tara brooch and the Ardagh chalice are other triumphs of craftsmanship. The Christians of Ireland, under leaders whom it has become customary to call Saints, spread their influence to some extent on the Continent and traces of it are found in Gaul, Switzerland, Austria, and the Rhineland.

Barbarian conquerors established local sovereignties in western Europe and these were based on rural life which developed considerably in this period of distress in the cities; thence there evolved the feudal system, so well known that it needs no enlarged description here. During Roman times iron-smelting had become more general, and iron axes could attack the forest and increase the area for food crops and pasture. Forest clearing and village development became features of European life in this phase.

Frankish conquerors in Gaul, overawed by Roman tradition,

and largely groups of young warriors without their own women, soon became Latinized through intermarriage. Slavonic conquests and forest clearance in east-central Europe spread this family of languages westwards to the Oder and Bohemia, eastwards into Russia, and south-westwards to the Balkan peninsula. We note, however, that Slavonic had to compromise with provincial Latin in the old imperial province of Dacia, where Roman soldiers had been settled in the third century A.D., and so we have the Romanian language, partly Latin and partly Slavonic. Slavonic pressure on Germanic peoples may have been a factor of the emigration of Angles and Saxons to Britain in family groups.

We have next to follow out some of the social consequences the larger ploughs, and of the clearing of the erstwhile oak woods of the lowlands, mentioned above.

Firstly, as already stated, the brown-earth soils, and still more the podsols or grey earths, needed deep ploughing to bring up to the surface the lower layers of the soil. This made enlargement of the ploughs necessary and gave a great advantage to those possessing a coulter to cut the sod in advance of the ploughshare and a mould-board or some alternative to throw down on the surface at the side of the plough the soil that had been brought up by the ploughshare. Often the laying of this soil at the side of the plough made the ploughed field a succession of ridges and furrows which might have value for drainage and for subdivision of the land into strips. In some regions the furrows once created became semi-permanent and might grow weeds or become marshy.

In a little rural group not everyone could own an enlarged plough or sufficient oxen to pull it. Nor would it have been practicable to use the big plough on very small enclosed patches of land such as appear to have been widespread in pre-Roman times. By this time, too, it had become realized that land must rest to renew its fertility and that dunging by folding animals on the resting land was of great value.

So there arose the system of open fields in which the householder held strips that, in some cases, might be reallocated from time to time. The open fields were used in rotation, and two main schemes of rotation were worked out.

On some lighter soils, especially if there was considerable grass-land for animals at hand, the fields were used for crops one year in two. Thus half the arable land produced crops in each year.

On the lowland loams, especially if there was little grass-land for animals, the beasts were folded more continuously on the resting fields, and it was found possible to grow crops on any given field two years out of three. After a year's rest the exacting and exhausting crop of wheat was grown. Then from harvest until the severities of winter became too acute, animals were folded on the stubble. It was ploughed at the end of the winter and spring corn (oats or barley) was sown, to be reaped in the ensuing summer before the field entered upon its year of rest. Two-thirds of the arable land was therefore, under this system, producing crops in each year. Beans might be an alternative to spring corn. Probably systems of strips were not applied very fully in many cases, and even family farms may have existed here and there.

All schemes of management of the land and beasts of a group entailed organization and brought a considerable measure of compulsion. The German name for it is *Zwangflur* (*Zwang* implying compulsion). The harvesting must be completed by a certain day in order that the animals may be driven on to the stubble, ploughing and sowing must be so arranged that each household may do its share, the number of beasts allowed often had to be regulated, and so on.

All this lent itself to the development of authority, especially if that authority owned the large plough and perhaps the oxen to pull it, as well as the mill for grinding the grain. We may therefore say that, where the three-field or even the two-field rotation system prevailed in western Europe, a local lord was either present from the first or developed as the scheme became organized. Moreover the rural group must be ready for defence and this implied a commander. So lordship became a feature if it was not already characteristic, and a hierarchy of lords right up to a regional king or count developed.

In several regions of grey soils (podsols), with too much moisture or too little sun for successful wheat-growing, the system of three-field or two-field rotations was modified. In the rainy west of the British Isles and Scandinavia more stress was laid on cattle which might be taken to hills or moorlands whilst the cereal crops, most often oats or barley, were growing. This scheme of transhumance is very different from that of Mediterranean lands, and, in parts of Ireland for example, the cattle might be folded even for a good part of the winter on the land that was to bear an oats or barley crop next summer. It was thus possible to crop one patch year after year for a long time because of this manuring, and such a patch might be called the in-field in contrast with the out-field, a patch cleared and cropped for a few successive years in the rough pasture usually farther from the hamlet or homestead. This scheme of farming might at times be worked by a single household, but more usually was maintained by a small group of households, often related by descent or marriage. Such a group is called in Ireland a clachan when the households are close set as a small hamlet. The clachan, or even the single household, might be allowed to develop as much of the rough land as it could.

Neighbouring clachans might be fellow members of a clan, especially in Scotland, under a military leader who was not quite like a lord of a manor. He must in a greater degree try to secure the consent and fervent loyalty of those under him because the law was, often at least, a custom of vendetta. It was important in the days of continual wars and vendettas for the chieftain to have a large number of willing followers, while the lord of the manor in the regions of the three-field system was more of an economic master of serfs or at least subordinates. It became characteristic of Scotland after the middle of the eighteenth century that, as law and order became established, the chieftain no longer needed so many men. Evictions became common and the victims tried to squat on marshy coastal patches. By growing potatoes and fishing they obtained a bare subsistence until, in the mid-nineteenth century, the potato disease and the opening up of the grass-lands across the ocean combined to cause a heavy emigration which continued for many years. It should be mentioned that, in the Scottish Highlands and even in the Hebrides, the winter was in many parts too severe to allow the cattle to remain outside. Winter fodder was scarce, and so starveling beasts often had to be carried out to the pastures in early spring. The creation of deer forests for hunting and grouse moors for shooting, as a pastime of seasonal visitors to the Highlands, aggravated the decline of population in the nineteenth and twentieth centuries.

In Norway, physical features influenced custom towards a different solution. The high land could be used in summer, when grass grew quickly after the snow melted and the melt-water soaked in. The fjords are sharp cuts in the high land with small arable patches along the fjord-side here and there. As men learned to build stouter boats with iron tools, the society of farmer-fishers developed in the fjords, but this involved restriction on the division of arable land, of which there was so little. The scheme of inheritance by the eldest son established itself, and the younger sons must adventure out (must go i-viking). Clinker-built boats, that is, boats with each board overlapping the one next below, made maritime adventure more practicable, and the Norsemen spread terror along the west of Europe. Later they were under the Hanse for a while, and, in the last 100 years, they have developed an important mercantile marine. Attempts to organize the people of the fjords, made for example under Harold Fairhair (late ninth century), led inevitably to discontent and resistance, and resulted in emigration to Shetland, Orkney, Caithness, Hebrides, Man, east Ireland, and Iceland and Greenland. The Norse kingdom of the Hebrides and Man later gave place to Scottish and English lordship, but the name of the diocese of Sodor (Sudreys or Hebrides) and Man preserves a memory of the olden time.

Farther east, in north Europe, oats were in general less successful, and rye has been the characteristic crop from the Early Iron Age to the present day. It needs less sun than wheat and less rain than oats. The flour of rye makes food with good heating power, so it is specially valuable in this region. But development of population has been slow in face of the environmental difficulties of winter cold, pine forests, and wild beasts (especially wolves) on the great plains, with their long duration of snow cover and their floods and mud as the snow melts, as well as the insect pests of the short summer. As farther west, so in the development of the north-east the monastic orders—in this case especially those of the Orthodox Church—played a considerable part.

This very brief survey of Europe brings us to the edge of recorded history and only a few points of special relevance for comparisons can be added regarding later times.

The final separation of the Roman from the Orthodox Church must be mentioned as a fact with the most serious consequences. It brought into prominence a zone of lasting conflict between east and west in Europe and facilitated Islamic penetration along that zone. It should be realized that Poland and Hungary and, with reserves, Bohemia, along the loess zone, adhered to the medieval west.

The decline of Roman towns in western Europe during the Dark Ages has already been mentioned. Medieval, feudal organization gradually developed into larger unities and the menaces from Norsemen correspondingly diminished, while possibilities of exchange with the Islamic civilizations were opened up by diminution of fear, and, to a slight extent, of prejudice. Towns then began to grow again. This occurred not only in Mediterranean lands, but also farther north, beginning in the latter part of the tenth century and increasing in the eleventh and especially in the twelfth century. In France the town grew chiefly as the centre of a rural district, a *pays* in common French speech. Especially if the town had had a bishop or archbishop during the Dark Ages, its redeveloped centre would be the cathedral on an open space, typically the market place. Its streets might be named after the various crafts, the men of one craft being concentrated in one street, and working to fulfil orders rather than for chance sales. Sometimes a castle might dominate the town, as in the Norman case of Falaise, but often the nobleman's castle in its situation evidenced rather the rural tradition of the Franks. The cathedral or town-church seems usually to have served also as a meeting-place for purposes other than the performance of the Church ritual, and few towns in France, except towards the Flemish border, have a really old town hall.

In Flanders and the Rhineland long-distance trade played a greater part than in many French towns and so there were influential and wealthy merchants often able to lend money to needy nobles or bishops and to get privileges in return, not seldom in lieu of repayment. Lack of building-stone in several areas of the Low Countries led to the redevelopment of the idea of burning brick and this technique spread fairly quickly. In

Flanders we find the town hall, often also guildhalls or woolhalls of great dignity alongside the cathedral. La Grande Place at Brussels is later in date than some others, being fifteenth century for the most part, but it illustrates the general idea specially clearly, as well as magnificently. In this case the fine cathedral of S. Gudule is some distance away.

At Köln, again, the cathedral is away from the old centre, which had public buildings of immense historic interest until they were destroyed in World War II. Disagreements between the archbishop and the merchants at Köln led to the residence of the former at Bonn for a long period. The domination of the city by the cathedral is much less marked on the Rhine than it is in the Paris basin.

Falling water was used as a source of mechanical power in Roman Britain and, more, on the Continent. Little was done in this line after the fall of the Roman Empire for some centuries. In the very general revival from the late tenth century onwards water-mills became more numerous. Most were used for grinding corn, but, by the end of the twelfth century, there were water-mills working bellows to give a strong and steady draught through smelting-furnaces. It thus began to be possible to cast iron, but wrought iron (shaped by hammering when hot) retained its predominance until large-scale casting developed in the nineteenth century.

Another technical development in which the twelfth and thirteenth centuries were concerned was the building of chimneys which, in due course, came to be mostly of brick. Chimneys mark a great advance in cleanliness and in warmth of a room over the old smoke-hole scheme. They also meant that there could be fires in different rooms, that there was more privacy, and that social refinements could develop.

The towns of France were growing especially when enterprising Cistercian monks were helping to clear woodland and to found villages. Village and town life were thus growing together in a region where it is possible to do farm-work nearly all through the winter. Village crafts were thus less developed there than in regions of long winter frost; and so town and country, for this reason also, were more closely linked in France than in most parts of Germany.

The German town developed beyond the Rhine eastwards and beyond the Danube northwards from the tenth century onwards. Sometimes a town grew under the protection of a castle and the smiths' and armourers' trade was emphasized. Sometimes a town was built around an ecclesiastical centre founded by a missionary bishop or abbot. Sometimes merchants extracted a concession from some noble and built a town primarily for trade. A maze of small sovereignties thus grew up in the complex tangle of hills and valleys just east of the Rhine from Mainz to Köln, and the idea of the city spread farther eastwards primarily along the loess zone, so that Prague and Cracow stand out, and had respectively the first and second universities established north of the Alps and east of France. Prague, Cracow, Poznan, and other cities set in regions of Slavonic speech were however still more apt to be distinct from their rural surroundings. In pre-urban days on the European plain, especially in the Polish loess zone, there were earthwork-refuges here and there, and the fortifications of some of these later became nuclei of cathedral towns to which came commercial German, and often also Jewish, immigrants. The merchants laid out a large town with public buildings such as a woolhall or a town hall on a great market-place dominated by a town church contrasting with, and often rivalling, the cathedral which was typically in the early fortified enclosure (the Wawel at Cracow). Slavonic people were drawn in from the country round about as labourers, so the city might have several rather distinct quarters—an aristocratic centre, a merchant centre, a Slavonic quarter, and often a Jewish ghetto.

On the Baltic urban development was not without partial analogies to that on the Aegean long before. The fisher-traders formed the Hanseatic league of trading cities. Lübeck became the chief of them, thanks partly to its fine situation twenty miles up a navigable river and so fairly secure from maritime pirates, and partly through possessing a good supply of salt in the Lüneburger Heide to the south. It could thus salt the herrings, netted chiefly off south-west Sweden, and was in a good position to sell them to the German towns as Lenten food. The Church had wisely instituted abstinence from meat in Lent to try to keep the peasants from slaughtering their cattle. At Lübeck the Rathaus (town hall) and the town-church were dominant, and the fine cathedral is at one end of the town, which was surrounded by water, a feature which other Hanse towns tried to repeat. The outstanding fact here is that the town was more or less autonomous except in so far as it formed a league with other towns of similar type, and all were busy with maritime commerce chiefly in fish, fur, and salt.

The decline of this league of merchant cities may be mentioned briefly. The Muscovite power took possession of Novgorod, the erstwhile Hanse agency for furs; and the fur trade thereafter tended to avoid the league and to send its goods by land (and river) to Leipzig, which thence developed its famous fair and its great university and publishing activities from the fifteenth century.

Also the island of Oléron on the Biscayan coast of France developed the salt trade through evaporating sea-water. Its salt came to the Baltic by sea via Copenhagen, which became more important while Lübeck and the Hanse declined. Further, from the early fifteenth century the herrings, which for a long time had spawned in enormous numbers off the south-western corner of Sweden, came to frequent in greater numbers the coasts of Holland and its islands. Dutch towns grew and were outside the Hanse tradition. In the sixteenth century ocean voyages became more important, and both the Mediterranean and Baltic seas lost a good deal of prestige. Though Hamburg and Bremen, both Hanse towns, grew later on, in connexion with ocean trade, this growth was outside the Hanse scheme. Finally, regional rulers, notably the great Elizabeth I of England, shook themselves free from what had been Hanse domination. The idea of the city-state thus had only a relatively short blossoming in the Baltic as compared with its unique history in the Mediterranean.

The rise of ocean navigation has just been mentioned; its early phase was accompanied by another revolution, the introduction of printing, and this brought a freshened insight into classical and especially Greek learning and literature. A partial spread of literacy, associated with printed books and with the need for written commercial agreements, brought criticism of the medieval world. Its maps were superannuated and soon Copernicus and others were putting its cosmogony out of date. Abuses in the Roman Church at the same time led to a theological revolt more widespread than any of those which had broken out in the Middle Ages. And this revolt had at hand a new and powerful instrument in new translations of the Scriptures into the various vernaculars. It is interesting from our point of view to note that, with some exceptions, it was especially the parts of Europe which had been within the old Roman Empire that now remained in the Roman Church, while many parts outside that Empire gave up their allegiance to the Papacy. England had been in the Empire, but was on the whole less Romanized than Gaul; she gave up her relation to the Pope but adopted in her Episcopal National Church an attitude that was in some ways less different from the Roman than that in Scotland. In Ireland loyalty to the Papacy accompanied and reinforced opposition to British rule. In Germany east of the

Rhine and north of the Danube there were and still are islands, as it were, of Romanism, especially where some early missionary abbot or bishop had taken his stand in the tenth or eleventh century. This distribution of centres of Romanist and of Lutheran sites was much promoted by the advocacy of the principle *Ubi regio, ibi religio*, which may be said to have been one of the factors of the Thirty Years War (1618–48) that so disastrously affected German life. The Papacy maintained its hold on a good deal of the loess zone, what is now Czechoslovakia, Hungary and Poland and upper Silesia remaining mainly Romanist, Poland especially so, partly because of the great part it had played and was playing in resistance to Mongol and Turk.

In spite of these exceptions, however, the secession of non-Roman north-western Europe from the Roman Church and the maintenance of allegiance to that Church in regions that had been in the Roman Empire is a fact that has been of very great importance even in revolutions after World War II.

Of later phases we can say only a few words. In the sixteenth century, especially in the Netherlands, the windmill came into widespread use and was applied in several ways, and notably to pumping water off the land. Land was reclaimed on a large scale, and was used to some extent for root crops by the early seventeenth century. Holland had given some hospitality to refugees from Romanist persecution. She thus gained a spiritual *élite* which had much initiative, and in the seventeenth-century Netherlands there was a remarkable blossoming of the fine arts, science, and scholarship, as well as great economic development. The traditional three-field and two-field systems were everywhere showing the weakness of the element of compulsion they involved. Custom lay upon those systems as a dead or dying hand, and enterprising cultivators sought to use their strips for special purposes. Parsnips had been grown in parts of western Europe as a garden crop from Roman times. They were spreading and interfered with the pasturing of cattle on the stubble fields after the grain harvest, because they remained in the ground until autumn. So it was enacted by various lords of manors that a peasant must get permission before enclosing a piece of land for parsnips. Parsnips, turnips, swedes, mangel wurzels (German for roots to meet scarcity) spread and the custom of stubble pasture declined with serious consequences for the humbler peasants, but greater freedom of initiative for the richer cultivators. The old order however persisted with modifications in several areas until well into the nineteenth century.

The Netherlands and Britain also took a considerable part in making ships easier to manœuvre in regions of variable winds (with fore-and-aft sails), and in reducing bilge-water, once a disastrous source of disease on long voyages. With these improvements and their initiative, the two countries rose to prominence in trans-oceanic enterprise, and began to learn how to diet seamen so as to diminish scurvy. The French were also very enterprising for a short time, from about 1625 to 1650, and Guadeloupe and Martinique, French Canada, St. Louis in Senegal, Reunion, and Mauritius became French stations. The Bourbon system of autocracy made the French effort lose its momentum. In spite of Dupleix in the eighteenth century, the declining autocracy was more concerned with European prestige. Religious persecution also gravely reduced initiative and drove an *élite* into exile or prison. Commerce by the mid-eighteenth century was bringing materials from many lands to be worked up, especially in Britain, and soon the great experiment of the industrial revolution was to gather the derelict humbler rural folk into factory towns. These have grown to enormous size, so that the rural basis of our region's life has in several areas been almost forgotten, and schemes of control from the mammoth cities are still developing in a region of rural origins.

India

KNOWLEDGE has so increased in the last twenty-five years
that further developments of ideas about India are very probable. The Indian region lies south of the great east–west mountain zone of the northern hemisphere of the Old World, and
peninsular India is largely south of the Tropic of Cancer. The
Himalaya had as many as five major ice phases in the Pleistocene
period but the Indo-Gangetic lowland and the peninsula were
not glaciated. Pebble and rough flake implements here give the
earliest traces of man. Most finds, so far, have been made on the
terraces of the river Soan in the north-east Punjab, and the name
used is the Soan culture. It existed during the second or great
interglacial, more or less parallel with the Mindel-Riss interglacial of Europe, but it lasted on for a long time and finds have
been made in the Bombay area, north of the Narbada, and in
parts of central and south-east India. Many of the pebble and
core tools are of indifferent quality. As the industry evolved,
pressure with wood, bone, or horn was used in shaping core
tools, suggesting a parellelism and a probable relationship with
the Acheulian industry of western Europe and Africa. In a late
phase tools were made from bone, sometimes the bone of animals
now extinct. Menghin at one time thought of India as the primary home of core tools but he later gave up this idea and at
present North Africa and the immediately adjacent parts of
Asia are generally thought to have been the place where the
more skilled shaping of core tools began. The art probably
reached India from the west, and seems to be associated, from an
early stage, with our own species, *homo sapiens*, rather than with
any of the near-men or hominids. But skulls and bones from the
early phases have not yet been found in India.

The fact that India, apart from the towering Himalaya, has

not had much ice during any Pleistocene period means that man could survive ice phases there, so there is a presumption that the peoples of India may include survivals of groups who drifted in in very early times. Another basic fact about India is that forests have long been very large and very dense, so groups retaining very early and lowly modes of life have been able to retreat into this relatively unfavourable environment to avoid subjugation by better-equipped folk occupying the better, more open lands. India thus offers dramatic contrast in mode of life and thought between lowly groups, usually in forest and jungle, and groups at various higher stages of equipment on the open lands. The sea and seafaring have apparently not been important, except at a few periods, in shaping Indian development.

In the last major retreats of the Pleistocene ice sheets and glaciers, deluges of melt-water must have flowed down the southern slopes of the Himalaya, and, indeed, they have left many traces of their work. They dumped huge quantities of gravel and mud on the floor of what is now the Indo-Gangetic lowland, which has an enormous thickness of these deposits. The lowlands and lower slopes of the mountains became covered with dense forest, so population was probably very sparse.

In the Indian peninsula rocky outcrops stand out in many places and have not been forested. Some of these spots were occupied by people making very small flint tools. This type of equipment was widespread in Africa, Asia, and Europe and is called in western Europe the Tardenoisian or pigmy-flint culture. The little implements of flint, quartz, or quartzite were probably mounted in wood, bone, or horn. It has been thought that in most of the Indian peninsula this continued to be the typical equipment until iron was brought in, during the last millennium B.C. At any rate, few finds have been made that suggest cultures intermediate between that of the pigmy-flints and that of the Early Iron Age, and such finds as have been studied are from the north-easterly limiting province, Orissa. For the north we have rather more evidence that brings in relations of India with lands farther east, and of Pakistan with lands farther west.

In Further India and Indonesia core tools were made by flaking on one face only and some think this type of tool per-

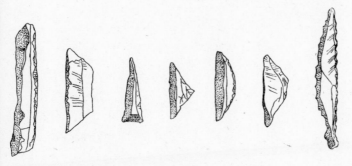

FIG. 53. Epipalaeolithic implements, India.

sisted in widespread use into the second or penultimate millennium B.C. with many transitions to a type shaped by grinding and rubbing. Ground-stone axes, more or less cylindrical, with a roughly oval cross-section, are known from various places in north India and south China. This primary Neolithic equipment spread to Japan via Formosa, also to the Philippines, eastern Indonesia, and Melanesia, but left only traces in Further India and did not reach Java. It probably came to east and south-east Asia from south-west Asia, and it has a wide distribution as a primary Neolithic tool in Europe.

At some time near the middle of the second millennium B.C. there developed in Further India and spread to south China a ground-stone axe with a large tang, sometimes called a shouldered axe (German: *Schulterbeil*). It spread to India, reaching Orissa and (one specimen) the Godavari, also Assam, Chota Nagpur, and Bengal and (one specimen) near Allahabad. There is some, not very conclusive, evidence for associating rice cultivation with the people who made these axes. If so, rice is probably of Further Indian origin as a cultivated plant. Later

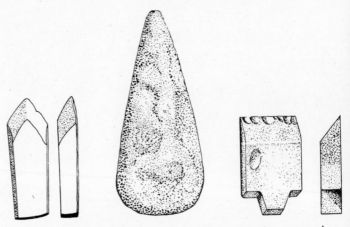

FIG. 54. Indian ground-stone axes (*a*) with rectangular cross-section, (*b*) with oval cross-section, (*c*) shouldered axe.

still there developed the fine stone axes, typically highly polished, with a rectangular cross-section. Some students believe they spread south from China; at any rate they seem to have reached India from the east or north-east, and the fashion penetrated to the Santal Parganas and Chota Nagpur. It has been suggested that there is a cultural link between these last stone axes and the Munda languages still spoken in Chota Nagpur.

Pakistan yields larger evidence of early cultures based on food-production, as is to be expected from its position in relation to the primary home of cereal cultivation (wheat and barley, and perhaps millet) in south-west Asia. It seems to have been after the development of an enclosed oven for cooking food, for firing painted pottery, and for rudimentary metallurgy of copper and bronze that the practice of cereal growing spread to the hills of eastern Baluchistan and reached the Indus basin. By that time south-west Asia had developed a high-grade technique and was casting as well as hammering bronze, making shaft-holes in bronze axes for insertion of a wooden handle. The eastward migrants appear not to have taken this full achievement with them and their casting remained a rough process. The Bronze Age cultures of western Asia had enormous influence in Europe and China as well as in Mediterranean lands, but Africa south of the Sahara and Abyssinia had no early Bronze Age at all; the condition is still more extreme than that of India. But there is a partial analogy, and, in both India and intertropical Africa, partly as a result of the paucity of early experience with copper and tin, partly as a result of great forest-areas and partly as a consequence of their southerly position, we find more survivals of early modes of human life than we do in western Asia, Europe, and China. The two cases differ in that India also has high developments of culture matching Europe and China.

In the years after the Second World War a new chapter in the early Indian story was opened out. Attention had already been called to ruins of an ancient city at Harappa in the Punjab, and in 1922 Mr. R. D. Banerji examined a Buddhist stupa on a part of the site of another ruined city and realized that it stood upon the remains of something far older. This gave Sir John Marshall a clue and there ensued years of organized excavation, continued later under the late Mr. Ernest Mackay, the site being called Mohenjo-daro. Since then work has been extended to many more sites, notably by the late Brigadier Ross and by Stuart Piggott and Sir Mortimer Wheeler, while Gordon Childe has visited the region and helped in the interpretation of finds.

It now appears that a number of village sites were occupied

by food-producers in the lower Indus region and eastern Baluchistan, probably before 3000 B.C.; and that later on, about 2500 B.C., there developed some large-scale organization on the Indus with a northern capital at Harappa in the Punjab, and a southern one about 350 miles away at Mohenjo-daro in Sind.

Among the first traces of early village life are some sites in the Bolan pass, and the culture these exhibit has been named after Quetta, the later city near the western end of the pass. These sites have yielded buff pottery painted in purple-brown with geometric patterns. The affinities of this pottery appear to be less with that of other Indus-region sites than with that of Persia (Tepe Sialk, third phase) and southern Mesopotamia (Susa, first phase), and these are now both usually dated before 3000 B.C. Links between the other early villages of the lower Indus and east Baluchistan and Mesopotamian culture are indicated in designs on pots and several other details. The early link with Mesopotamia is clearly a link of the villages of southeast Baluchistan; links with the Indus cities come much later. These connexions were probably by sea from the Makran to Ur. Ross followed out a sequence of settlements at Rana Ghundai (Zhob valley). The earliest layer had ashes showing where hearths had existed, and there were hand-made pots (unpainted save one specimen), flint blades and bone points. No buildings could be traced and it would seem that this was a temporary site of an occupation by some semi-nomad people with humped ox, sheep, and ass; and, curiously, four animal teeth found here have been identified as belonging to the domesticated horse. From the probable dating of later phases at Rana Ghundai this first settlement can hardly be dated later than the earliest part of the third millennium B.C., and is possibly older still, so these teeth may be the earliest known trace of the domestic horse.

In southern Baluchistan and Sind the village sites yield buff pottery, mostly wheel-made and often very fine and thin, covered with a fine white slip which at one site (Nundara) is painted with various designs in red. At another site, Nal, farther north among the Brahui mountains, painting on pots includes blue, yellow, and green colours as well as red, but these additional colours were not well fixed. Designs at Nal include items derived from plants and animals as well as many inter-secting circles.

At Kulli and related sites in southern Baluchistan have been found figurines of women in which attention has been paid to bangles, necklaces, head-dress, and other adornments rather than to the features of the people concerned. There are also small vessels shaped in soft stone, probably to hold rather pre-cious substances such as medicaments and cosmetics. The villages in several cases may have lasted on until the days of the cities of Harappa and Mohenjo-daro, as one finds in some villages, for example, fragments of models (? toys) of carts, a great feature in finds from the cities.

At the sites in the Zhob valley the pottery is at first buff or terra-cotta but later much of it is red, and the red of the northern sites comes to stand out in contrast with the buff of the villages of Sind and southern Baluchistan. As the cities made red ware, this may mean that they are more related to the Bolan and Zhob villages than to those of the south. The rise of the cities is, how-ever, still full of mystery, and it would not be wise to be con-fident about any particular relationship as yet.

The villages have yielded a fair amount of bronze as well as copper, and an analysis of a piece of an axe found at Nal showed no tin but some lead and nickel. Nickel occurs in copper ores in north India and Afghanistan, but it is possible that the Nal metal was found in Baluchistan. The bronze objects from the cities are sometimes rich in nickel but usually also have arsenic, of which only a trace was found in the axe from Nal. In the cities seals, probably for marking property, were very important, but only two seals have been found at Nal. One is in soft stone (steatite), the other is in copper but is probably quite late and appears unrelated to any other finds at this site. Again, the cities made great use of burnt brick, but it is not found in the early villages which we are reviewing. Stone and sun-dried brick are the general materials. The early villages came to have some trading relations with the cities as these latter developed but, for a good while, it was not a case of cultural domination by the cities.

On the whole it seems that Sind and eastern Baluchistan must have been less arid in the third millennium B.C. than they now are, and Stuart Piggott has developed the attractive idea that the monsoon then reached farther west than it does now. Whether it was stronger or whether its location has drifted eastwards is a further question; but the former possibility is the more likely. The Indus cities used burnt brick on a large scale, and this suggests not only the presence of wood fuel at hand but, probably, also a need felt to protect building sfrom the rain which would have washed away sun-dried brick. The cities' drainage systems also imply rain and river floods, the latter danger to some extent fended off by dams. The representation of the tiger rather than the lion on seals further suggests jungle rather than open semi-arid grass-land. In parts of this region we may, however, have one of those cases in which a forest existed under moister Pleistocene or early post-Pleistocene conditions and lingered on but could not replace itself when destroyed. This is the case with some areas of loess in Europe, though in others bush and small trees do grow again after clearing.

Harappa and Mohenjo-daro are the two large cities and the two which have been most studied. Others, perhaps of less importance, await examination in a dry area of the south-west Punjab, Bahawalpur, near the dry course of the ancient river Sarasvati, famous in early Hindu literature.

The two cities, 350 miles apart, front rivers in situations which gave water on a considerable part of their perimeters, and each had a number of smaller towns and villages in its region, but between them a long stretch of the Indus has yielded nothing. Harappa and Mohenjo-daro seem to have been mutually supplementary rather than in rivalry, and Wheeler and Piggott think of them as respectively northern and southern capitals of a kingdom. We lack here the continuous ribbon of arable between the capitals of Upper and Lower Egypt. The two cities show similar plans, with streets laid north–south and east–west, and both had citadels, now represented by mounds higher than those of the rest of these cities. That at Harappa has been sadly plundered for bricks for railway-track beds, and that at Mohenjo-daro still has on it a Buddhist ttupa of about A.D. 300, so we do not yet know what may be beneath. At Harappa a great platform of mud with a centre of sun-dried brick was faced with burnt brick, and on this platform was built the citadel with northerly and westerly entrances up to which led processional ways. Wheeler has found that late in the city's history the facing of platform and walls had to be reconstructed, and that then the westerly entrance was more or less blocked, an indication of troubled times. At Mohenjo-daro, near the area occupied by the stupa, there is a great bath with dressing-rooms, also a large building around a courtyard and described by Wheeler as probably a collegiate institution, also a hall in which the roof was supported on a number of brick pillars. Even though we await examination of the ground under the stupa we cannot doubt that the citadel was the seat of authority. Wheeler has found what must have been a grain store under control of the authorities, with a long platform for loading and unloading. The better houses had baths and many were probably two-storied and flat-roofed. They also had chutes for throwing refuse into bins along the streets, whence it was apparently collected. Drains

FIG. 55. Street with brick drain. Mohenjo-daro.

in the house walls lead down to brick-lined covered conduits under the streets and so carry sewage out to pits; to add to all this sanitary scheming there are removable brick covers to man-holes over the street conduits. No ancient cities known else-where had anything as elaborate as this, and no modern city in the east is comparable in this respect. With the streets running in the directions of the cardinal points the built-up blocks were either rectangular or parallelograms nearly rectangular. The houses presented to the streets windowless walls unless there were windows in upper stories, and the frontage lines seem to have remained unaltered for centuries. Near the granary there are rows of small two-roomed buildings that are supposed to have been a barrack-like housing scheme for servile labour, some of which was employed in crushing grain in great mortars with heavy pestles at Mohenjo-daro. At Harappa we know that the city was preceded by a small settlement with red pottery, apparently therefore related to the more northerly rather than to the more southerly villages of Baluchistan. Barley may have been the most important grain crop, but bread-wheat was also in use. There is no indication of rice cultivation. Cotton was grown and there is evidence that it was woven. Perhaps it was an object of trade but its perishable nature makes investigation difficult. Cattle were very important and included the castrated ox for work. The cattle were often the humped variety so charac-teristic of India but there was also a short-horned humpless beast. Sheep, goats, pigs, buffaloes, asses, and elephants were also known, and chickens may have been domesticated or half-wild. Some bones of the one-humped camel and of the horse have been found, and these give a contrast to finds of the third millen-nium B.C. in Mesopotamia, which do not include evidence of these animals. These facts about the camel suggest that it was domes-ticated first somewhere in Inner Asia rather than in Arabia where its later breeding has become a feature. Some researchers think the two-humped Bactrian camel was used for work in Mesopotamia before the one-humped dromedary.

The people of the cities seem to have prospected eastwards, in Rajputana, for copper and lead, and they learned something of the smelting of copper and tin for making bronze, as well as a little of the art of casting. Some of their copper contained arsenic in appreciable quantities and this made casting much easier, as a little arsenic or tin prevents bubbles of oxygen from forming in a closed mould filled with molten copper reduced from a copper ore. It has been thought that supplies of tin were not very assured. The early excavators, Marshall and Mackay, between them claimed that as against thirty-four blade axes of copper they had only nineteen of bronze, but several bronzes now known have about a normal proportion of tin. The copper axes are mostly flat; and spearheads, hooks, arrow-head tips, and so on are usually simple. There are, however, some more elaborate objects: a mirror with a woman's figure as the handle, and the mirror itself (a metal surface) as her enormously enlarged head, a model of a curtained wagon drawn by oxen, a number of vessels and a figure of a girl dancer of southern Baluch character are examples here. In spite of these finds it is nevertheless broadly true that the art of metallurgy did not attain very high general achievement in the Indus region. Not only are handle-holes unknown, save in a clay model in one case, but sockets also were not used, though Mesopotamia had developed them by the time the Indus cities became important. A good deal of the casting in the Indus cities was rough and the product was afterwards further shaped by hammering.

The external relations of the Indus cities touched materials other than the metals and timber already mentioned. Beads are usually preserved on ancient sites and so these items are apt to loom more largely in our discussions than they did in actual fact. Cornelian beads, some etched, seem to have been a link with

Mesopotamia, that region and the Indus being apparently the two places where cornelian beads were etched. Lapis lazuli apparently came from Persia, Pamir, or Badakshan in the north-east Afghan ranges to both Mesopotamia on the one hand and

Fig. 56. Bronze figurine of a dancing girl.

the Indus on the other, but was much less used in the latter. Jadeite came perhaps from Tibet or north Burma, silver from Persia, turquoise and other bead materials from Afghanistan, or, in some cases, from the peninsula of Kathiawar, which also sent sea-shells. A few bead materials may have come from south India, as well as a green stone from which a cup was made. Gold is thought to have been collected from Persian streams, and red haematite, used as a pigment, came from the Persian Gulf. Stags' horns, used as a medicament, appear to have come from Kashmir. The coast of Sind is occupied by the Indus delta, which did not favour early settlement or trade, so merchants traversed southern Baluchistan and made Sutkagendor a fortified station fairly near alternative coastal landings. In western Europe at Santiago da Compostella, Canterbury, and St. David's we have analogous stations. Traders must also have gone overland to Persia, Afghanistan, Turkestan, and perhaps Tibet, as well as into Rajputana and possibly south India. Stations along some of these routes have been tentatively identified.

Methods of transport of goods are not known in any detail. There may have been both human porters and pack animals, and, probably mainly for the shorter distances near the cities, ox-carts were used. They apparently had solid wheels and were often pulled by a pair of oxen. Model carts, some apparently used as toys, are a feature among the finds at Mohenjo-daro. One should keep an open mind concerning the extent to which camels and horses may have been used as pack animals pending the finding of more evidence. It seems that there is no evidence of the use of the horse as a draught animal in the Indus civilization.

Unpainted, undecorated pottery was wheel-made in the cities of the Indus in large quantities for general use, but when painted it is usually in black on a red ground and thus in relation with north rather than south Baluchistan villages. But the pots from the cities are less orderly and less formal in their decoration than those from the early villages; the decoration may include plant or animal forms and is mostly of rather poor quality. A few cases of painting on pots in several colours are known and are thought to suggest links with Nal in the Brahui range of Baluchistan discussed in an earlier paragraph. Some of the un-painted pottery is thought to be related to the grey ware of western Asia (Turkestan). There is little change in quality or style of the pottery of the cities throughout their history. The kilns were apparently outside the cities, as is natural in view of danger of fire, but, in the times of danger and decline, some kilns were made within the cities, whether because regulation had weakened

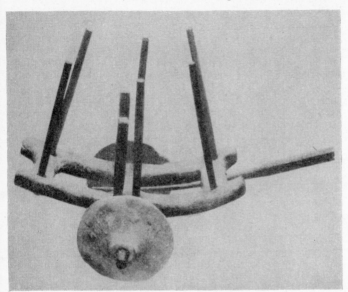

Fig. 57. Model cart, probably a toy.

or because safety from raiders demanded it we do not know. Figurines, chiefly of women and of cattle, are numerous and some of them have heads or other parts in separate pieces fastened on. Some are toys, some probably fertility emblems or charms. Engraved seals are a noteworthy feature of the Indus cities and, though they have not been found in Baluchistan settlements related to the cities, several occur in Sumer at datable sites, mostly in the last two or three centuries of the third millennium B.C. These seals may indicate that Indian merchants or their agents were in commerce at Ur and other Sumerian cities. Perhaps the absence of seals from Baluchistan indicates that the people there were carriers for the trade of the Indus cities rather than themselves merchants, but it is well not to argue too much from absence of finds. The seals are often rectangular and intended for stamping soft material, probably an equivalent for

FIG. 58. Seal showing a bull.

our marking of various belongings with special ink. The seal usually has a carefully cut decoration, a humped bull or a tiger or an elephant in profile. Accompanying this design is an inscription, usually limited to a few signs. The execution of the seals and, apparently, the style and language of the inscriptions, still unread, remains almost unchanged through the centuries. The cities have no long inscriptions and no public statues or analogous monuments so far as is known at present. No temple or shrine has yet been found, but we do not know what may be under the stupa at Mohenjo-daro or what may have been utterly destroyed by the brick plunderers at Harappa.

Apparently the cities were unusually exact in the matter of controlled weights and measures. Multiples which are most used are 2, 10, and 16. In this matter again there is little change through the centuries.

The indications are that regulation of production and trade in the Indus cities was carried very far and that change was frowned upon; it has been suggested that this ultra-conservatism was an accompaniment of rule by priest-kings enforcing religious sanctions.

The people themselves mostly, at any rate in the earlier centuries, were representatives of what Sergi called the Mediterranean race and Elliot Smith named the Brown race. They are typically long-headed and had oval, longish faces with fairly prominent noses and not very strongly built bodies. This type nowadays varies in colouring from the paleness characteristic of Europeans to a brownish tinge in North Africa, Arabia, and India, and it has wavy hair. In parts of western Asia and central Europe at the present time people with broad heads are the characteristic type, and this type also occurs in India. It was present in the population of the Indus cities.

Skulls of another type have also been collected from the cities, the type of what may be called the aborigines. Very long heads with prominent brows and retreating foreheads, small broad noses, rather large mouths. Very dark skins with wavy or curly hair seem to have been conspicuous aboriginal features, and, so far as information from skulls goes, the type occurred in some of the people of the Indus cities. The bronze figurine of a dancing girl of Baluch style illustrates the type. Probably a good deal will be known when full reports on recently examined cemeteries are available. But the 'aboriginal' type is very interesting already in connexion with the end of the Indus cities. Stuart Piggott and Wheeler are pointing the way to a reinterpretation of the Rig Veda poems, now thought to have been composed about 1400 B.C., as evidence of the conquest of the Indus civilization by Aryan barbarians. This may be a most interesting field of research for Sanskrit scholars in the coming years. The Rig Veda poems despise the Dasyus, the conquered people, with black faces and no noses. Had this type become fairly numerous in the Indus cities, or have we here a case of fixing on one type that is conspicuously different and therefore an object of dislike? The Rig Veda also gives us contrasts in ritual and belief between conquerors and conquered.

If the cities of the Indus really lacked temples and shrines, ritual must have been largely a family affair. A god with at least three faces was thought by Marshall to be an early form of the god known in much later Hinduism as Siva. In Hinduism the cults of Siva, of the mother goddess, of trees and animals, and ideas of Yoga take present shapes after the Aryan conquest. It is quite probable that there was a resurgence of pre-Aryan ideas after the conquerors had settled down. Indra, the Lord of Hosts of the Rig Veda, not without analogies with the Jahweh of the Book of Joshua, fades into the background, much as, for a time, Jahweh did in Israel, when crop-growers' fertility rites were competing with the traditions of the herder-raiders of an earlier time.

The Indus civilization, as that of crop-growers, naturally emphasized fertility rites and sex. The phallus and conical stones probably derived from it were important emblems, and on the female side we have the yoni sometimes modified into a large ring stone. These ring stones are widespread features of ancient cults, often placed in a passage and used for a purificatory rite, the subject having to crawl through the ring (being born again). The invading conquerors were great beef-eaters who sacrificed animals to Indra and their other gods (of fire, sky, storm, &c.) and who despised the cults of the cultivators and city dwellers, but nevertheless sometimes married their girls, and so, in the course of some generations of settled life, came under the influence of a modified version of the old religion. The old cults of the Indus show other forms of symbolization of women, pregnancy and so forth, and a mother goddess, apparently very different from an earth goddess of the name Prithivi who was worshipped by barbarian, possibly Aryan-speaking, conquerors.

The Indus cities were overwhelmed by barbarian invasions that are still not very closely dated. Dates of 1700–1500 B.C. are usually given for a period of movement of peoples in south-west Asia and a recurrence of change and disorder is supposed to have occurred about 1200–1000 B.C.

In the Indus region, Chanhu-daro in Sind gives evidence of a ruined city of the Indus culture occupied subsequently by barbarians. These incomers seem to have acquired fragments of the older civilization, especially of its more rural Baluch elements, but they also give evidence of contact with south-west Asia in seals and other details. Professor Heine-Geldern, in unpublished lectures (1952), emphasizes the relation of these seals to some used by Hittites in Anatolia towards 1200 B.C. He also points out parallels between scattered finds from north-west India and objects from Transcaucasia, Anatolia, Kuban, &c., datable 1200–1000 B.C.

It is thus possible that, even if barbarian invasions began to destroy the Indus culture before 1500 B.C., they continued or were repeated from time to time during several centuries, perhaps even a long time after 1000 B.C. At what stage in this process the Indo-Aryan languages began their Indian evolution it is better not to try to guess at the moment. With the barbarian invasions we get evidence of battle-axes with a hole for the handle, and of the war-chariot drawn by horses. The horse has been mentioned for an earlier time, but it appears to have gained more widespread importance when the chariot came to be used in war as a vehicle for an archer. The charioteer-conquerors ended the effective life of the Indus cities and have left indications of massacres.

The barbarian conquerors, highly mobile if not completely nomadic, have left little direct trace of their early story; they no doubt specialized in work in wool, fur, and leather, all perishable. They were beginning to know something about the sword as a weapon and would soon learn about iron. Their dispersal from the great steppe between the Pamir and the Dnieper has, however, left important linguistic results. Among these mobile peoples it is probable that a widespread similarity of language without too much complexity of inflexion grew up, and we have the early Aryan language of India (Sanskrit) and the languages of Europe, and some languages of Anatolia and Iran all related to a common origin or common origins in a group of related modes of speech. For India we have especially the views of the eighteenth-century scholar Sir William Jones and of the twentieth-century scholar Sir George Grierson. The latter grouped the Aryan languages of India into two classes, the Dardic family spoken in parts of the mountains of India's western border and in a belt north of the Indian peninsula and south of the Ganges basin, and the Vedic family in the basins of the Indus and Ganges. It is not quite clear whether Dardic is to be considered as basically Aryan or whether it results from mutual influences between Aryan speech and older forms presumably of the Dravidian or the Munda family. The theory that the barbarian invasions of the Indus culture may have been repeated perhaps over several centuries suggests a possibility of two or more waves of Aryan speech and so relates itself to Grierson's hypothesis.

It has been suggested that the people of the Indus cities spoke a Dravidian language and one language of this family survives as Brahui in the hills of eastern Baluchistan called the Brahui range. Dravidian languages are now spoken in the Indian peninsula, which does not seem to have been much influenced by the

Indus civilization, and an alternative suggestion has been made that the Dravidian languages, which appear to have Mesopotamian relationships, were brought by sea to the Indian peninsula in the last millennium B.C. As Baluchistan was concerned with commerce between the Indus cities and Mesopotamia, a linguistic link is possible from Mesopotamia to both Baluchistan in earlier and the Indian peninsula in later times. Until the script of the Indus cities has been read much must remain in suspense, and even the reading of the script may help only a little, because no long inscriptions and no hint of a literature have been found, at any rate as yet. The inscriptions available are short ones on seals. It seems that most of the Aryan invasions of the Indus region were movements of barbarian warriors, in whole groups of men, women, and children, against groups of merchants and cultivators living in cities that had long passed their prime. As the conquerors penetrated deeper into India among village cultivators and perhaps cities east of the Indus group, they seem to have fractionated into families of lordlings dominating villages of cultivators, but at the same time needing to consider the traditions and prejudices of those villagers. Of some of the incidents in the process of conquest one finds glimpses in the Mahabharata, for instance, when a warrior walks into a mirror, of which he has never before seen an example. Of the conquerors' later adjustment of themselves to their new surroundings, we hear that, while it is right to sacrifice animals and especially cattle to the gods, yet it is not expedient to do so because it angers the people.

The Aryan conquerors recognized priests, soldiers, and their own people—Brahmins, Kshatriyas, and Vaisyas. The people of the conquered groups were servile Sudras. The conquerors did not come in with a caste system fully developed, but there is the germ of it in this classification if we further realize the Aryan contempt for the people with black faces and no noses, and the conquerors' anxiety, as they became more or less separate and isolated clans of lordlings, lest they should be swamped by intermixture. Such fears strengthened prohibitions of commensalism and intermarriage and also prescription of occupation by heredity.

In Hindu literature of a period long after the conquest the ideas of a god like the Hindu Siva, of a mother goddess, tree-worship, Yoga, the phallus, and yoni, and transmigration of souls, all appear. They are probably revivals, with alterations, of pre-conquest Indian ideas, most likely of ideas which had found some expression in the Indus cities.

The Brahmins or priestly class, as has so often happened in different parts of the world, were the people who learned how to extend their power over both conquerors and conquered by adapting what they could not displace from local cults. So they became expositors of both traditions, and there probably was some infiltration of priests or officiants from the older tradition into that brought in by the conquerors. The Brahmin group persisted and made its position strong in relation with both the Aryan and the pre-Aryan civilized folk. There were no doubt, as there are now, jungle groups and others outside the system, pariah, as they are called in modern times, and some so far outside the developing scheme that they were considered as 'other peoples'.

The Kshatriya as a group lost its identity and became a collection of ruling clans, known in history as the Rajput clans. The Vaisya were those most subject to losing their separateness through intermixture with the craftsmen of the conquered people, some of whom were no doubt superior in knowledge and technical skill to themselves. The Vaisya lose their distinctiveness as a group in the later story of Indian society.

The young people were required to marry within certain group limits, to marry, that is, within the Gnyati, which was based largely on occupation or ritual or both together, with a background of relationship. At the same time marriage of close blood relations was condemned; one must not marry within the Gotra. For a girl to be married to some man of a 'lower' group than her own was, as usual, looked upon as a disgrace to the family. Marriage of young men was more difficult to control and there arose the saying: 'A wife from the east, a husband from the west.' This implies the tendency for some of the descendants of the conquerors to take wives from among the conquered, or from descendants of earlier mixed marriages. The tendency towards hypergamy among girls is almost world-wide and in some high-grade Brahmin groups in India it has made normal marriage difficult for their girls.

Helping this elaboration of a social hierarchy with accompanying effort at fixation of hereditary grades is the general principle of avoidance of unpleasant or dangerous contacts. Often the lowlier groups with their crude dwellings may be careless and unclean; and more careful neighbours will seek to avoid the many dangers of infectious disease from pollution of wells and crude methods of food-preparation and eating. Especially is there danger from flesh food in a hot climate with a long, hot, wet season.

It has become characteristic in India that some of the higher groups eschew flesh food altogether, a scheme made more practicable by the fact that rice was made available as a food procurable in large quantities and, on the whole, possible to prepare in clean fashion without elaborate equipment.

Groups which developed rituals of cleanliness and care and eschewed flesh food have been apt to rise in the social scale, especially if their occupations have not meant too dirty hands. The social hierarchy therefore, in some ways, has a certain fluidity, though India suffers from the attempt to fix occupation in hereditary fashion and to limit too strictly commensalism and possibilities of marriage.

Outside the recognized groups of Brahmin, Kshatriya, Vaisya, and Sudra were, and are, as already stated, the pariah or untouchables, namely those who have disgraced themselves in some way or those who belong by descent to aboriginal jungle groups but have become hangers-on of better equipped folk. One can have little doubt that much of this social grading is very old, but it probably became more a matter of conscious thought and organization after the Aryan conquests, when physical contrasts in skin colour, in mouth prominence, and nasal development became more conspicuous and more widely observable. The high position of the Brahmins has to be remembered alongside the elaborate subdivision of this grade according to occupation and ritual. The Sudra have elaborated their subdivisions almost beyond belief, with many grades of mutual avoidance. European connexions have brought educational opportunities to some of the pariah, so that they may now sometimes be more hygienic and better informed than the descendants of some of what have been the higher castes.

In matters of thought the sequence from the Aryan conquests has been as momentous as it was in social grading and organization. Two rituals confronted one another: (1) that of the descendants of conquering pastoralists committed thenceforth to fitting themselves into a routine of cultivation and to settling down, often without the horse which had played such a large part in the lives of their forebears; and (2) that of the cultivators pressing itself on the local princelings and lordlings. Clashes and the increased predominance of the cultivators' ritual were inevitable but, as elsewhere, one also finds a stimulus to thought trying to find a way of easing the clashes and of making an overriding harmony between the two. The prophetic thinkers and teachers appear in India within perhaps five or six centuries, or less, of the conquests and continue to emerge during another five centuries or more. Their attitudes vary, some inclining to incorporate in their systems more, others less, of the older

traditions. The most famous of these teachers was Gautama
Buddha, who concerned himself less with gods and goddesses
and more with the helping of mankind towards a final consummation which he set forth under the name that has come down
to us as Nirvana. He accepted and utilized the ancient and
widespread belief in reincarnation, including the idea of reincarnation in animal as well as in human form. The particular
reincarnation of the individual was held to be decided according to that individual's conduct. All individuals could attain
ultimately to Nirvana, and it was enjoined upon believers that
they should do nothing to hinder a spirit on its upward way.
This involved abstention from killing animals and from flesh
food, and this may have helped to strengthen such abstention,
which is a feature in Indian society quite apart from Buddhist
belief and ritual nowadays.

About two centuries after Buddha a great ruler, Asoka,
established his power over nearly all peninsular India, save
Travancore, as well as over the north, and then sought to spread
the teaching of Buddha by peaceful means. He ordered the
building of a great monument in honour of Buddha at Sanchi,
from which had come his favourite wife. This great stone-faced
mound, surmounted by a sacred building and encompassed by a
stone palisade with gates, is of great interest in several ways.
Stone bars are fitted into sockets after the fashion of wooden
beams and the structure gives the impression of a carpenter's
technique applied to stone. The analogy in this respect with the
British Stonehenge is most noteworthy. At Sanchi the stones are
finely dressed and the gate-posts are carved in relief, sometimes
with representations of steppe herdsmen in costume, suggesting
the original Aryan invaders, and yet this monument, called a
stupa, was built probably a thousand years after the supposed
date of the invasion. There is no doubt about the building of
Sanchi in the third century B.C. Were there other older stupas

and had wood been used in some of them? These are questions for the future. For the present we may suppose that in Asoka's day there was some knowledge of the peoples of the steppe and perhaps some surviving tradition of their invasions of India long before.

We must now go back, in time, in order to consider peninsular India. There, it seems, in many areas the lowly Epipalaeolithic mode of life, with small flints in wooden or bone mounts, persisted for ages, as it probably also did in some parts of Europe. There is, as yet, little evidence of contact with the Indus valley culture or of a bronze-using age, though gold, silver, copper, and tin occur in the peninsula. It is with the coming of iron that one finds new developments, evidenced especially by megalithic tombs. One must not argue that because they are megaliths they have close relationship with the megalithic cultures of, for example, western Europe. The use of large stone blocks is natural enough and simple enough to be invented, or perhaps one should say evolved, independently in various areas; especially is this a likely hypothesis when the accompaniments of the cult belong to, or at least begin in, such different ages as the third millennium B.C. in the west and the early part of the last millennium B.C. in India. At the same time we should remember that the megalithic cult in the west continued into early Christian times and even later in some places; and at any time evidence may be forthcoming of the actual building of a megalith in the west long after the period of the early ones.

Here it may be relevant to refer to megalithic structures of the Khasia and other peoples of Assam. These are more typically groups of standing stones, especially stone circles, and so are probably not closely related to the megalithic tombs of the peninsula.

A legend tells of the 'churning of the ocean' by a god armed with a great stone, and this suggests a possibility that the people who brought the megalithic cult to the Indian peninsula and spread there the use of iron and of pottery may have to some extent come by sea.

It is permissible for the present to think that, when these new activities spread in the peninsula, the people came into contact with the north and acquired a good deal of the religious tradition of the north, or at least of its older lowlier elements. Saivite Hinduism then, or possibly later, became the general ritual of the south. It was stated above that Asoka spread his power over the peninsula, apart from Travancore where, a contemporary record states, people were engaged in commerce by sea. Presumably he tried to spread Buddhist ideas in the south as well as in the north, and Saivite Hinduism (worship especially of Siva) may be a hostile reaction to his efforts—we have as yet little evidence of any kind.

In the course of time the prophetic phase, illustrated most clearly in Buddha, gave place to the institutional phase with men following a religious life as a profession, i.e. with a priesthood and monastic scheme. With this added equipment Buddhism spread to Ceylon, Burma, and Further India and also to Tibet, Inner Asia, China, and Japan. The spread to Ceylon and Burma and Malaya is called Hinayana Buddhism (the lesser Buddhism), while the other is known as Mahayana (or greater) Buddhism. In India itself the ritual institutional phase of Buddhism was not able to hold its own against the older agricultural ritual, and it practically disappeared as a distinctive worship; but one finds that Buddha is widely revered nevertheless, though for some centuries Buddhists were persecuted.

After the rise of Islam in south-western Asia struggles for power between its rival princes brought Islamic invasions into India, a most notable instance being the conquests in north-western India in the eleventh century A.D. under the leadership of Mahmud of Ghazni (Afghanistan). The Islamic world was deeply affected by the Mongol invasions of the early thirteenth century, but these did not penetrate into India. The second series of Mongol invasions, on the other hand, led in the late fourteenth century to the foundation of the Mogul Empire, which took over as its capital the city of Delhi, near the entry into the Ganges basin from the north-west. The first of the two great Mongol conquests was a pagan, the second an Islamic, effort. The Mogul Empire in India was thus Islamic, and, under it, an Islamic administrator was established at Hyderabad, Deccan, most important of former princely states of India. The headship of the state of Hyderabad became hereditary. Some other small princely states acquired Islamic rulers, but for the most part the Hindu princes maintained their positions or regained them as the Mogul Empire weakened. In the controversial case of Kashmir, a Hindu ruler has governed a population with an Islamic majority. Eastern Bengal became to a large extent converted to Islam. Opposition of one religion to the other has emphasized contrasts in ritual practices between them and this has remained to the present day a major social problem. Islam has apparently had little influence in modifying Hindu belief and ritual, but Hindu social rules have had considerable influence on Islam in India in those regions in which followers of the two religions live more or less intermingled.

From the sixteenth century A.D. onwards Europeans founded commercial ports in India, and maritime trade with Portugal, France, and Britain became an important aspect of Indian life, which had previously long been highly self-contained and from time to time deeply affected by overland relations.

Under the new conditions India tended to become in large measure a producer and exporter of raw materials, to be worked up in Britain and, in the twentieth century, also in Japan. The ports of Calcutta, Bombay, and Madras became the three most populous cities of India and still hold that rank.

The resurgence of Indian life has, however, led to the re-establishment of Delhi as the capital of the major division of the new autonomous India, with Karachi, a port, as the capital of western, and Dacca, another port, as the capital of eastern, Pakistan. Industries are growing on modern European lines and the export of raw materials is no longer such an important factor in Indian life.

Modern communications by rail and bus as well as by steam-ship and aeroplane, and large-scale commercial contacts, are deeply affecting the structure of Indian society and its caste system, causing on the one hand far-reaching changes, and on the other hand hostile reactions to change among many of the more conservatively minded people of India and Pakistan.

9

China

UNTIL well into this century it was widely believed, even in China, that all Chinese history before about 850 B.C. was mere mythological fancy. It is true that Terrien de la Couperie much earlier had claimed, on slender evidence, that China had received the beginnings of its civilization from south-west Asia, and F. von Richtofen in his famous studies of China had given a summary of legendary Chinese history from before 2000 B.C. He attached much importance to these legends, and excavation since 1928 has confirmed his views in considerable measure. In the case of China, as in those of Crete, Troy, India, prehistoric Britain, and the west Baltic, therefore, legend has been shown to have a considerable amount of truth, usually mixed with elements of fancy.

It has been thought by many students that the art of cultivation, or at any rate of cereal cultivation, arose somewhere, perhaps at several places, between the Caspian Sea and the western desert of Egypt, and that it spread thence to all the lands in which it has later been practised. That it did arise very early (before 5000 B.C.) in that region and that in other lands its beginnings are later, rarely much before 3000 B.C., is fairly generally agreed. But the theory of one origin and dispersion from one centre must not be overpressed; the evidence is not sufficient.

It seems that in the last retreat of the ice sheets of the Pleistocene period, and perhaps in the last interglacial phase also, peoples spread over many regions. In areas with trees, these migrants learned to cut branches by making stone axes with transverse edges and began to shape stones in part by rubbing, perhaps using them for digging up roots for food (see Chapter 5). This phase of social evolution is often called the Epipalaeolithic or Mesolithic; and it is just possible that people who dug up

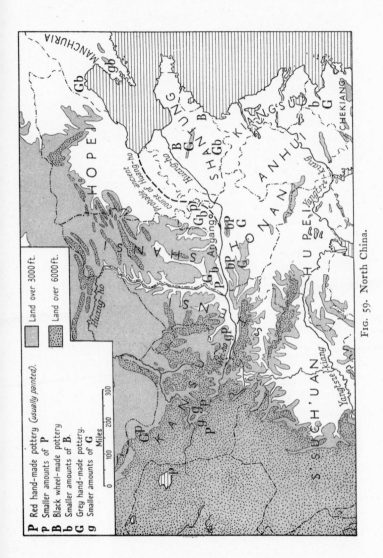

FIG. 59. North China.

Legend:

P Red hand-made pottery (*usually painted*).
p Smaller amounts of P.
B Black wheel-made pottery
b Smaller amounts of B.
G Grey hand-made pottery.
g Smaller amounts of G

Land over 3000 ft.
Land over 6000 ft.

Miles
0   100   200   300

roots for food made some attempts at cultivation. Cultivation
may thus have several different birthplaces, and it is better for
the present to think of the south-west Asiatic and Egyptian area
above-named as the prime home of special cultivation of wheat
and barley, long the world's most widespread cereals. That the
cultivation of these cereals in Europe was started by influences
from south-west Asia and Egypt is universally agreed, the same
is probably true for the Indus basin. The case of China is not so
clear. Here the earliest cereal was millet.

China has been considerably isolated from the west through
most of human time, until the age of steam. In Pleistocene
times, Inner Asia must have had immense ice sheets on its great
mountains and ice-melt would be slow, so that conditions in
Inner Asia long remained very difficult, especially on or near the
Tibetan highlands. Even towards the south, China was bounded
by the high hills of north Burma and the Shan states. Memories
of the Burma Road in the Second World War tell us of the difficulties here. So China, on geographical grounds, almost suggests
a likelihood of a measure of autonomous evolution in early human
affairs, but whether this could apply to cereal cultivation is very
doubtful indeed. The caves of Chou Kou Tien, thirty miles
south-west of Peiping (Pekin), have yielded remains of several
individuals of a hominid (a near-man) whom we call *Sinanthropus*, and they are accompanied by very rough stone tools.
No specimens of *Sinanthropus* are known from any phase after
a fairly early Pleistocene date, but there is the curious and probably very important fact that *Sinanthropus* and many modern
Mongols, Chinese, and even American Indians, have some special
characters, of which the best-known are the shovel-shaped
incisor teeth. This makes it possible, even probable, that
Sinanthropus has contributed to the physical heritage of Chinese
and Mongols, just as Neanderthal hominids may have contributed to the physical heritage of Europeans. We must be

cautious about ideas of unitary origins. In Late Paleolithic times upper layers at Chou Kou Tien cave show occupation by people akin to Europeans of that time, and in Hokkaido (north Japan) the Ainu, with hairy bodies, whitish skins, often wavy head-hair and very long heads, suggest an ancient link with Europe.

Fig. 60. Prehistoric painted pottery. North China.

After much discussion there has arisen a preponderance of opinion, still by no means unanimous, in favour of a hypothesis that Neolithic tools and arts of cultivation of the soil and of pottery entered China from the west. In the third millennium B.C. the art of painting pottery had spread far and wide from its probable primary home in north Mesopotamia or adjacent parts of Anatolia. It spread eastwards to Kansu, Shensi, and

Shansi, and a little beyond into Honan. Its quality in China is often superb with a bold spiral scroll design on a plain ground, a style which indicates skill and taste. The stages of evolution of style in painted pottery in western Asia and in China are a complex affair and the resemblances in the two areas strengthen the general hypothesis of western origins. This particular style disappeared from north China after a few centuries but, probably from some area west of Kansu, it came to be distributed over parts of south China, whence it, in a sense, spread to Further India, but there the decoration was incised on the surface instead of being painted, though the designs were akin. A date about 2300 or 2200 B.C. is often assigned to the painted pottery of north China and a date about the middle of the second millennium B.C. to the spread, with modifications, into Further India.

Apparently following it, there spread eastwards also a type of fine grey ware from the Turkestan area east of the Caspian Sea about the end of the third millennium B.C. or later. In China it was first known chiefly in Honan and Shantung, that is, to the east of the area of painted pottery, and, because of this and because some local forms of pots become highly characteristic, some students believe, or believed, that the grey ware is a Chinese development, perhaps with a general stimulus from the west. Other considerations have, however, been brought in.

The grey and black polished ware of south-west Asia goes back into the fifth millennium and in Anatolia into the fourth. The painted pottery styles of Halaf displaced the grey ware to some extent in Mesopotamia, but farther north and in Anatolia the making of grey ware continued and the idea spread to south-east Europe, to Sumer (as a contributor to the Uruk culture) and to the east Caspian area in the third millennium B.C., whence it extended its influence to the Indus cities. Later it reached China, some time after the painted pottery. Pot forms, the polishing of the pots, the fatty feel of the surface of the pots, and some very fine thin ware all connect the western Asiatic with the Chinese grey ware. Thus far only a little fine black pottery has been found with the grey in western Asia as against a good deal in China. In China, also, the grey ware and related types have now been found in Shansi, Shensi, Kansu, and Szechwan, also in Anhwei and Chekiang. In some places it is in layers over-

FIG. 61. Fragment of incised grey ware.

lying those with painted pottery, in others here and there the two types may be mixed.

Some pot forms are uniquely characteristic of China. The Li-tripod is a special form which may originally have been made by placing three pots with pointed bases against one another for mutual support. The Hsien has a lower part which is an ordinary broad-mouthed bulbous pot and an upper part with a perforated base so that steam from the lower part can cook what is placed in the upper one. Apparently these special forms, characteristic of north-east China, did not spread to south China and Further India. The fine black ware above-mentioned, and some of the grey ware as well, was made on the potter's wheel.

The earliest cultivators in north China seem to have grown

millets and it has been queried whether some varieties of millet may not have come into cultivation in this region. In the course of time wheat and barley were added and, probably during the period of either the painted pottery or the grey ware, rice spread northwards in China to about latitude 34° 30′ N.; its present limit of general usefulness is now about latitude 32° N. Cattle were important, bronze came in only towards the end of the phase with grey ware.

The domestic horse had probably spread from Inner Asia into Mesopotamia at some date not far from 2000 B.C., so it may well have been domesticated by man somewhat earlier in Inner Asia and this would increase interconnexions and cultural exchanges. Fine wheel-made pottery, including also some made from fine white clay (practically porcelain), and domestic cattle and horses might well be among the cultural imports of China under such circumstances. It is known that this was a time when sheep of Inner Asiatic breed were spreading into Europe (see Chap. 8).

The Chinese at this stage, and even later, seem to have had no brick and to have done little building in stone, but they achieved a good deal in wood and in stamped loess earth. They stamped this so hard that it is still firm to this day. They had a fortified settlement protected by a stamped earth rampart in the north-west of Shantung, near the later Tsinan, and no doubt many others could be found.

Legendary history speaks of a Hsia Dynasty traditionally dated from about 2300 B.C. to 1765 B.C., translating Chinese dates into our own. We do not know whether either the painted pottery culture or the black-ware culture is linked with this, or whether the black pottery is linked with the early part of the succeeding dynasty—the Shang, which is traditionally dated 1765–1123 B.C.

There is a possibility that these dates may have to be reduced a little (to about 1550–1000 B.C.) but provisionally they are useful. The black-ware phase with its fortification may have been able to attain to statehood. Its dwellings seem to have been rudimentary for people of such skill (they still are, in the same area of China), but there are many other cases of a discrepancy of this kind in other parts of the world, not least in early Anglo-Saxon England.

Before proceeding farther it seems appropriate to indicate a deep contrast between north China and India. India lies to the south of the major mountain zone of the northern hemisphere in the Old World. China lies largely to the east-north-east of that zone. We have seen that probably *homo sapiens* originated quite early in the Pleistocene and made the Acheulean hand-axes, spreading possibly from North Africa and south-west Asia. His spread to India would be relatively easy especially when, in the ice-phases of the Pleistocene, sea-level was lower and the coastal plain of south Arabia and Baluchistan spread farther out and also the west coast of India was farther out into the Arabian Sea. The present edge of the western Ghats in India is probably due to Late Pleistocene or post-Pleistocene uplift and faulting. India thus could receive very early drifts of peoples from farther west, and those who could not maintain themselves in full competition with later immigrants could find refuges in the forests and jungles. India has many refuges for descendants of very early immigrants, and remains to this day a region of immense social contrasts. Jungle tribes with rudimentary agriculture, even recently a few still dependent on hunting and collecting, contrast with highly sophisticated philosophers at the other end of the scale, and between these is an intricate gradation almost too complex for orderly analysis.

China probably had less numerous early immigrations from the west, and may have had a heritage from the *Sinanthropus* hominids. More important still is the fact that the entry into

China was via the Hwang Ho in Kansu, and also its tributary the Wei-ho in Shensi. Here we are in a loess region without much large forest, and with cultivation by irrigation as the main means of livelihood. Both possible aboriginal stocks and immigrant peoples were, in this region, subject to the same conditions; there was little opportunity for primitive folk to hide away even if they had drifted in. North China therefore has little of the contrast in social development that is a feature in India, its contrast is between wealth and poverty in the same social unit. The jungle, in other words, is not a social factor of any importance here.

According to legendary history, Yu, founder of the Hsia Dynasty, introduced the idea of irrigation canals into China at some time not far from 2300 B.C., long after irrigation canals had been developed on a great scale near the Nile and Euphrates. Some scholars think this statement is a propagandist invention of the days of the Chou Dynasty, and there is no evidence at present for a serious conclusion. The very fine pottery made on the wheel, cattle (including the water-buffalo) and horses, stamped-earth ramparts, and probably irrigation canals may give effect to imported ideas, but there was an indigenous element of quality that is remarkable in all the achievements of people in this area.

On the Hwang Ho in Kansu and Shansi and the Wei-ho in Shensi irrigation involved especially the bringing of water to the cultivated patches of loess. In the lower Hwang Ho region and the coastal plain it involved rather the draining off of surplus water from seasonally, but irregularly, flooded land. This latter region lacked the regularity of conditions found along the Nile or even the Euphrates.

Other features of ancient and recent Chinese life are linked with this uniformity of dependence on intensive cultivation of loess or, in the coastal plain, alluvium derived from loess. Where water is brought to the loess, and that soil is available in inexhaustible quantities, the same patch can be used for many years and can be enriched by bringing loess soil to it from some cliff side not far away. On the flood plain, the ditches must be cleaned and this is done by heaping the rich mud on to the land and thus helping to raise it above flood-level; again the same patch may be cultivated year after year. The attachment of the cultivator to the soil is thus very old and very intimate, laced around with tradition and ceremonial, a god of the earth parallel with a god of the heavens. Until the last phase of the Imperial régime the sacred emperor ceremonially inaugurated the spring ploughing of the soil of China. The emphasis on god and emperor contrasts with that on a mother goddess in some other regions of early cultivation, but whether this has some connexion with the legendary late introduction of irrigation into China cannot at present be ascertained.

With agriculture for thousands of years the main, almost the sole, means of subsistence, especially on the featureless flood plain with few trees and only cultivated bushes, the little plots of land were in danger of too frequent subdivision as the families increased. So the family clung together and put off the dreaded division of the inheritance. The family sentiment has been a main feature of Chinese life and with it has been long maintained the effort to do all that was possible, the making and mending of tools and utensils for example, with materials obtainable on the farm by the family itself. Implements have therefore tended to remain relatively simple, but skill has reached rather high levels. The family has in this way become a main feature of Chinese life in a sense rather different from what we have in the west. It is a compound family, father and sons and their wives and children, in wealthier households formerly a wife and some fully recognized concubines for the head of the family and perhaps for some of the other men. The large household might send out one of its members into government service and to become a scholar as well, but he would tend to return to the family in retirement or in the event of misfortune. So the family is the basis of the traditional social ethic of China, and loyalty to the family has mostly taken precedence over loyalty to the larger unit, the empire for example. The position of the chief wife in the household, provided she has borne sons, is a very important one; she has typically been the conservative influence, maintaining the traditions of the family while leaving the performance of ceremonial to her husband or eldest son, whose power over the members of the family has been very great.

Why centuries round about 2000 B.C. should have witnessed so many important developments and perhaps very specially important ones in Inner Asia is an interesting problem. Ellsworth Huntington long ago imagined climatic cycles in Asia with damper and more arid phases alternating. Further study has not lent support to this idea. Recovery from glacial conditions of the Pleistocene must have meant melt-water on a large scale at various times and the Mesopotamian flood or floods tentatively dated about 4000 B.C. are well authenticated. Probably others may have occurred and may have given special opportunities from time to time in Inner Asia.

We should remember that the herding nomads of that region are most probably descendants of cultivators who have become foot-loose and have survived if and when they were able to make some exchanges with cultivators to supplement their food-supply. Complete separation from cultivators and their products is a very specialized condition apart from Arctic and near-Arctic regions where peasant cultivation is impossible, but even there some vegetable food is collected if it can be found. It is possible, even probable, that people had to have a good deal of experience of cultivation before they could settle to any considerable extent in Inner Asia, so groups may not have become specialized nomad herdsmen very early. Some, however, may have graded into herding in this region from hunting and collecting.

It may be that the latter part of the third millennium B.C. in Inner Asia was a period that favoured the herders and may have led to the acquisition of the horse as a domestic animal, or, if it had been tamed at an earlier period, to its acquisition as an animal to be ridden, a very great acquisition from the point of view of development of an aristocracy.

Herding is, in modern times, inevitably quite a minor activity on the alluvial plain of north-east China, where land for crops is so precious, but the pig consumes waste material and does not need much space. The contrast between the Chinese peasant of the irrigated lands and the stock farmer or nomad herdsman of the arid borders is therefore extreme, and is made the sharper because the transition is so rapid as one proceeds up the valleys of Wei-ho or Hwang Ho. The herders, especially of course the semi-nomadic ones, are ready for war and to defend their flocks and herds at any time; they are an army moving with its own commissariat. The peasants traditionally are unwarlike, though tenacious in defence and liable to outbursts of violence at times.

Repeatedly during the centuries the herders of the dry lands on the border have invaded north China and set up their rule there, usually settling in and becoming an administrative group that loses its identity and vigour for war and so is conquered in its turn. It seems that this relation of herder conquerors and conquered peasants established itself as a normal cycle when the military power of the herders was vastly increased by the acquisition of the horse for riding or the spread of its use for this purpose, probably about the end of the third millennium B.C.

Relations of China with south-east Asia need to be considered as well as those with Mongolia and Inner Asia. In China, as in most other regions, the full Neolithic phase is characterized by the use of smoothed stone axes, typically oval in cross-section.

This type of tool can be traced through south and south-east China to Formosa, the Philippines, eastern Indonesia (but not Java), and Melanesia. A few are known from Further India, where a later type became very widespread and important. This type has a long and broad rectangular tang and, because of the angle between the side of the tang and the end of the axe-body, it is often called the shouldered axe. It spread into south Yunnan and also via the coast of south-east China to Formosa, the Philippines, north-east Korea, Japan as far north as Yezo, and to north Celebes. It also occurs in New Zealand. In Further India it is often found mixed with another type that has a rectangular cross-section but no specialized tang. This last type is widespread in China and appears to have an association with the painted pottery. It spread into the Mekong basin and is widely found also in Polynesia.

The black-ware phase in north China came to an end at some time in the second millennium B.C. and the next phase, though apparently in continuity with it, has not yet been linked with it by inferences from excavation. The people who made the fine black ware handed on the idea of the Li-tripod to the next phase, and also the idea of using flat bones as oracles by heating them and making inferences from cracks resulting from the heat. Oracle bones and oracle shells and carapaces of tortoises became abundant and important in the period 1400–1100 B.C., which has been identified with the later part of the legendary Shang Dynasty.

Chinese scholars have been able to make considerable progress in reading inscriptions incised on oracle bones by the diviners, and this may be taken as evidence of a considerable continuity of culture from Shang days to the classical Chinese period and so to modern times.

The traditional dates for the whole Shang Dynasty are 1766–1122 B.C. and for its later part about 1400–1122 B.C., but it should be noted again that dates before about 840 B.C. in China are rather tentative though not likely to be much more than a century too high.

The period from 1400 B.C. onwards is illustrated by the excavations at Anyang in Honan on a defensible promontory above the ancient course of the Hwang Ho on the border of Honan

FIG. 62. Shang oracle bones.

towards Hopei. This royal centre of the later Shang rulers has yielded evidence of culture and craft-skill including cast bronzes of elaborate design, apparently datable 1400–1100 B.C. The technique of this casting bespeaks considerable experience, but we have, as yet, little evidence of the preliminary stages. Anyang had been occupied earlier by people who made the fine black-ware pottery mentioned above, but whether these were the forebears of the bronze-casters or their predecessors, either immediate or earlier, is not yet known. The bronze-casting under the Shang Dynasty reached a height of elaboration hardly approached in other regions of the world until much later. So far, we have every reason to suppose that bronze-work was introduced into China before it became so elaborate, but long after

FIG. 63. Shang libation cup.

the first development of casting in south-west Asia and Egypt round about 3000 B.C. It is therefore probable that the arts of metallurgy came into north China from the west, but, in spite of all the investigations of Dr. Andersson, no evidence has been obtained from Kansu, the traditional way into China from the west. It is possible that the gap between the Neolithic black-ware phase and the Shang bronze phase at Anyang may some day be partly filled by finds elsewhere. For the moment, however, we have to think that bronze work, like the painted pottery of a much earlier time, was introduced but quickly attained to a unique quality of expression in north China. There is some doubt about the method of casting, which was in any case remarkably efficient.

In the Shang period the country was by no means so closely settled as it has since become, and the lords of that day hunted not only deer and wild boar but also elephant, rhinoceros, and tiger. The city might have some stone as paving for a terrace or as a socket for a pillar of wood, but the main dependence was still on stamped earth and timber, with here and there some use of bronze for pillar bases. Though the best pottery was wheel-made, a great deal was still made by hand. Chariots were used for war and no doubt for ceremony, and a man with a very long spear stood in the chariot, which was drawn by two, or later sometimes by four, horses. We have no evidence of cavalry or of swords. The bow and arrow, with a specially powerful double-curve bow, was the weapon most widely used, but axe-daggers of bronze are also known. Hard stone, of the type broadly known as jade, was rubbed down and polished for ornament.

Apparently men rather than women did the routine work of cultivation, but women reared silk worms, and the use of silk may be linked up with the high quality of so much of the other work. We have as yet no evidence of the plough under the Shang Dynasty. It is uncertain whether there was a mother goddess connected with cultivation, and this suggests a contrast over against south-west Asia. Sacrifice of animals and of human captives was on a large scale and wives and servants were sometimes buried to accompany an important man into the spirit world.

Whereas in Europe, Persia, and India at this time Aryan languages were spreading from the lowland steppe of the west of Inner Asia and what is now south Russia, there is no evidence of anything of the kind in China. Whether the Shang language, as well as pottery and other fashions, was derived from the people who made the black ware is not certain, but on grounds of the various heritages passed on to the Shang phase it is probable. The Shang language has developed, with many changes, into later Chinese. Much has been learned about this from inscriptions incised by diviners on the oracle bones and shells of tortoise in reply to questions put, usually by kings, as mentioned in an earlier paragraph.

A group of royal tombs at Anyang has been interpreted as belonging to the last twelve kings, and the last of the series was found empty, suggesting that it had been prepared during the life of the last king. Legend says he was a degenerate who was killed in an uprising supported by Chou warriors from the Mongolian border who had settled in the valley of the Wei-ho (south Shensi) and had acquired a good deal of the Shang culture. This is likely to be a fiction made up by the Chou conquerors. The Chou conqueror of the Shang died a few years later, leaving a son too young to take responsibility. So a brother became the ruler as guardian of the boy, and this guardian, with the title Duke of Chou, has often been described as the most notable statesman in all Chinese history as well as a pioneer in philosophy. A site near the modern Loyang in western Honan became a secondary capital and rulers of minor states, as well as Shang and Chou princelings, were placed in charge of many provinces subject to the oath of loyalty and service to the Chou king. This feudal scheme naturally led to attempts at independence and conquest, and the Chou prestige declined in a few generations, though there were temporary revivals of it when a determined and able ruler emerged. From soon after 700 B.C. to the end of the Chou period in 221 B.C. there was little unity in north China. The early Chou kings had, however, given a measure of

unity under their authority exercised through a feudal nobility
to a much larger area than the Shang had ruled. If we make it
include parts of Shensi and Shansi and most of Honan, Shantung,
and Chih li (Hopei), we shall probably not overestimate it.
Mencius, writing in the third century B.C., gave an idealized
picture of Chou organization. He said that a given area of land
would be divided into nine parts of which eight would be cultivated by subordinate proprietors for themselves, but the ninth
would be cultivated by the eight for the benefit of the lord of
the whole area. It would be too much to expect that such a
scheme was at all generally carried out, but we may guess there
was some division between the shi'h or lord and the subordinates.
On the whole it seems that there was often greater security and
more justice and social welfare in the better parts of the Chou
period than under the Shang; and there is practically no
evidence of human sacrifice under the Chou, nor do we find
real evidence of immolation of widows at their husbands'
funerals. There are also indications that scholars were often
made administrators under the better rulers, and they were not
always or necessarily aristocrats, so the boundaries of social class
were weakening a little. The Chou kings seem to have tried to
make the feudal lords dependent on them, as creations by the
king, rather than as provincial rulers on a basis of hereditary right,
but this idea would remain largely theoretical in many cases.

We do not at present know, and we are probably likely to
remain uncertain, whether iron-smelting was developed in
China independently of its discovery in Anatolia, but the fact
that it appears during the Chou period, so far as present evidence
goes, seems to make it a little later in the east than in the west,
and so makes somewhat more probable the hypothesis that it
spread from western Asia. It was a simple craft that could spread
rapidly, as we know it did to Europe. The Chou people acquired
the plough. We gather from legends that some of the people

under the early Chou were not very definitely settled as yet, for the story tells of a vast migration eastwards caused by pressure of the Demon tribes (Hsiung Nu). It is probably best to understand this as a migration of the emperor's court, no doubt with a mass of servants. The peasants were kept at work cutting timber, building, hunting furs, weaving, collecting mulberry leaves and so on for their lords; but under the early Chou there was a measure of security and justice, apparently including some care for the aged.

Cities, trading over considerable distances, coinage, and comfort developed considerably, though, as the dynasty lost its virtue through luxury, there came, about the seventh century B.C., a phase of complex difficulty made all the greater by the developments that had preceded it. Professor Heine-Geldern in recent lectures in London has suggested that some time after 700 B.C. maritime activity was for a while important among peoples of China south of Honan, and that Chinese styles in various objects can be traced right out into the Pacific.

It seems also to have been after 700, and probably after 400 B.C. that the idea of wet cultivation of rice in seasonally flooded enclosed basins spread in eastern Asia. Its probable connexion with a development of Chinese culture in regions south of Honan should be noted. There is little doubt that this advance in methods of cultivation not only increased population but made possible the extension of Chinese power in Indo-China in the last few centuries B.C.

It was in this phase that there arose the great teachers, broadly contemporary with those of India. It is of special interest that the Chinese and Indian teachers, especially Lao Tzu, Confucius, and Buddha, were not specially concerned with the hypothesis of a deity, in fact Confucius seems to have very deliberately avoided this problem. Buddha was specially concerned with human fate and the culmination of his vision was the idea of

Nirvana, the final universal consummation to which men move one by one. The Chinese teachers, on the other hand, were concerned mainly with the welfare of society. Lao Tzu held that men should be content to live in harmony with nature, that is, should go on as they were in his day, at least among the simple folk. He deprecated elaboration, movement, love of power and riches, interference of one community with another. He thought that there were many and diverse approaches to, and aspects of, truth and that it accordingly behoved men to be respectfully tolerant of differences of doctrine. Confucius was essentially the conservative sage, concerned to find guidance in the past for proper conduct in the present, in a hierarchical society in which virtue was, for him, especially the characteristic of the nobility.

Craft skill was supposed to be handed on from father to son, so the son was supposed to follow his father's trade, and the difference between noble and simple, corresponding generally with rich and poor, was firm and sharp, but there was never the elaboration of the caste system that was so marked in India; and one reason undoubtedly is, as has been stated in the chapter on India, the absence in China of the striking contrasts one had in India between, for example, Vedic-Aryan-speaking princes and jungle tribes.

The decay of the Chou Dynasty was accompanied, as that of the Shang had been, by pressure from the borders of arid Mongolia. Various rulers in different parts of what had been the Chou state had become precariously independent and on the western border the Ch'ins gained more and more power until eventually in 221 B.C. Chin Shi'h Hwang Ti made himself master of most of northern China, after the Chou had moved their capital eastward, out of the way of immediate Ch'in pressure. The new master aimed at absolute rule and wished to destroy the books of historic records and much of the teaching of the sages and to make penal all criticism of his government. He abolished the idea of the ninefold division of land and the hierarchy of rank, and he made all dependent on the emperor and his officials and all liable to military service. History and its supposed guidance were to him misleading, and he must confine thought to defined limits, so he must limit contacts; and, in pursuance of this idea, he ordered the building of the Great Wall, by soldiers, criminals, and political and intellectual offenders. Previous dynasties of local states in the phase of Chou decay had built walls, but the Great Wall was on a much larger scale and only here and there utilized previous ones; and it fairly closely marked a boundary between fertile and arid land. The conqueror also built roads within his empire, offering an analogy to the effort of the Romans a little later within theirs. He ruled a large part of what is, after him, called China, and probably a good deal of the east of the peninsula we now call Further India. His organizing power must have been very great and ruthless but the scheme broke down under his son, who was killed by the revolt that ushered in the Han Dynasty in 206 B.C. This was in some ways a conservative reaction including some measure of revival of feudalism and, after a period of peace and prosperity, the accumulated resources were spent on imperial expansion that took the emperor's power far to the west in Chinese Turkestan (Sinkiang).

Meanwhile the west had been active, and Alexander the Great had spread his conquests into what is now Turkestan, founding cities ruled by the descendants and successors of his generals. The Chinese merchants of the Han period came into trading relations with these, and silk was sold to the west by traders who went along the silk road. The power of the Han, at the same time, pushed back the nomadic Hsiung Nu and, as the Huns, these turned westwards towards Europe, which they ravaged as Rome declined. It is probable that this development of trade, with roads and stations right through Inner Asia, accompanied a period of reduction of mountain glaciers that gave a temporary increase of water to the otherwise arid lands below. As we have evidence that before and just after 500 B.C. there was a phase of cold wet summers in Europe, and that this condition passed away, more or less, after a couple of centuries, there is just a possibility that moisture from ice-melt in Inner Asia would increase about 200 B.C. or so, and that these wetter conditions might last for a few centuries.

The Han Dynasty, like its predecessors, went through the phases of luxury and decay and was brought to an end in a revolt in A.D. 208.

In the earlier Han period the Confucian teaching was restored to a place of honour and new copies of the sacred books were made supposedly from old ones which had escaped the destruction ordered by Chin Shi'h Hwang Ti, but, as usual, the thought later became formalized and the ritual lost its meaning, especially during and after the Han decline, following which came a long phase of 360 years of disunity and nomad attacks.

Reorganized unity under an emperor called Yang led to the great enterprise of building the Grand Canal, which gave a much-valued link between the Hwang Ho and Yangtze but which cost an enormous amount in lives and in treasure. Yang's extravagances in connexion with this and with vainglorious display led to the downfall of his family, and in A.D. 618 the great T'ang Dynasty began its mighty work. Under Yang a start had been made with the selection of civil servants by examination on the Confucian doctrines, and this was organized under the T'ang to destroy the power of hereditary governors of provinces. Tea began to be grown on a large scale in suitably warm parts of China. We do not know whether it had one primary home or more than one and whether, if only one, that one was on Himalayan slopes in Assam and Darjeeling or in some part of China. It had great value as a flavouring for water that was often procurable only from muddy canals or pools and tanks; and it did a little to soothe for a time the rheumatic pains that were inevitably prevalent among rice-growers working in flooded fields. But relief was sought still more in opium.

In early T'ang times a flat stone surface was incised with characters that could be read. Then the surface was inked, leaving the incised grooves white. Copies could be taken off and had characters in white on a black background. This seems to be the first stage of the invention of printing. Later on, probably after the end of the T'ang Dynasty, hard wood with incised carving came into use for blocks for printing. Then the characters were modelled in clay or some other material that could be baked hard and, in this way, movable type came into use. Much later still this was done in metal. Needless to say, for ease and rapidity of printing, as well as of learning to read and write, our western rather crude alphabetic systems were much easier to learn to use than the highly specialized ideographic system of Chinese tradition with its endless attempts to simplify and schematize the tens of thousands of characters. It is fairly generally thought that typesetting and printing were introduced into Europe from China in the late Middle Ages.

The T'ang period also saw great developments of poetry, landscape painting, including large pictures on rolls of silk, modelling of horses and men in clay, which was afterwards baked, and porcelain making. The modelled horses and men show minute study of types and equipment and are of very high quality, but neither the painting nor the modelling spread from China to the west. Porcelain did spread to Holland and Europe generally many centuries later.

The T'ang Dynasty, like all others, declined, and it came to an end in A.D. 907. Then, after a relatively short period of unsettled government, the Sung Dynasty established itself but on a weaker basis involving appeasement of the north-western barbarians. The *Corvée* (to use a French term) or system of forced labour was modified by allowing men to pay instead of giving work. Art seems to have taken on a reflective or introspective turn as contrasted with the vigorous extrovert minds of the T'ang artists. Sung work is often very graceful and delicate in colouring as well as in form and some Sung pottery is thought to represent the highest achievement in that art. The northern territories of the Sung fell more and more under Mongol influence as the dynasty declined. The Sung Empire, persisting for a time in the south, developed maritime trade which spread around south-east Asia, and brought Sung porcelain (Celadon ware) eventually to East Africa and South Africa. It has been found notably at the ruined Islamic port-city of Gedi, northeast of Mombasa, and also fragments were found by Miss Caton Thompson under stamped granite-earth floors at Zimbabwe, Rhodesia. Maritime trade was very busy during the later part of the Mongol Dynasty's rule, as we know from Marco Polo, and transcontinental land-routes were also much used. Some of this activity was continued under the Ming Dynasty from the fourteenth century onwards and it spread not only trade but also people to south-east Asia and Indonesia. So some of the more or less Chinese population in those regions may be of fairly old standing, though the bulk of those who speak Chinese there are modern immigrants into Malaya and Indonesia.

The conservatism of the compound family, its effort to provide all its needs from its own lands, and its self-contained life have operated to keep Chinese life what we should call old-fashioned, with home-made tools and reverence for the ancestors and their ways. And the compound family has been one of the greatest powers in Chinese society. Emperors have hesitated to weaken a father's authority over his household. It has sometimes been said that China, as a country, has been the least governed land in the world, so much being left to the family.

Inevitably a concomitant of this has been the frequent sacrifice of the public welfare to family advantage by officials, but this is a feature under all systems of government.

It has been the fate of one dynasty after another, in China as in many other lands, to decline after a promising beginning under some able leader, in the case of China not always of aristocratic birth. One cause of decline and downfall operating again and again has been, as elsewhere, palace intrigue through the harem and its attendant eunuchs. Harem, primarily, means simply women (in Arabic), but it has come to be applied to the group of wives and concubines belonging to a magnate. A favourite concubine might solicit the succession to the throne or title for her son, and she could exercise influence without responsibility. A clever eunuch, without children to think of, could and often did intrigue for power. Usually both concubines and eunuchs were evil, even disastrous, influences, but there are a few exceptions.

It is notable that China has contributed in many ways to the world's life. We all think of silk, tea, citrus fruits, probably in or before the T'ang period, the loadstone, said by some to have been known in Shang times, which is the origin of the mariner's compass that became known in Europe in the period of expansion of Chinese maritime trade, porcelain, the igniting material, which in western hands became gunpowder, printing, and paper, perhaps banknotes, and the examination system. The soya bean is a recent addition. The art of painting, so highly developed in China, seems to have brought little influence from China to Europe. It is difficult to think of definite material contributions of western Europe to China before the days of steam and machinery. On the intellectual side the early Jesuits sought to combine their teaching with the Chinese reverence for the family and with the veneration for Confucius and his ethical ideas. These efforts were later stopped by the Roman Church as tending towards a compromise with non-Christian religion.

10

South-east Asia and the Pacific

FROM a phase preceding the more definitely Neolithic period in south-east Asia there are various evidences of the use of stone points and blades, but also, as in North Africa, of tools of core types, save that the cores are apparently chipped in detail on one face only.

At Guwa Lawa and Bodjonegoro in Java von Stein Callenfels made finds which Heine-Geldern has since interpreted as being early arrow-heads, occurring there without any Neolithic axes; he also infers from the form and toothing of the arrow-heads that they may have come to south-east Asia from Japan. It has been suggested that, among some groups in Malaya, both cores and the flakes chipped from them were in use by the same people.

Leaving these rather dim and confused beginnings, we may next consider finds of the implements which in so many areas of the world represent the advent of fully Neolithic culture. These are stone axes with surface and edge shaped by grinding, and with an oval cross-section. German scholars use the name *Walzenbeil.* They are well known from India, China, and Japan. Some few have been found in Further India, probably spreading from China. But a more important spread took them from south China, via Formosa, to the Philippines and thence to eastern Indonesia and Melanesia and perhaps even Micronesia and beyond. An important and curious fact is that, at least until a few years ago, in spite of the collection of large numbers of Neolithic axes from Java, no example of this type had been found there. It is widely thought that this phase of development in south-east Asia was not reached until 2000 B.C. or even later, so pre-Neolithic life lasted a long time in that region. We may suppose that cultivation was practised by the people who made the axes just discussed.

The next type of Neolithic axe in order of age in south-east Asia is flatter faced and has a very definite stalk narrower than the axe, so that the junction of stalk and axe proper may be compared to the junction of a man's neck and shoulder. These implements have often therefore been called 'shouldered' axes. The stalk was bound by thongs to a wooden haft. Further India seems to be a primary home of this type of implement and it is thought to have spread thence to India, where it occurs in Orissa, Chota Nagpur, Bengal, and up the Ganges as far as Allahabad; one has been found near the Godavari. As it is also known from the Naga region of Assam, it might have reached India via Assam, but this route is notoriously difficult because of forest and mountain barriers, so it is well to hesitate about such a conclusion on the slight evidence available. It is also thought that the same type of implement spread northwards into Yunnan and the Chinese coast near Hong Kong. It may be thence that it spread to Formosa, Korea, and Japan, even as far north as Yezo, as well as to the Philippines and the northern peninsula of Celebes (Minahassa) and North Borneo. It does not appear to have reached southern Malaya to any extent, as only one specimen has been found there, in Pahang. The people who used shouldered axes were cultivators, but evidence of domestic animals, even pig or dog, is lacking. The shouldered axe is not known from Sumatra or Java. Its

Fig. 64. Early stone axe, Borneo.

distribution among the Pacific Islands is of special interest and
will be mentioned below. The shouldered-axe people valued
pearls and made shell rings and shell ornaments of other
kinds.

The next, and most important, type of Neolithic axe is one
with, usually, a chisel-like form and a rectangular section, but

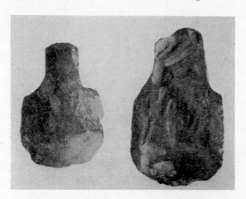

FIG. 65. Shouldered stone axes, Annam.

without the shoulder arrangement. It is highly characteristic
of China, including Kansu, Honan, Shensi, Shantung, Fengtien,
and Yunnan. It spread from south China into Further India,
including Tongking, Laos, the Mekong valley, and Malaya. From
either south China or Further India it spread into India as far
as Chota Nagpur and the Santal Parganas. From Malaya it
became important in Sumatra and Java, where some axes are
almost triangular in section through grinding away of two of the
four corners of the primarily rectangular cross-section. From
east China it spread via Formosa to the Philippines and Japan,
and from Java it spread through eastern Indonesia but not to
any extent into Melanesia. In Borneo and eastern Indonesia these
axes sometimes have a ridge along the middle of one face and

some of these have been collected among the Pesechem in Dutch New Guinea.

These axes and their distribution in south-east Asia seem to be older than the use of bronze, which began at a late date not yet satisfactorily estimated. They are associated with painted pottery in north China and with incised ornament of pottery in Further India. Perhaps the phase known from north China spread to and survived for some centuries in south-east Asia after it had passed away in the north. In north China there were triple pots, each with a pointed base, three together giving mutual support. There were also pots with an upper part fitted into a lower part in which water was heated for cooking by steam what was placed in the upper part, which had a perforated base.

Fig. 66. Chisel-shaped stone axe, Java.

As these types of pots do not occur in south-east Asia it is possible that the northern culture spread south via perhaps Szechwan from some area rather farther west than those from which this phase is best known in north China. But triple pots are well known from the Fiji Islands.

The makers of stone axes with rectangular cross-section seem to have sawn grooves in a stone block and then to have separated the pieces with blows directed into the grooves; and this

type of axe spread to America and over Polynesia. Cattle
and pigs were reared by these people in south-east Asia, and
rice was probably cultivated but not as yet by the 'wet' method
(of enclosures seasonally flooded). Millet was also cultivated. It
has been rather speculatively suggested that the canoe with
double outrigger was a device first used on rivers in Further
India, and, if so, perhaps among the people who made shouldered
axes, and before the advent of the finer stone axes with rect-

FIG. 67. Incised pottery.

angular or more elaborate cross-section. The double outrigger
may have promoted stability in the water but made management
difficult, and the single outrigger is more general. Another suggestion has been that the shouldered-axe people were active in
the spread of the Munda group of languages. The survival of
Munda languages in Chota Nagpur, India, is an indication of
this possibility.

It is clear that India did not influence early south-east Asia
much, and indeed the peninsula of India seems to have remained
in a very backward state until the Iron Age. In the early centuries of our era, Indian groups spread to Cambodia, however,
and Java and, later on, built the great temples of Angkor Vat in
Cambodia and Barabudur in Java.

Incidental reference has been made above to Japan. The early type of ground-stone axe with an oval cross-section is found in numbers in Japan, and the shouldered axe also occurs, as well as the chisel-like form. These types of tool may have reached Japan via Kyushu, the Ryukyu Islands, and Formosa from south-east China, or, less probably, from Indonesia. The possibility of navigation helped by the Kuro-Siwo current should be borne in mind. At least in later times there were important cultural relations between China and Japan via Korea and, if one may trust legend to some extent, Kyushu.

The prehistoric monuments of Japan include dolmens related to those of south-east Asia and Indonesia. As the idea of monuments of this type spread from Indonesia to the New Hebrides, and something akin to it reached the Caroline Islands, it is natural that one should find it also in Japan. In India and south-east Asia dolmens appear to be not earlier than the spread of iron in the last millennium B.C., and in Melanesia some are quite recent constructions. So those of Japan may not go back far beyond our era. A special Japanese type of monument of pre-historic date is the misasagi. This consists of a circular and a triangular mound which merge into one another and are sur-rounded by one or two fossae. The misasagi contains a vault of unhewn stones, i.e. practically a dolmen or, more strictly, a corbelled chamber. The way into the chamber is through a passage roofed by stone blocks. The analogy between these misasagi and the prehistoric corbelled chamber tombs of the Iberian peninsula, Brittany, Ireland, and north Scotland is interesting. It is said that Japan lacks evidence of a bronze age antedating the introduction of iron, a strange fact in view of the remarkable development of bronze-casting in the China of the Shang dynasty, but the paucity of development of prehis-toric bronze-work in the parts of India which have rough-stone monuments of the Iron Age is a noteworthy point here.

Japanese chroniclers made the first emperor reign at a time

which, translated into western dating, would be 660 B.C. This emperor, centuries later, became known as Jimmu Tenno, and some stories associate him with the south Chinese or Indonesian element and he is said to have been buried in a misasagi. Stories of the early period (until about A.D. 500) tell of fighting with earlier peoples of Japan, remnants of whom still survive as the Ainu. These Ainu, now living in Yezo (Hokkaido), Sakhalin, and the southern Kurile Islands, differ conspicuously from the Japanese. They are long-headed—sometimes extremely long-headed—people of short stature, men over 1,600 mm. (5 ft. 3 in.) being relatively tall; but, unlike the many Japanese people of short stature, they are thick-set. The men have abundant hair on head, face, body, and limbs; women have some on their limbs but not on the body. The hair is black, coarse, and inclined to curl at the ends, whereas Japanese hair is typically rather fine and straight. The nose-root is deepset, and the cheekbones stand out, but the face is not flattened as it is in most Japanese. The eyes are brown and look European. There is at most only a trace of the Mongolian fold of the eye-lid. All in all, therefore, the Ainu are very different from the general population in Japan, Korea, and China: they are non-Mongolian. This, and their habitat in the remote north, as well as their persistence in an Epipalaeolithic mode of life largely dependent on hunting and fishing, all suggest that they are an ancient remnant. This view may get slight support from the finding of very long-headed skulls of Late Palaeolithic date in upper layers of the caves at Chou Kou Tien in north China. Individuals with Ainu traits occur all over Japan and make it probable that Ainu once were the main population of the islands. The conquest of these early peoples by later immigrants from Korea or south China or both is a large part of Japanese history.

Legends or early chronicles speak of a Japanese invasion of Korea under an empress of about A.D. 200, but Chinese history does not mention this, and its occurrence is doubtful. There must have been cultural, if not military, relations well before A.D. 500 with Korea and north China, so invasions are not ruled out entirely and Korean chronicles do mention wars with early Japan. The Chinese of these centuries speak of Japanese weavers. The use of iron for spears, swords, knives, hooks, and sickles seems clear. Silk and the mulberry may have been introduced from China into Japan before A.D. 500, and the cultivation of rice was old-established. The straw raincoat and animal pelts were in early use, as well as woven hemp for clothing. The horse seems to have been in use for riding, and cattle are mentioned, but not sheep or pigs. Shipbuilding developed and the art of writing was brought to Japan not very long before A.D. 500 from China. It is a strange feature that, in spite of the high development of pottery in China from about 2000 B.C. onwards, and in spite of the introduction of the potter's wheel fairly early into Japan, the latter country did not become interested in artistic pottery until the tea-drinking habit was introduced about A.D. 1200. At that time the beautiful Sung pottery was being made in China.

In the sixth century A.D. Buddhism spread via Korea to Japan, and with it came an increased influence of Chinese civilization as well as development of the arts and crafts, including architecture.

In the seventh century A.D. laws were written and an attempt was made to build up an administration, while the ancient practice in so many lands of constructing enormous tombs for nobles was restricted.

By the eighth century the old idea of a new palace centre or capital built for each sovereign on accession gave way to the custom of a fixed centre, and Kyoto became the national capital at the end of that century. This change from a shifting to a fixed capital has been a feature of the evolution of many peoples.

The long struggle of the power focused on Kyoto against aboriginal Ainu and other elements was generally a struggle on a narrow front, a concentrated effort, and it contributed to the growth of a nationalist sentiment with a military setting and the creation of the Samurai, a hereditary military knighthood. In this way Japanese social development came to contrast dramatically with Chinese social evolution, and the subsequent stories of the two countries are strikingly different as a result.

Cultural evolution in south-east Asia is traceable in the stone monuments of the region, monuments which it is difficult to relate in any detail to the various cultures indicated by the stone tools discussed above. These monuments, possibly related to those of western Europe, are found in Assam and west Burma, and in Assam their erection has been continued down to modern times. In Laos and Tongking they were connected with ancient ritual. They are absent from the Nicobar Islands but occur in parts of the Malay peninsula, Sumatra, and Java. Off the west coast of Sumatra lies a series of islands, among which Nias is specially notable for its stone monuments, but they are absent from the southerly members of the series, which are known as the Mentawei Islands. East of Java these monuments are important in Sumba and Flores and in parts of Celebes, but they are absent from most of Borneo and the Philippines.

The monuments include what in western Europe are usually called dolmens, i.e. a horizontally laid large stone block resting on a number of uprights. In a number of cases the uprights have been so arranged as to leave an oval opening between two adjacent ones, or an opening has been carved out through one of them. This has often been called the port-hole, but the German name *Seelenloch* may be better, if, as is widely believed, the opening is to allow the spirit of the person, or spirits of the persons, buried in the monument to come out, probably for rebirth.

In dealing with India, mention has been made of dolmens in the Indian peninsula, some of which have yielded objects belonging to the Early Iron Age, subsequent to about 800 B.C. It is worth noting that long ago Elliot Smith gave that approximate date for the spread of the idea of megaliths to India from farther west. In his view it was a spread from the Egypt of the XXIst Dynasty, and part of the spread of a 'Heliolithic' culture helped by Phoenician commerce and collecting various features on its way. Elliot Smith's full claim is generally held not to have become established, but that is perhaps all the more reason for mentioning points in which he was partly right.

The monuments of the Naga and Khasi districts of Assam differ considerably from those of the Indian peninsula. They are part of the series found in the East Indies, and it is by no means certain that the cultural spread was from Assam south-eastwards. A spread in the opposite direction is at least as probable. The types of construction with great stones in Assam and south-east Asia include, once more, dolmens and stone boxes or cists, and standing stones (menhirs in western Europe). These standing stones may be set in groups sometimes with the form of alignments or circles, sometimes massed together on an artificial mound. In the latter case they may commemorate the slaying of enemies and one stone may be set up for each enemy killed. The peoples concerned hunt enemy heads to get more 'spirit-power' (vital essence) into their group for rebirth, so we have here a variety of fertility cult involving death. Circles of standing stones may also be places of ceremony or of discussion among the headmen of a group, and these may sit on the stones of a circle for the purpose of selecting a chief and other matters of communal importance.

Among the Angami Nagas Hutton noted four categories of other stone monuments. The dahu is a more or less rectangular pyramid of stones which can be used as a defence centre in a fight with another village. The pyramid appears to mark the burial place of ancestral chiefs and it is held to be specially sacred. Hutton thinks that something of the nature of a large dahu was a feature of the great stone buildings at Tiahuanaco and Sacsahuaman in Peru. The tehuba is a raised levelled space for

Fig. 68. Pyramidal skull receptacle.

dancing that may be surrounded by a circle of squared stones on which men sit drinking, but it often has a wall at one end of the flat space and this wall has tiers of seats; there may be recesses in the wall for holding the men's drinking-cups. The wall may have wings, with more tiers of seats, at each end, and the extensions may be in wood. Polynesian analogies with dahu and tehuba have been noticed by various observers.

Hutton notes that the syllable *hu* is associated with some kinds of buildings of great stones in south-east Asia, Polynesia, and Peru. The kwĕhū is a mound of earth levelled at the top and surrounded by a circular wall; and sometimes it is paved over the top. It may also have a wooden effigy of the dead man whom it commemorates (it is a memorial rather than a grave), and if so there is likely to be a standing stone behind the effigy to continue the memorial after the wood has decayed. Something

FIG. 69. Tehuba over grave.

like the kwĕhū occurs in south India, North Africa, and Etruscan Italy. The fourth category is the bāzĕ, a name without the syllable *hu*. It is a rectangular stone platform with steps leading up to it and sometimes seats around the top or, sometimes, rows of seats one behind and above another. The stone structure may be continued above as a wooden scaffold, and sometimes platform and all is of wood. Hutton asks whether we may not here have one of the many examples from various parts of the world (Sanchi in India, the Parthenon at Athens, Stonehenge in Britain, &c.) of a scheme of wooden construction going to be modified into a stone one, and whether the fact that in this case wood is still used may not be a reason why the syllable *hu* does not come into its name. Henry Balfour long ago drew attention to some similarities between a Dahu of the Angami Nagas and an Ahu of Easter Island; and in the Marquesas Islands there are ceremonial dancing places called Tahua, not unlike the Tehuba mentioned above, so there may be a link between monuments of Polynesia and south-east Asia, doubt-fully via western America (Heyerdahl).

It may be that in Polynesia and western America we are dealing with a complex interweaving of cultural elements largely based on heritages from south-east Asia. The routes and methods of the spread of those cultural features will be the subject of notes later in this chapter.

Among the Khasi of Assam the treatment of the corpse has led to another form of monument. The body is first cremated and the ashes preserved in an individual grave, then they may be transferred into a family grave, and finally into a clan grave. These family and clan graves may be distant from one another, and the ceremonial transfer from the one to the other may be held to involve giving the soul a rest on the way, at a sacred place with a standing stone and a few stones laid around its base as a temporary seat of the soul. Memorial standing stones are set up, usually later on, to the number of 3, 5, 7, 9, or 11 with the tallest one central. Some stones are laid flat, on supports, in front of them, and the top of the flat stone may be as much as $2\frac{1}{2}$ feet above the ground surface. The menhirs which stand are in some cases said to represent the male relatives of the dead man's mother. The chief stone set flat is said to represent the ancestress of the group, and the next one the grandmother of the family concerned. This representation of the two sexes by stones in different positions has also been found far away in the Gilbert Islands in the Pacific, as well as in Madagascar south-westwards.

The special mention of the male relatives of the mother implies a connexion with a matrilineal system; but sometimes the central stone is said to represent the father and the others brothers and so on, suggesting a patrilineal scheme, which, some think, may be older than the matrilineal one in this region. These are opinions that are controversial. In Malaya monoliths of granite are known, with platforms in front of them. Their age is problematic, though it is fairly generally thought that they antedate the advent or, at any rate, the triumph of Islam in this region. It is thought that they are memorials rather than grave stones.

In the East Indian Islands, Nias, west of Sumatra, has drawn much interest in view of its retention of many presumedly ancient features, undoubtedly related to those just mentioned for parts of Assam, but showing a higher degree of elaboration than is common in the latter region. These ancient features include numerous great stone monuments, often with the stones carefully dressed, and provided with carved decoration. They are principally memorials, standing stones being often considered male and prostrate ones female; a monument usually having them in pairs. Prostrate stones may also be seats for the spirits, or sometimes for the living, meeting in council. Some seats, often in front of the houses, are large and canopied or elaborately carved. Standing stones behind these seats are sometimes described as for the spirit to lean against. In view of Hutton's notice of the syllable *hu*, above-mentioned, it is appropriate to add that a standing stone against which the spirit of the dead may lean is in Nias called *tedro hulu*. Some platform seats, with a menhir at each end, in Nias, may be used as thrones, and these menhirs are often carefully shaped. Platforms of this kind, but with stones left rough, occur among the Konyak Nagas, whose traditions show that they came from much farther south than their present home in north-east Assam.

Nias has the walled fortification of the village and the paved paths uphill like the Naga country of Assam, but the work in Nias is often much more elaborate.

Building with large stones is, or has been in the past, widespread in the East Indian archipelago, and in general includes the types

Fig. 70. Great Stone Monument, Nias, in front of Chief's House, S. Nias, Indonesia.

mentioned above for the Nagas and Nias, but it does not occur in most of Borneo or the Philippines, and there are other gaps in the distributional scheme. It is generally held to be a cultural feature introduced by immigrants of some past period. Heine-Geldern, one of the best-informed specialists on this region, holds that the great stone monuments of Indonesia and south-east Asia are related to those of western Europe in considerable part, and mentions the cup-markings and the port-holes (*Seelen-löcher*) of the dolmens in both areas. For those who connect the western European monuments exclusively, or almost exclusively, with the latter part of the third millennium B.C. this raises difficulties. The dating of the great stone monuments of the Indian peninsula is usually given as within the last millennium B.C., and there is at present no evidence for their greater antiquity in Indonesia. If, however, we keep in mind that great stone monuments in western Europe remained as ritual centres down to the Middle Ages in some cases, and that many are undated as regards construction, the difficulty of the possible relationship is somewhat less. We have, nevertheless, to remember that Reygasse considers the great stone monuments of cemeteries in French North Africa as having little relationship to those of western Europe, and those cemeteries date fairly definitely from the last centuries of the last millennium B.C., if not, in some cases, later. They are thus more nearly contemporary in construction with most of those of south-east Asia than are the majority of the great stone monuments of western Europe. It may be added that seats for councils, chiefs, and so on are a large proportion of the monuments of south-east Asia whereas, so far as we can infer, they do not occur in western Europe. Apparently these monuments on the Island of Sumba include a number in which the stones have been elaborately worked, as well as others in which the stones have been left rough. It has been suggested that the latter may be tombs or memorials of commoners and the former may commemorate chiefs, but this seems to be speculation. Another speculation emphasizes the importance in some regions, such as Minahassa (north Celebes), of having for each village a pair of stones, one placed upright (male) and one lying flat (female), usually on small supports.

Turning now towards the Pacific, we note in the first place that the Early Neolithic axe (with oval cross-section) spread from Asia via Formosa and the Philippines to eastern Indonesia and Melanesia. Beyond Melanesia it has been found in Tonga, New Zealand, Tubuai (Austral Islands), and Pitcairn.

The shouldered axe occurs in Tubuai. With the specialization of the stem to a position at the side rather than in the middle, it has been found in Pitcairn and the Society Islands. With the stem thinner than the axe, but usually central, it has a wide distribution in the Pacific including New Zealand, Chatham Island, Niui (Savage Island), Cook Island, Tubuai, Society Islands, Marquesas, Pitcairn, but also Tikopia just east of the sea-passage between the Santa Cruz Islands and the New Hebrides (Melanesia).

This distribution in the Pacific, together with the fact that in Indonesia it is connected only with North Borneo and Minahassa (north Celebes), and with the Philippines, suggests that it did not get to Polynesia via Melanesia, but that the type reached Tikopia from Polynesia.

The axe with rectangular section is found very generally in Indonesia and in Polynesia, with a few in Melanesia. The peoples who had it as part of their equipment appear to have been able to navigate almost anywhere.

Fiji has the triple pots (often glazed), but the potter's art either did not get to most of Polynesia or died out quickly beyond Tonga, as well as in most of the New Hebrides. Samoa had no pottery. The absence of pottery, or the loss of the potter's art, in Pacific islands is very notable. Wooden bowls, tightly braided fibres, gourds, and sometimes stone vessels are substitutes. Another feature is the absence of weaving or the loss of the art in many islands. Looms are used, by women, in the Caroline Islands, but not in the Marshalls and the Gilberts beyond them. Weaving is unknown in Papua and Melanesia, save in the Santa Cruz Islands, where it is done by men; women there braid but do not weave.

Bows and arrows and their utilization are another feature with a patchy distribution. The Admiralty Islanders, for example, have bows and arrows but use them for hunting only, though they are widely used in Melanesia. The Bismarck archipelago (now New Britain, New Ireland, &c.), however, lacks these weapons, and so does New Caledonia; but Santa Cruz has them. They are known for Tahiti, and were in use in Tonga for war, but the Marquesas islanders have used clubs.

The art of hammering the bark of the paper mulberry into sheets for apparel (Tapa) is widespread in Pacific islands of low latitude.

In the interior of Papua and the Solomon Islands, with traces elsewhere, there are short dark peoples who may have kinky hair and seem, like the Tasmanians, to be related to the Negrito remnants in the Andaman Islands, Malaya (Semang), and the Philippines (Aeta). There are also taller dark-skinned peoples, often with more marked profile, and sometimes with curly or wavy rather than kinky hair, also beards among the males. These have some kinship with the Australian aborigines, and both these racial strains represent early dispersals at a time when the level of the ocean was lower, probably because masses of water were locked up as ice-sheets at various periods of the Pleistocene era. Wood-Jones has suggested that the Tasmanians were a chance drift by sea from Melanesia. But Atkinson (1890) photographed some special Australian aborigines in north Queensland, and similar ones have more recently been found in the rain-forest area near Cairns by Tindale and studied by him and Birdsell. It is claimed that they are related to elements in the extinct Tasmanian people. It is also claimed that neither the Tasmanians nor the Australian blackfellows are a unitary breed.

The Negrito element is strongest in Papua, the Australoid most marked in Melanesia. There is no doubt about a spread from the Papuan direction to Melanesia; and that continued after the Pleistocene period and the rise of sea-level.

From what has been said above, there is no doubt that the idea of pottery and bows and arrows spread through Melanesia and as far as Viti Levu and Tonga.

The ground-stone axe with oval cross-section also spread through Melanesia to Viti Levu and Tonga, and some have been found in New Zealand and suggest possible Melanesian contacts. But, in the case of stone axes, it is advisable to speak cautiously as a type of axe may have long remained in use and is easily portable.

The loom, mentioned above, used by women in the Caroline Islands of Micronesia and by men in the Santa Cruz Islands on the Polynesian side of Melanesia, but unknown in the Marshall and Gilbert Islands or in Papua and Melanesia (apart from Santa Cruz), has apparently spread eastwards and south-eastwards from the Celebes Sea. Apparently a definite current sets from the Celebes Sea eastwards to the Carolines for most of the year, and the equatorial counter-current sets eastwards from the latter, so this is in theory a possible route out to the Pacific. The way from the Caroline Islands to the Santa Cruz group does not seem, from highly generalized maps, to be favoured in the matter of currents, but a zone between the counter-equatorial and the southern equatorial current apparently gives a good deal of variety. Voyages from the Celebes Sea or the Caroline Islands to the Santa Cruz group would, however, seem to be a considerable adventure for indigenous navigators. According to generalized maps, navigation along the south-west side of the Solomon Islands would have less current opposition than along the north-east side.

What has just been said about a few culture features can serve to introduce the subject of the great stone monuments of the Pacific islands. Monuments which can be described under this name have been found in both Melanesia and Polynesia, with, on the whole, marked contrasts between the two regions in this respect. The monuments of the New Hebrides have been studied in some detail, especially in Malekula Island, by Layard. He has drawn special attention to the occurrence there of standing stones (monoliths) which he thinks represent the male principle, and dolmens (a tabular block resting on a few upright stones) which represent the female principle. The former has some relation to a patrilineal succession and the latter to a matrilineal succession, but the two types of monuments may occur together, and there may also be circles of standing stones as well as, sometimes, built-up platforms.

In south Malekula near the coast there are monoliths and small stone circles, some monoliths being carved with representations of faces. North central Malekula, on the western side of an isthmus linking the north and south of the island, has stone circles and avenues of standing stones. The 'Small Islands' off the north-east coast of Malekula have dolmens and also, in some localities, monoliths, and stone-built platforms, but no stone circles have been found. In north Malekula there are both monoliths and dolmens. In Atchin monoliths seem to have superseded dolmens, a patrilineal system is strongly established and the families sometimes have long genealogies, whereas in Vao (Small Islands) patrilineal ideas seem to be fairly recent introductions and there are recently made dolmens and the genealogies are relatively short. In Espiritu Santo Island and the Banks Islands the characteristic monuments are dolmens. The chief ritual goes under the name of maki and it is based on the idea of ritual rebirth. It is probable that the patrilineal scheme of society extended itself northwards from south Malekula. The latter district has a tradition of light-skinned culture leaders who ultimately sailed away. In the south-west of Malekula one of these culture leaders was buried in what, on European analogies, would be called a chambered round barrow with a stone seat on which the leader was supposed to sit, a chamber that may be a dolmen and a covering mound of earth and loose stones.

The Caroline Islands have already been mentioned as being approachable along a current from the Celebes sea, which has great stone monuments. Ponape, the most important island of the Caroline group, has an islet Nan Matal on its eastern side. There a terrace of massive basalt blocks stands more than 6 feet above the shallow water. Above the terrace is a building of large blocks with 'headers and stretchers' (i.e. some set vertically and some horizontally). A gateway leading into an enclosure is 25 feet high on the left side and even higher on the right. The enclosure is about 185 by 115 feet; its wall is 15 feet thick and in places up to 40 feet in height. Steps lead up to a courtyard around a terraced enclosure 85 by 75 feet, the thickness of the wall being 8 feet and its height 15–18 feet. Within this inner enclosure is a vaulted chamber tomb of the Chau-te-leur (Kings of Ponape).

The Polynesian monuments are especially stone platforms and terraces which often resemble a truncated step-pyramid and suggest some analogy with the Maya monuments of central America and the early monuments of Peru.

Samoa has carefully built rectangular constructions of stone over chiefs' graves, and these monuments may be covered with white pebbles (quartz or flint) or bleached shells.

Tonga has grave-mounds of coral rock covered by a platform which was originally surrounded by a stone wall. Some graves have great blocks set in terraces rising altogether 15–20 feet. Tonga, again, has trilithons, pairs of standing stones with a horizontal stone beam laid across the top of each pair.

Several islands have a type of monument often called Marae (sometimes written Marai). These are usually rectangular enclosures often with a fence of standing stones in which small gaps occur.

On Tubuai (Austral Islands) the stone fence occurs on three sides of the rectangle, the fourth side being left open and the side opposite to this having the largest stones of the fence. On Rarotonga (south of Cook Islands) the rectangle lacked the stone

Fig. 71. The Great Vault, Nan Tauach.

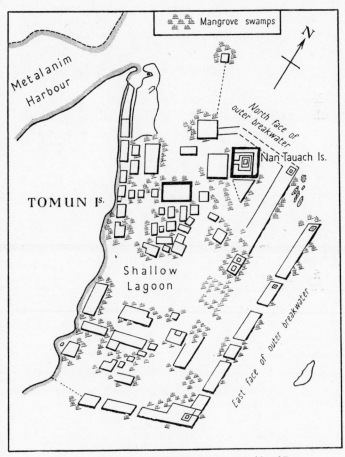

Mangrove swamps

Metalanim Harbour

N

North face of outer breakwater

Nan Tauach Is.

TOMUN Iˢ.

Shallow Lagoon

East face of outer breakwater

FIG. 72. Nan Matal, one of the islets on the east side of Ponape (Caroline Islands).

fence, but had seats in rows, with back-rests, also a stone for human sacrifices and a high stone used in ceremonial.

On Tahiti the sacred rectangle was fenced by stone walls on three sides; the fourth side (one of the narrower ones) had a stepped rectangular pyramid. Stones for the heads of families stood in rows in the enclosure, which was a place of council and judgement. Tahiti also had larger enclosures called Ahu which included a stepped pyramid, in one case arranged in eleven tiers on a base 71 by 26 metres and over 13 metres high. The great Ahu at Mahaiatea has an enclosure with the longer side of the rectangle 110 metres in length. The pyramid contains a specially sacred grave. Tahiti, the Marquesas, and Easter Island have what may be said to be the most remarkable of all monuments of Polynesia.

In the Marquesas there are remains of platforms built of great basalt slabs with stone statues on them. A maze of artificial coastal islets, some surrounded by walls 10 feet thick and up to 30 feet high, was described by F. W. Christian (1910). Some of the monuments of these islands are called Ahu and some Me'ae. There are also Tohua, places for dancing and other ceremonial; these consist of a paved rectangle with platforms rising tier above tier for onlookers, sometimes on one or more sides of the rectangle, sometimes on all.

The Ahu of Easter Island are in some cases triangular, as though the otherwise typical rectangle had been cut diagonally. In other cases a terrace 100 metres long and 3 metres broad rises gently from the land to the extent of 5 metres until it reaches a sharp edge facing a steep drop to the sea. Great stone figures stand on the platforms.

In Viti Levu there are Nanga, rectangular enclosures with a fence of standing stones in which there are many narrow gaps. Truncated pyramid-terraces of stone set transversely, according to one description, divided the enclosure into three parts.

Fig. 73. Ancient Statue from Marquesas.

FIG. 74. Shell adze,
Caroline Islands.

The fact of the spread of the loom
to the Caroline and Santa Cruz Islands, and its use in the latter by men
only (probably therefore a not too
remote cultural acquisition from immigrant navigators) points to the use
of the current from the Celebes Sea
to the Carolines archipelago, but it is
better not to speculate on the route to
the Santa Cruz Islands. The shouldered
stone axes of the coasts of the Celebes
Sea might be supposed to have spread
by the same route to Polynesia, where
they are important in various islands
(see pp. 292–3), but they have not
been found in the Carolines, in which
sharp shell edges are used, so this is
in doubt.

Recently the Norwegian, Heyerdahl,
has given the inquiry into Polynesian
cultures new life by his adventure
on a balsa raft. Balsa is a fairly soft
absorbent wood found in the equatorial
rain forests of South America. Following the ancient Peruvian pattern,
Heyerdahl lashed logs together longi-
tudinally with hemp rope to form the
raft, and laid bamboo flooring over
the logs in the centre of the raft.
Coniferous wood was thrust vertically
down between the central logs to make
a keel. A mast scheme was made of hard
mangrove wood, and a mangrove oar

was used for steering. A sail was hoisted. No metal nails or wire ropes were used as these would have rusted in the sea. On this remarkable craft the voyage was made from Callao, 4,000 miles to Tuamotu in the Low Islands, following the Peru current, the south equatorial current, and the latter's southward branch to the Low Islands. Heyerdahl thus makes a strong claim for the possibility of migrations from western South America to the Pacific islands, and he doubts the possibility of a voyage by Polynesian navigators in the reverse direction, against wind and current. He notes especially the fact that the sweet potato under its name Kumara is widely distributed in Polynesia and he claims that it was brought from South America. He also thinks the great stone structures of Tiahuanaco in the Peruvian highlands may be a part of the story of the spread of culture from South America to Pacific islands.

In the discussions on Heyerdahl's adventure, a further point has been brought out by that author. He thinks navigators may have followed the Kuro Siwo current past Japan around to western America, where the coast of what is now British Columbia offered large trunks of fir-trees from which dug-out double canoes could be made of a far better quality than was possible in N.E. Asia. With these better canoes voyages to Hawaii and on to Polynesia generally were undertaken, probably by groups escaping after defeat. Heyerdahl dates this supposed movement near A.D. 1200 and thinks it conquered islands previously occupied by migrants, possibly again defeated groups, from Peru, who had travelled by raft.

Questions of Polynesian cultures have been given increased interest by Heyerdahl, and the problems concerned are far from settled. At the moment it seems likely that ways via Melanesia, via the Celebes Sea and the Carolines and via western America may all have been used by voyagers in the Pacific, and Polynesians have probably visited adjacent parts of Melanesia and Micronesia.

It is probable that the ancestors of the Australian aborigines reached Australia when sea-levels were lower in some part of the Pleistocene, probably the Late Pleistocene, period. It is possible that kinky-haired peoples spread in Papua and parts of Melanesia, also in the Pleistocene period, and mention has already been made of Wood-Jones's view that the Tasmanians were strays from Melanesia, but it is generally thought that the Tasmanians are an early spread through Australia. A few strays appear to have reached Australia since it was cut off by the rise of sea-level; and the use of boats by the aborigines of the Cape York peninsula, perhaps also some traces of what is called Neolithic culture, is evidence of such connexions.

The spread of full Neolithic culture from Asia into Indonesia is usually thought not to have preceded the second millennium B.C., and the art of building monuments of great stones is believed to have spread in south-east Asia and Indonesia not earlier than the last millennium B.C. In western Europe it was apparently this art that accompanied early maritime navigation and we may guess that the architectural skill of the monument-builders was accompanied by technical knowledge of other kinds, perhaps including skill in boat-building and navigation. There is thus little reason at present to suppose that the remoter islands of the Pacific Ocean received population much before the beginning of our era, if as early as that. Heyerdahl's dates seem as useful as any. The best known of the voyages is the migration of the Maori fleet to New Zealand in the fourteenth century A.D.

There seems little doubt that the arts of pottery and weaving were never used, or early lost, by Polynesians, and that the arts of hammering tapa-cloth, making feather cloaks, boat-building and wood- and stone-carving had considerable development, though they did not always maintain themselves in the small inbred communities of the islands. Whether those island communities were generally able to maintain their numbers by reproduction in pre-modern times is not quite certain, but at any rate many islands had dense populations (for their economic status) when contacts with European ships began. These brought epidemics to which the islanders had not acquired immunity, and venereal disease added to the mortality. So, for these reasons alone, population would apparently have decreased, at any rate for a time. But there was added to these disturbances of mortality rates a further one which is still only partially understood. A social order based on the life of mainly self-sufficing communities with highly evolved reproductive customs and rituals was undermined by intrusive commerce and a new outlook in many directions. There has undoubtedly been a marked decline in birth-rate connected in some way with the social and biological revolution the island peoples have undergone. It is thought that, in the case of the New Zealand Maori, the decline may have been arrested and that the Maori people, with some European admixture, are tending to increase once more. This is not the case in several parts of both Melanesia and Polynesia, and old skills are disappearing as European goods and trade become more important.

II

Africa South of the Sahara and of Ethiopia

AFRICA has recently yielded a number of specimens of higher apes and possible hominids (see Chap. 1), thanks to the enterprise of Drs. Broom and Dart in South Africa, while Dr. Leakey in Kenya has added greatly to knowledge concerning early man and his work. The whole chapter of the story of the Old Stone Age in Africa south of the Sahara has been enormously amplified, and its chronology has been much discussed, keeping in mind the possibility that the Old Stone Age's types of life may have continued in some parts of Africa much later than in Europe.

When we come to the later periods and the spread of food-production into intertropical and South Africa we find the problems still obscure.

A relatively small number of Neolithic tools has been collected from Nigeria, from the Congo basin, and from south-east Africa, but they are not really common nor generally distributed. A find of well-chipped barbed flint arrow-heads at Umtali (south-east Africa) has remained isolated in its region, though, if it had occurred in Britain, it would have been considered good evidence for the presence of people on the threshold of Bronze Age equipment. Africa south of the Sahara and of Ethiopia has so far yielded no clear evidence of the preparation, use, or importation of bronze in prehistoric times. A pre-iron Bronze Age apparently did not occur in this region. Tin is an important modern product of Nigeria, and has been worked on the Bauchi plateau for centuries, and Northern Rhodesia is now one of the world's chief sources of copper, but there is no good evidence that these products were brought together to make bronze in prehistoric or, shall we say, pre-iron days in Africa south of the Sahara.

Iron is found in many regions in low-grade ores. A soil in a hot country with a long dry season is likely to have iron oxides brought to the surface by the upward movement of soil water on the way to evaporation. Especially if lime is also present there may be a crust formed at or near the surface, and the seasonal rains may wash out a good deal of the accompanying non-ferrous clay, leaving the crust only slightly reduced. Thus even without large mineral deposits there may be useful sources of iron.

Iron needs for its treatment longer heating than does copper but, once a blast could be developed, the process of smelting, especially with wood fuel, would be simple and would not involve the organization of trade and skill needed to make bronze from copper and tin, so often obtainable only at long distances from one another and from the smelting place.

There have been theories suggesting that iron-working originated in Africa several millennia ago, but evidence is unsatisfactory. It seems, on the whole, advisable to adopt for the present the hypothesis that iron-working, apart perhaps from fragments of meteoric iron, became very important among the Chalybes of Anatolia after the middle of the second millennium B.C. As soon as the method of driving an air blast through the furnace was known, the smelting of iron could spread, so it may not have taken very long to get into intertropical Africa. On the other hand the fact that iron has been so much more used by African peoples north of the Congo Forest than by peoples of South Africa (at any rate before modern European contacts) suggests that the use of iron in Africa may not date back very far. There is also the fact that the smiths in intertropical Africa are often wanderers from group to group, sometimes looked upon almost as magicians, sometimes rather as strangers and therefore under suspicion. One must, however, mention that Sir Leonard Woolley found an iron spearhead in a twelfth dynasty tomb at Buhen, just below the second cataract of the Nile; and he wonders whether it may not have come from ironworkings in intertropical Africa before 1800 B.C.

The penetration of ideas of food production southward in Africa was subject to considerable difficulty. Already in the fourteenth century the Islamic philosopher Ibn Khaldun emphasized the absence of cities in the torrid zone (of Africa) and ascribed the lack of civic development of this kind to the effect of the excessive heat on men's minds. There seems to be no doubt that humanity in general is most comfortable and efficient in environments with day temperatures 60°–70° or 72° Fahrenheit and occasional cooler spells. This suggests that mankind, *homo sapiens* shall we say, originated in a fairly temperate environment and that adaptation to great heat, especially moist heat, between the tropics, has been a difficult process which has probably remained incomplete. One should recall the activity of an African kraal at sundown and during the night. The human constitution seems liable to many diseases in intertropical lands, and there are many insect and other troubles. But, however this may be, there were other difficulties. Wheat and barley are not adapted to torrid conditions and did not spread far south of the Sahara in Africa. Millets did spread over the continent and became the traditional African 'mealies'. They may have originated as cultivated plants in south-western Asia or Egypt, but this is not securely decided as yet. They neither require such skilled cultivation as wheat, nor do they yield as good food. In south-western Asia and Egypt cultivation was, from very early times, based on irrigation, and success was achieved where there were regular annual floods from melting snow, as in Sumer and Akkad, or from the Ethiopian summer monsoon in the case of the Nile. In Africa south of the Sahara climatic regions rarely lent themselves to early and rural methods of irrigation; it is in fact only now, in the middle of the twentieth century, that water-control is being planned seriously in many parts of intertropical Africa. Water-control exercised a vast influence tending towards social organization from early times in Egypt; intertropical Africa lacked this factor of evolution, and cultivation thence remained on a low level. The spread of flood-rice could do a great deal for Africa's soil and social life. In intertropical Africa it seems that native food plants were few and poor; in fact a poor kind of yam and perhaps a bean were the only ones of which we know. We must add to this the very important geographical fact that the ways into Africa south of the Sahara and of Ethiopia were through arid belts or the swamps of the Sudd, and, consequently, only trickles of population would be likely to enter, and these usually because they were driven in that direction by pressure of better equipped groups. Occasional sea voyages were made as equipment for shipbuilding developed, probably from the third dynasty of ancient Egypt onwards, but for ages the ships do not seem to have ventured far beyond the southern part of the Red Sea and the Gulf of Aden. In Carthaginian times circumnavigation of Africa reached from the Mediterranean south-westwards as far as the Gulf of Guinea. But early traders seem to have voyaged mainly to take back certain products, and it is fairly clear that they had little influence on African life in the torrid zone. Torrid Africa has thus largely lacked the advantages of entry of ideas from other lands, whereas south-east Asia has had many stimuli from China.

Introductions of new food plants in early days must have been rare and the establishment of a new food plant in intertropical Africa must have been difficult. Millet (mealies) and bananas are two cases of successful introduction before European influence began, but the banana is probably an importation by Arabs. The introduction of domestic animals into the region also had to face considerable difficulties. Of native animals, the members of the antelope family were probably the least recalcitrant but, though related to the oxen, they are very swift of foot and it is doubtful whether any were anciently domesticated to an extent such as to make them really useful to man. At an early cemetery at Heliopolis outside Cairo, dated not far on one side or the other of 3000 B.C., have been found some six burials of small gazelles with offerings. They may have been sacred animals; whether they were kept by men we do not know.

Ruling out, therefore, the antelopes, we may say that domestic animals had to be introduced into Africa south of the Sahara by migration from the north. Cattle are so dependent on water that their routes of introduction were limited, but, more than that, it seems that the grasses of torrid Africa are for the most part inferior and tough, lacking especially in vitamin C, so the animals would not be at their best. Also, the tall tough grasses have much cellulose and relatively little protein, and as cattle need 15–20 per cent. of protein in their grass-food, for adequate feeding, they would need to eat huge amounts of the tall tough grasses of many parts of torrid Africa. Moreover, insects and ticks and other pests abound in the region; and cattle rearing would need great care to make it a real success and to provide animals useful to man for work. It may be stated with some confidence that cattle for work were unknown in intertropical and South Africa until modern contacts and methods changed the situation, except in some areas near the Niger. Sheep are essentially animals of cooler climes and do not thrive well in African equatorial regions, so, apart from modern spreads to South Africa, they are of little account in our region. Goats manage better and are of some importance in parts of Africa, and so are chickens; but neither has been bred with much skill. The camel has no record in Egypt until Islamic times (seventh century A.D.), though it was apparently used in Arabia about 1,700 years earlier, and one must mention that a few bones, identified as belonging to the camel, have been found with pre-Dynastic objects (before

3400 B.C.) in Upper Egypt. Its slight extension into Africa south of the Sahara is a quite recent event. The horse reached Egypt with the Hyksos or Shepherd Kings in the seventeenth century B.C. and did not penetrate into intertropical and South Africa, apart from Ethiopia, until modern European contacts spread its use into South Africa.

Domestic animals have thus been a limited source of help to Africans, and it is probable that the very slight extension of the plough, before eighteenth- and nineteenth-century changes, into Africa south of the Sahara, in northern Nigeria, was quite a late event.

Early torrid African cultivation was therefore without irrigation and without the plough, and so was on a low level of equipment, skill, and social organization, and such it has remained. Ploughing is, however, apt to expose the soil to scorching by the sun in many parts of intertropical Africa and in semi-arid African areas outside the tropics. There is the further difficulty that, whereas in temperate lands the cattle manure their pastures, in intertropical lands termites eat the dung, tropical rains wash it away, and during droughts it quickly decays into a powder dispersed by wind. Lowly cultivation is apt to follow certain customs which are destructive in the long run. An area is cleared, by axe-work and burning, is cultivated at most for a few years, and is then left to itself for a time. It may be cleared again after some years and once more cultivated for a time. An area of grass may be burnt frequently with a view to cultivation, and often the area burnt will exceed the area cultivated, so a surface may be left exposed without vegetational cover. It may then be ravined by a rainstorm; and these are frequent as afternoon thunderstorms in several regions; or it may be exposed to strong evaporation that will bring up water with lime and iron to the surface. As the water evaporates the lime and iron may form a hard crust. So one may eventually get what may be called an armour-plated desert where once was a grass-land, or one may get dongas, ravines with soil washing down into rivers and out to sea at an appalling rate. Even where these calamities do not occur on a great scale, repeated burning of a grass cover leaves the advantage for regrowth to those, generally very tough, grasses which have underground food storage of some kind; these grasses, mainly tough cellulose, are of very limited value for pasture, as the animals would have to overeat seriously to get a reasonable supply of protein. In the case of forest land, clearing, cultivating, and leaving for a time often means that a poor jungle grows in place of the original forest and may invite a second clearing too soon because that is easier than tackling the virgin forest. It is estimated that a cleared forest area should have twenty years' rest to recover more or less, as there is a large loss through leaching of the uncovered soil under heavy rains. Typically nothing is done to manure the soil of intertropical Africa under African schemes, apart from the ash derived from the burning. Insect, arachnid, and other pests also give rise to large-scale problems. It should, however, be borne in mind that the application of European methods of cultivation in many African environments may be harmful to the soil. Valuable elements in the soil are in some cases leached out, in others they are destroyed by the scorching rays of the sun.

Not only is cultivation therefore on a low level, but in some areas, especially in the forest, the settlement must be moved from time to time. Timber huts decay and become too verminous, and the group moves to a new clearing. The area required by a small group under these wasteful systems (and as territory for supplementary hunting) is a large one, and a visitor may get an erroneous impression of the occurrence of considerable tracts of unused land. Nevertheless, one must recognize a certain amount of craft-skill in the building of huts with local plant-material in several areas.

Fig. 75. Hut construction in Parklands of the Niger region.

In some areas, for example in parts of West Africa, large permanent settlements have grown up with more skilled systems of hoe cultivation, but the plough, apart from European influence, has not spread beyond northern Nigeria, and indeed its further spread would involve a revolution in social ideas. Cattle are kept to be exchanged for wives, and it is their number rather than their working strength that matters. Moreover, the furrowing by the plough is a danger in a warm wet region, and deep ploughing is out of place where plant food is near the surface.

Often, the small local group manages most of its little affairs and has been largely self-sufficing. There may be tribute payable to a chief presiding over a number of groups, and sometimes, as in Uganda, there is a king of a fairly considerable territory and an aristocracy, largely of herders, dominating cultivator-underlings.

It has been typical for most of Africa south of the Sahara and Ethiopia that, except in parts of Nigeria, of the Sudan and Uganda, there has been little development of the administrative state, or of institutions with arrangements for passing social heritages on from generation to generation save as regards the group-life in general. There is typically no writing and no serious record. Even where there is some succession of a chieftainship, that succession is often a matter of dispute and actual strife.

A sparse population at a low level, coping inadequately with a difficult environment may be taken as a fairly general account of the region, allowing for a few special concentrations apart from those enforced by Europeans.

On the east side circumstances changed to some extent when Arab mariners, probably about the time of the rise of Islam, learned to use the monsoons of the Indian Ocean for navigation and commerce. Boats from the Red Sea and the Gulf of Aden could thenceforth reach Oman, India, and Malaya and so make contact with China. Landings on the East African coast, especially on a return journey, were probable. It is likely that in this way some ideas and probably objects were brought from south Asia to East Africa. Whether this is how the banana spread to Africa or whether it was known earlier is an unsolved question. But it is quite possible that plants were introduced and perhaps some of them were lost or forgotten in Africa. These new contacts meant that a slave trade developed, at any rate with Arabia, but various skills touched at least the coasts of East Africa.

North of Mombasa are the remains of various ports and stations of medieval Islamic times, and at Gedi, for example, the foundations of a palace and a mosque are known. Finds of pottery suggest contacts with Oman and, perhaps indirectly, with China, going on well into our Middle Ages as the Chinese Celadon (Sung) ware shows. These contacts should be remembered when the famous Rhodesian monuments, Zimbabwe and others, are discussed. Dr. Randall McIver and Miss Caton Thompson both found much evidence at Zimbabwe for the hypothesis that the place came into existence, or at any rate developed considerably, in our Middle Ages, fragments of Celadon and other ware being found under stamped-earth pavements. They may well represent the southward extension of influences spreading from coastal traders to African peoples of the interior.

On the west side one has to consider the carving and metal-casting of Benin and of Ife and other Nigerian sites. It has long been known that bronze-casting, ivory-carving, and terracotta-modelling were being carried on at Benin at the time of the Portuguese voyages of discovery (fifteenth century A.D.). A famous ivory head, now in the British Museum, is decorated with a number of miniature heads of Portuguese, and other specimens give analogous evidence. How long this art had been active in Benin or even whether it had been developed as a consequence of the Portuguese contact is not strictly decided, but it remains probable that this art existed in Benin before the Portuguese came. Some of the casts are in bronze, a unique fact for Africa, but one which may be related to the notable occurrence of tin on the Bauchi plateau to the north. Any tendency to ascribe the origins of this art to the stimulus imparted to the Niger region by the spread of Islam probably about the eleventh and twelfth centuries A.D. faces the difficulty that the art concerned itself specially with representations of men, and that is a form of art which was not approved by Islam, or at any rate by the Sunni Muslim. We are dealing with something that is to all appearances non-Islamic.

In recent years at Ife a number of finely modelled heads made of an alloy related to bronze have been dug up, and the ruler, called the One, of Ife has taken care of them and brought them to England for treatment by specialists at the British Museum. They were exhibited at the Museum in 1948 for some time before their return to Africa. They belong to the same group as a number of terracotta heads found in connexion with metal workings on the Bauchi plateau.

The fine modelling and expert casting of naturalistic representations of various types of men's heads, including the reproductions of what are to all appearances tattoo patterns, has led to much thought concerning origins which, one confidently supposes at present, are non-Islamic. This is a field in which inquiry is in progress and the time for conclusions has not yet arrived, but the possibility of its being an indigenous development should be borne in mind.

Islam, as is well known, spread by conquest westwards along North Africa in the seventh and eighth centuries A.D., and Arab domination met Berber resistance again and again. By the eleventh century North Africa had been largely Islamized but Berber and Arab were nevertheless still at enmity. The decline

of the Umayyad aristocracy and government of Islamic Spain
led to the rise of a Muslim reform movement in the eleventh

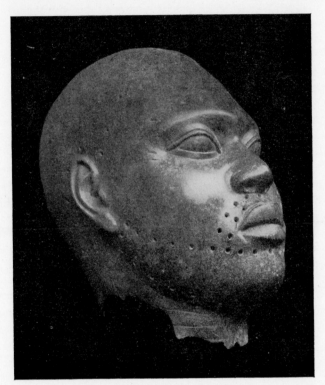

Fig. 76. Bronze head from Ife, Nigeria.

century in North Africa, and the reformers, who became known
as the Almoravides, established themselves on the Senegal, thus
bringing Africa south of the western Sahara into active contact
with Islam. It is probably from that time onwards that Muslim
Emirates came into existence on the lands south of the Sahara,

with cities of sun-dried brick, markets, camels, and, near the bend of the Niger, the plough.

There has since been a general tendency for groups belonging to the latitude of northern Nigeria to feel pastoralist pressure from the north and to dominate cultivator-peoples farther south.

The discovery of America by Europeans has been one of the most fateful of all events for Africa. It caused a huge development of the slave trade and the transference of thousands of West Africans to the West Indies, Brazil, and the southern United States of North America. In their new homes the slaves and their ultimately freed descendants have multiplied and now number millions, mostly to some extent of mixed African-European descent, especially in U.S.A. The quest for slaves undoubtedly had a disastrous effect on West African life, so that what we see is probably far below what might have been had this awful trade not developed.

But the discovery of America had quite other influences on African life. It led to the introduction of a number of American food plants into intertropical Africa. Two of these are of special importance because of their widespread cultivation in Africa. These are maize and manioc, both easy to cultivate without ploughing. Whereas there may be ritual concerning the growing of mealies (millets), the old traditional food crop, nothing of the kind has come into existence concerning the new foods. In addition to maize and manioc, there were also brought in varieties of yam new to Africa, tomatoes, and a variety of other plants, including the potato and sweet potato.

The population of Africa with these new food-supplies could increase considerably and no doubt would have done so even more had it not been for the growth of the slave trade and its attendant misery and disorder.

We must also notice that whereas, before the sixteenth century, a new impetus in African life was likely to come from North

Africa southwards over land or from Arabia by coastwise voyage to East Africa, after that time intertropical and South Africa became open to the direct impact of foreign ideas. In the nineteenth century the outside influences enormously increased their powers of penetration into Africa and of changing African life, and many African peoples have to face a sudden transition from their old life to a new one that they have not desired. The attendant problems are among the most serious in the world of today, and especially of tomorrow. Up to the present European influence in Africa has continued, even perhaps sometimes worsened, the deterioration of soil that went on, more slowly, under native systems. Control of water, growing of flood-rice in suitable areas, tree cultivation and, above all, protection of arable soil from exposure are among Africa's urgent needs, apart from reduction of tsetse flies, locusts, ticks, mosquitoes, bilharzia and other pests.

A Selection of Studies for further Reading

Chapter 1 and general introduction

BREUIL, H. 'Pleistocene Succession, Somme valley', *Proc. Prehist. Soc.* 1939.

BROOM, R., and SCHEPERS, G. W. H. *S. African fossil Ape-men*. Pretoria, 1946.

CLARK, SIR W. E. LE GROS. 'Fossil Anthropopithecinae', *Yr. Bk. Phys. Anthrop.* 1947. Publ. New York, 1948.

COON, CARLETON S. *History of Man*. 1955.

DE GEER, G. *Geochronologica Suecica*. Stockholm, 1940.

MARSTON, A. T. 'The Swanscombe Skull', *Journ. Roy. Anthrop. Inst.* 1937.

McCOWN, T. D., and KEITH, SIR A. *Stone Age of Mt. Carmel*, vol. ii. 1939.

Chapters 2 and 3

BREUIL, H. *Four Hundred Centuries of Cave-Art*. Montignac, France, 1952.

CLARK, J. G. D. *Mesolithic Settlement of N. Europe*. 1936.

—— *Excavations at Star Carr*. 1954.

DE TERRA, H., and PATERSON, T. T. *Studies of the Ice Age in India*. Washington, U.S.A., 1939.

GARROD, DOROTHY A. E. 'The Upper Palaeolithic', *Proc. Prehist. Soc.* 1935.

LEAKEY, L. S. B. *Stone Age Africa*. 1936.

WINDELS, F. *Lascaux*. Montignac, France, 1948.

ZEUNER, F. E. *Dating the Past*. 1946.

Chapter 4

BURTON, BROWN, T. *Studies in Third Millennium History*. 1946.

CHILDE, V. G. *New Light on the most Ancient East*. 1934.

FRANKFORT, H. *Kingship and the Gods*. Chicago, 1945.

GARROD, DOROTHY A. E. *Stone Age of Mt. Carmel*, vol. i. 1937.

LLOYD, SETON. *Twin Rivers*. 1943.

PERKINS, A. L. *Comparative Archaeology of Early Mesopotamia*. Chicago, 1949.

SCHAEFFER, C. *Stratigraphie comparée et Chronologie de l'Asie occidentale*. Oxford, 1948.

WOOLLEY, SIR C. L. *Ur, the first phase*. 1946.

—— *Alalakh*. 1953.

Chapter 5

AMER, M. (with MENGHIN, O.) *Excavations at Maadi.* Cairo, 1932 and 1936.
BREASTED, J. H. *History of Egypt.*
CATON THOMPSON, GERTRUDE, and GARDNER, ELINOR. *The Desert Fayum.*
HUZAYYIN, S. *The Place of Egypt in Prehistory.* Cairo, 1941.
SMITH, W. S. *History of Egyptian Sculpture and Painting in the Old Kingdom.* 1949.

Chapters 6 and 7

ATKINSON, R. J. C. *Stonehenge.* 1955.
CHILDE, V. G. *Dawn of European Civilization,* 4th ed. 1947.
—— *Prehistoric Migrations in Europe.* Oslo, 1950.
COGHLAN, H. H. *Prehistoric Metallurgy of Copper and Bronze.* 1951.
DANIEL, G. G. *Prehistoric Chamber-Tombs of England and Wales.* 1950.
FOX, SIR C. *Personality of Britain,* 3rd ed., Cardiff, 1938.
—— and DICKINS, B. *Early Cultures of N.W. Europe.* 1950.
HAWKES, C. F. C. *Prehistoric Foundations of Europe—to the Mycenaean Age.* 1940.
LEISNER, G. und V. *Megalithgräber der Iberischen Halbinsel.* Berlin, 1943.
MYRES, SIR JOHN L. *Geographical History of Greek Lands.* 1953.
NILSSON, M. P. *Minoan-Mycenaean Religion,* 2nd ed. Lund, 1950.
PIGGOTT, STUART. *Neolithic Cultures of the British Isles.* 1954.
WACE, A. J. B. *Mycenae,* Princeton 1949.

Chapter 8

DE TERRA, H., and PATERSON, T. T. *Studies on the Ice Age in India.* Washington, U.S.A., 1939.
MACKAY, E. *Indus Civilization.* 1935.
MARSHALL, SIR J. *Mohenjo Daro and the Indus Culture.* 1931.
PIGGOTT, STUART. *Prehistoric India.* 1950.
WHEELER, SIR R. E. M. W. *Cambridge History of India.* 1953.

Chapter 9

CREEL, H. G. *Birth of China.* 1936.
VON RICHTOFEN, F. *China, Ergebnisse eigener Reisen.* 1882.
STEIN, SIR AUREL. *Serindia.* 1921.
WU, G. D. *Prehistoric Pottery in China.* 1938.

Chapter 10

CHRISTIAN, F. W. *Caroline Islands.* 1899.
—— *Eastern Pacific Lands.* 1910.
HEINE-GELDERN, R. 'Megalithen Sudostasiens', *Anthropos*, vol. 23. Vienna, 1928.
—— 'Urheimat und Wanderungen der Austronesier', ibid., vol. 28. 1932.
HEYERDAHL, T. *American Indians in the Pacific.*
HOWELLS, W. W. (Editor). *Early Man in the Far East.* 1949.
LAYARD, J. *Stone Men of Malekula.*

Chapter 11

CATON THOMPSON, GERTRUDE. *Zimbabwe Culture.* 1931.
LEAKEY, L. S. B. *Stone Age Africa.* 1936.
GOUROU, P. *Les Pays tropicaux.* Paris, 1947.

INDEX

This index is chiefly one of names and includes materials only in cases of special importance. Countries are not indexed as the reader will easily find the chief references by perusing the appropriate chapters.

PRINTED IN GREAT BRITAIN
AT THE UNIVERSITY PRESS, OXFORD
BY CHARLES BATEY, PRINTER TO THE UNIVERSITY